Globalization and Culture

For my Mother

GLOBALIZATION AND CULTURE

John Tomlinson

The University of Chicago Press

The University of Chicago Press, Chicago 60637

Polity Press, Cambridge CB2 1UR, UK

First published in 1999 by Polity Press in association with
Blackwell Publishers Ltd.

08 07 06 05 04 03 02   3 4 5 6 7 8 9 10

ISBN: 0-226-80767-3 (cloth)

ISBN: 0-226-80768-1 (paper)

Library of Congress Cataloging-in-Publication Data

Tomlinson, John, 1949–
    Globalization and culture / John Tomlinson.
         p.   cm.
    Includes bibliographical references and index.
    ISBN 0-226-80767-3 (cloth : alk. paper).—ISBN 0-226-80768-1
(pbk : alk. paper)
    1. Culture. 2. Internationalism.   I. Title.
HM101.T633 1999
306—dc21   98-51046
                                                                 CIP

Typeset in 10½ on 12½ pt Palatino by Ace Filmsetting, Frome, Somerset
Printed in Great Britain by MPG Books Ltd, Victoria Square, Bodmin, Cornwall

This book is printed on acid-free paper.

Contents

Acknowledgements

This book has benefited greatly from discussion with many people – some friendly to the ideas it contains, others (friendlily) sceptical. Some of the arguments were first tried out as invited papers at various workshops and seminars and I am grateful to the following people for their kind invitations, hospitality and helpful comments: Jaap Verheul and Hans Bertens at the University of Utrecht, Ritva Levo-Henriksson and Kaarle Nordenstreng of the Finnish Association for Mass Communications Research, the late Vincent Tucker at the University of Cork, Frans Schurman and Detlev Haude at the Third World Centre of the University of Nijmegen, Clive Barnett and Murray Low of the Department of Geography, Reading University, Barbara O'Connor at Dublin City University, and Mohamed Salih and Jan Nederveen Pieterse at the Institute of Social Studies, The Hague. I am also indebted to the following people for the way in which they have, in various ways, influenced and enriched my thinking about globalization and culture: Martin Albrow, Ash Amin, Anthony Giddens, Luke Goode, Stuart Hall, Cees Hamelink, James Lull, Tony McGrew, Graham Murdock, Renato Ortiz, Jan Aart Scholte, Annabelle Sreberny-Mohammadi, Peter Taylor, Ken Thompson, Gillian Youngs. The Faculty of Humanities at the Nottingham Trent University has been an extraordinarily stimulating and supportive intellectual environment to work in during the last few years, and I have benefited enormously from many discussions with friends and colleagues in CRICC and the Theory, Culture and Society Centre, in particular: Roger Bromley, Deborah Chambers, Hugo de Burgh, Chris Farrands, Mike Featherstone, Richard Johnson, Eleonore Kofman, Ali Mohammadi, Parvati Raghuram, Chris Rojek,

Tracey Skelton and Patrick Williams. Terry McSwiney gave her usual superb secretarial support. Rebecca Harkin at Polity Press provided invaluable comments on early drafts. Finally, Anny Jones is always the most vital source of intellectual stimulation and incisive critique – Oh (other) fair warrior!

Peter Grimes: I am native, rooted here
                       By familiar fields,
                       Marsh and sand,
                       Ordinary streets,
                       Prevailing wind . . .
                       And by the kindness
                       Of a casual glance.
Captain Balstrode: You'd slip these moorings
                       If you had the mind.

Benjamin Britten/Montagu Slater: *Peter Grimes*

1

Globalization and Culture

Globalization lies at the heart of modern culture; cultural practices lie at the heart of globalization. This is the reciprocal relationship I shall try to establish in this chapter and explore in the chapters which follow. This is not a reckless claim: it is not to say that globalization is the single determinant of modern cultural experience, nor that culture alone is the conceptual key that unlocks globalization's inner dynamic. It is not, therefore, to claim that the politics and economics of globalization yield to a cultural account which takes conceptual precedence. But it is to maintain that the huge transformative processes of our time that globalization describes cannot be properly understood until they are grasped through the conceptual vocabulary of culture; likewise that these transformations change the very fabric of cultural experience and, indeed, affect our sense of what culture actually is in the modern world. Both globalization and culture are concepts of the highest order of generality and notoriously contested in their meanings. This book certainly does not aim at an exhaustive analysis of either: more modestly it tries to grasp the main elements of globalization in what might be called a cultural register. In this first chapter I offer an orientating understanding of the concept of globalization within this register, and then try to show why culture and globalization matter intrinsically to each other.

Globalization as Complex Connectivity

To construct this argument I begin with a simple and relatively uncontentious basic understanding of globalization as an empirical condition of the modern world: what I shall call *complex connectivity*. By this I mean that globalization refers to the rapidly developing and ever-densening network of interconnections and inter-dependences that characterize modern social life. The notion of connectivity is found in one form or another in most contemporary accounts of globalization. McGrew, to give a typical example, speaks of globalization as 'simply the intensification of global inter-connectedness' and stresses the multiplicity of linkages it implies: 'Nowadays, goods, capital, people, knowledge, images, crime, pollutants, drugs, fashions and beliefs all readily flow across territorial boundaries. Transnational networks, social movements and relationships are extensive in virtually all areas from the academic to the sexual' (1992: 65, 67). An important point to draw out here is that the linkages suggested exist in a number of different *modalities*, varying from the social-institutional relationships that are proliferating between individuals and collectivities worldwide, to the idea of the increasing 'flow' of goods, information, people and practices across national borders, to the more 'concrete' modalities of connection provided by technological developments such as the international system of rapid air transport and the more literal 'wiredness' of electronic communications systems.

McGrew writes from the perspective of international politics, but similar formulations – 'interconnections', 'networks', 'flows' – can be found in sociological (Lash and Urry 1994; Castells 1996, 1997, 1998), cultural studies (Hall 1992) or anthropological accounts (Friedman 1995). What this attests to is at least a basic degree of consensus on the empirical reality that globalization refers us to. It is these mul-tivalent connections that now bind our practices, our experiences and our political, economic and environmental fates together across the modern world. And so the broad task of globalization *theory* is both to understand the sources of this condition of complex connectivity and to interpret its implications across the various spheres of social existence.

One of the most striking features of the idea of globalization is just how readily and plentifully all manner of implications seem to flow from it. It is an extraordinarily fecund concept in its capacity to generate speculations, hypotheses and powerful social images and metaphors which reach far beyond the bare social facts. In one sense of course this can be counted to its credit, since the simple fact of increasing connectivity is limited in its interest and, without inter-pretation and elaboration, could remain an almost banal observation. Connectivity is thus a condition which immediately needs elaboration and interpretation. However there is also a danger of confusion arising from the tendency towards conceptual slippage that seems to attend the idea. Because of this, we need to exercise a degree of circumspection in the way we elaborate the core idea of connectivity. To illustrate both the need for elaboration and its pitfalls, I want to look at two ways in which the simple idea of connectivity shades into other themes.

Connectivity and Proximity

First the idea of connectivity could be taken to imply increasing global-spatial *proximity*: what Marx in the *Grundrisse* (1973a) talked of as the 'annihilation of space by time' and what David Harvey (1989) has referred to as 'time-space compression'. What is involved here is a sense of the shrinking of distances through the dramatic reduction in the time taken, either physically (for instance, via air travel) or representationally (via the transmission of electronically mediated information and images), to cross them. At another level of analysis connectivity shades into the idea of spatial proximity via the idea of the 'stretching' of social relations across distance (Giddens 1990, 1994a, b). The discourse of globalization is replete with metaphors of global proximity, of a 'shrinking world': from Marshall McLuhan's famous 'global village' to the United Nations' recent coining of the term 'Our Global Neighbourhood' to describe an emerging world-political context. All such metaphors and images derive their sense of increasing intimacy precisely out of the extension and the elaboration of different modalities of connectivity. But proximity/intimacy is not the same thing as connectivity: it is at best an elaboration, at worst a slippage.

Proximity has its own truth as a description of the condition of global modernity and this is generally of either a phenomenological or a metaphorical order. In the first case it describes a common conscious *appearance* of the world as more intimate, more compressed, more part of everyday reckoning – for example in our experience of rapid transport or our mundane use of media technologies to bring distant images into our most intimate local spaces. In the second, it conveys the increasing immediacy and consequentiality of real distanciated relations metaphorically. Here the connections that affect our lives (for example, the financial networks that tie our bank accounts into the global capitalist market or shared global environmental threats like 'global warming' which we confront) are made sense of *as though* they really bring us into closer contact. Proximity, then, takes us beyond the 'empirical' condition of connectivity. It is not that this language is misleading or invalid, but it is nevertheless important to maintain the distinction between this idea and the idea of connectivity.

For the condition of connectivity not only underwrites the notion of proximity, but places its own stamp on the way we understand global 'closeness'. Being connected means being close in very specific ways: the experience of proximity afforded by these connections coexists with an undeniable, stubbornly enduring *physical distance* between places and people in the world, which the technological and social transformations of globalization have not conjured away. In a globalized world, people in Spain really do continue to be 5,500 miles away from people in Mexico, separated, just as the Spanish conquistadores were in the sixteenth century, by a huge, inhospitable and perilous tract of ocean. What connectivity means is that we now experience this distance in different ways. We think of such distant places as routinely accessible, either representationally through communications technology or the mass media, or physically, through the expenditure of a relatively small amount of time (and, of course, of money) on a transatlantic flight. So Mexico City is no longer meaningfully 5,500 miles from Madrid: it is eleven hours' flying time away.

One way indeed of thinking about the particular sense of proximity produced by a 'technical' modality of connectivity is to consider the transformation of spatial experience into temporal experience that is characteristic of airline journeys. Planes are truly time capsules. When we board them we enter a self-contained and independent temporal regime which seems designed to remove our experience almost entirely from the business of ultra-high-speed movement through the air. The familiar sequence of take-off routine, distribution of newspapers, complimentary drinks, meals, sale of duty-free goods and in-flight movies all focus us on the internal time-frame of the cabin. So, phenomenologically, our 'journey' is one through this familiar sequence of time rather than through space. Going from London to Madrid is one mealtime; from Madrid to Mexico two mealtimes, a movie and a period of sleep. And so forth for the longer hauls. It is only when we occasionally look out of the window, perhaps to trace a coastline, that we might fleetingly grasp a sense of the vast tracts of distance that we are actually passing over. And the sense of the enormity of this space, linking quickly to discomforting thoughts of our vulnerability, probably discourages us from dwelling on this external reality.[1] Much more comforting to focus on the flight data display within the cabin, constantly translating thousands of kilometres into 'hours to destination': our true lived reality. It is only very rarely indeed that the territory we fly over intrudes at all into the experience of airline travel. Perhaps the flight crew may draw our attention to some particular physical feature – 'On our left you can see Cape Cod' – but examples of any deeper sense of human territory are so rare as to appear eccentric: 'When an international flight crosses Saudi Arabia, the hostess announces that during the overflight the drinking of alcohol will be forbidden in the aircraft. This signifies the intrusion of territory into space. Land = society = nation = culture = religion: the equation of anthropological place, fleetingly inscribed in space' (Augé 1995: 116). Marc Augé interprets this as the brief intrusion of the thickness of culture into the 'non-place 'of the airline's space, but we can equally see it as emblematic of the curious penetration of an enclosed journey through *time* by externalities of *space* (territory) which seem entirely remote from, indeed irrelevant to, this experience.

After a few hours of this enclosed time-journey we arrive, clear customs, walk out of the terminal building and magically 'there we are', deposited in the same clothes in which we boarded (the tangible attachments to our not-so-distant home) into a strange environment, a different climate, probably a different language, certainly a different cultural tempo. What sort of 'proximity' does such a process involve? How, precisely has the connectivity provided by air travel brought us closer ? It undeniably makes distant places *accessible* without a great expense of time, energy or (relatively) money. It makes physical relocation a matter of routine – something often to be fitted into a few hours, a day or so at most. But this proximity is also surely a problematic one, born as it is out of the technologically achieved compression of space by time. For the space we traverse in these journeys through the routine sequence of 'cabin time' is not just physical distance but the social and cultural distance (Saudi Arabia = Islam = no alcohol) that 'real' material space preserves. The connectivity of air travel thus poses for us sharply the question of the overcoming of social-cultural distance.

From the suspended animation of the flight, then, we have to confront the cultural adjustment of arrival. Our experienced journey though time rather than space has not prepared us for the new reality of this place. We have not experienced the sense of the traversing of 'real' distance: the gradual changes of scene, the gradations in climate, the series of social interactions, the *longueurs,* the interruptions and pauses, the symbolical moments of border crossings and the sheer physicality which travel in the 'real time' of, say, a railway journey affords. This compression of distance has left us temporarily dislocated and we need to adjust to a reality which is immediate and challenging in its otherness, precisely because it is so accessible. One measure of the accomplishment of globalization, then, is how far the overcoming of physical distance is matched by that of cultural distance.

There are various ways in which we can think about this. The most obvious is to ask *how* different the place of arrival actually is, in the modern world, from the place of embarkation. This is to enter the discourse of cultural homogenization. The homogenization thesis presents globalization as synchronization to the demands of a standardized consumer culture, making everywhere seem more or less the same. So to assert cultural homogenization as a consequence of globalization is to move from connectivity through proximity to the supposition of global uniformity and ubiquity. As I shall argue in chapter 3, this is a precipitate and in many ways an unjustifiable movement. However, we can see how it has a certain plausibility, particularly when thought through in relation to the example of air travel. For there is no denying the similarity between air terminals worldwide. The exits and entrances to different cultural spaces are, as has often been remarked, curiously uniform and standardized. However, this observation may be of limited significance, since airports are pretty clearly special kinds of places defined by the functional demands of their business, which is precisely to minimize cultural difference in the interests of a functional commonality, smoothing the passage of international travellers. To decide whether the homogenization thesis really obtains you have to venture outside the security of the terminal and get progressively deeper into the dangerous cultural hinterland. This may be something that theorists are unwilling to do. For the encounter with the messiness and particularity of actual cultural practices is of course dangerous for theories – like the homogenization thesis – established at the distance of broad abstraction. Noting different disciplinary tendencies towards progressive levels of theoretical abstraction, Néstor García Canclini wryly observes that 'The anthropologist arrives in the city on foot, the sociologist by car and via the main highway, the communications specialist by plane' (1995: 4). The assertion of global homogenization of culture is a little like arriving by plane but never leaving the terminal, spending all one's time browsing amongst the global brands of the duty-free shops.

So, leaving aside the suppositions of broad cultural homogeniz-ation for the present, let us pursue the idea of the relation between connectivity and cultural proximity by thinking about the process of adjustment that occurs outside the airline terminal. The accomplish-ment of globalization appears here as a function of the ease with which this adjustment can be made. And this reveals some of the intrinsic 'unevenness' of globalization. At one end of a continuum of experience we might find the accomplished business-class passen-ger who displays his (mostly, 'his') credentials with the insouciance with which he enacts the social-cultural adjustments of arrival: the swift location of the taxi, the easy transit to the pre-booked inter-national hotel whilst gradually, comfortably, absorbing the changed scene, the assurance of finding all the facilities – faxes, CNN busi-ness news, international cuisine – that will allow him to function independently of context. For the orientation of business travel is actually to *minimize* cultural difference so as to allow the 'universal' practices of the international business culture to function smoothly. This is connectivity working functionally to achieve a manufactured form of 'proximity' experienced as universality. Distant places are culturally close for business executives because they are carefully negotiated according to the business in hand: international stand-ardization in the hotel and the board room, enhanced, perhaps, by some local colour in the evening's entertainment.

From the instrumental point of view of capitalism, then, connect-ivity works towards increasing a *functional* proximity. It doesn't make all places the same, but it creates globalized spaces and connecting corridors which ease the flow of capital (including its commodities and its personnel) by matching the time-space compression of con-nectivity with a degree of cultural 'compression'. This is certainly an important dimension of globalization. But it does not grasp the whole picture, and risks exaggerating the shading of connectivity into cultural proximity. What the business-class traveller does not typ-ically experience is the fine grain of everyday cultural practices defined by *locality* rather than globality and maintaining cultural difference in the face of encroaching connectivity. This culture does not reveal itself in five-star international hotels, but in the streets, the houses, the churches, the workplaces, the bars and the shops that lie beyond the business or tourist centres.

Such 'localities' are quite simply the places where people live their everyday lives: the day-to-day environments of 'home'. For some they may exist pressed hard up against the perimeter fence of the airfield and yet they are part of an entirely different cultural 'world' from that of the connectivity of air travel. And they are clearly not governed by the same immediate demands of an instrumental connectivity and standardization that organize international business culture. Entering such environments means entering the order of social life which feels the sway of local affairs more than the demands of globality, and which exhibits the particularity – the cultural difference – of 'locality'. When discussions of globalization raise (as most do) the 'global–local' relationship, this is the vast order of everyday life that they invoke.

Few business travellers stray into these environments (until, of course, they are returned to their own comfortable localities). So this level of cultural difference is often invisible when viewed from the perspective of the smooth-functioning globalization of capital. It is more likely to be encountered by less well-organized or resourced travellers: by labour migrants or perhaps by independent tourists on a low budget. In the global space of the terminal such people may appear less accomplished in the rituals of arrival, but their lack of resources means that they quickly penetrate deeper into the culture of locality: the bus rather than the taxi, a basic hotel in a working-class neighbourhood lacking the cultural 'insulation' provided by five-star status, the need to shop in cheap local stores. These travellers quickly become more accomplished hermeneuticians, testing out the real extents of cultural proximity outside of the enclaves of a global business culture. The journey into localities then is a journey into the challenging reality of cultural difference, posing the question of how far connectivity establishes 'proximity' beyond the technological modality of increasing access.

At this point we have to move beyond the example of air travel. Tracing the phenomenology of this modality of connectivity pushes us towards a 'high-profile' understanding of globalization which is seductive but restricted in its application. Jet travel is an intrinsic part of connectivity and, in its increasing commonplace integration into everyday life, demands attention as cultural experience. But obviously it reveals only one aspect of what connectivity implies. First because, despite its increasing ubiquity,[2] it is still restricted to *relatively* small numbers of people and, within this group, to an even smaller, more exclusive, cadre of frequent users. Many people in the most developed countries of the world have never been on an aeroplane, and this obviously applies to many millions in less developed countries. Air travel, like the use of the internet, could thus be seen as merely the globalization available to the affluent. And if this were so, it would lose much of its claim to be a *general* condition of our time. But, more significantly, the sense of global connectivity implied by this sort of high-profile globalizing technology pushes, as we have seen, towards a particular and exaggerated sense of proximity.

If connectivity really does imply proximity as a *general* social-cultural condition, this has to be understood in terms of a transformation of practice and experience which is felt *actually within localities* as much as in the increasing technological means of access to or egress from them. Lash and Urry (1994: 252) suggest that 'modern society is society on the move', and that 'the modern world is inconceivable without . . . new forms of long-distance transportation and travel.' I don't want to disagree with this, but I think it is also important not to exaggerate the way long-distance travel figures either in the lives of the majority of people in the world today or in the overall process of globalization. 'Local life' – contrasted here with the transient 'global life' of the space of the air terminal (or indeed the computer terminal) – is the vast order of human social existence which continues, because of the constraints of physical embodiment, to dominate even in a globalized world. Local life occupies the majority of time and space. Although the increasing ability to move – physically and representationally – between places is a highly significant mode of connectivity, it is ultimately subordinate to – indeed derivative of – the order of location in time and space which we grasp as 'home'. Globalization *is* transforming this local order, but the significance of this transformation reaches beyond the technological accomplishments of communications and transport. Putting it simply, connectivity means changing the nature of localities and not just occasionally lifting some people out of them. So I think a statement like 'the paradigmatic modern experience is that of rapid mobility over long distances '(Lash and Urry 1994: 253) needs to be treated with some caution. It might be nearer the mark to say that the paradigmatic experience of global modernity for most people – and this is not of course unrelated to the correlation between income and mobility – is that of staying in one place but experiencing the 'dis-placement' that global modernity *brings to them.*

To understand globalization in this way is to pay attention to the other modalities of connectivity that we have mentioned. In particular it is to grasp the 'proximity' that comes from the networking of social relations across large tracts of time-space, causing distant events and powers to penetrate our local experience. It is to understand how someone may face unemployment as a result of 'downsizing' decisions made at a company head office on another continent, or how the food we find in our supermarkets is radically different today from twenty years ago because of the complex interaction between cosmopolitan taste and the global economics of the food industry, or of how our very sense of cultural belonging – of being 'at home'– may be subtly transfigured by the penetration of globalizing media into our everyday lives. It is these sorts of transformation that I shall mainly be concerned with in the chapters that follow.

Connectivity and Global Unicity

But now I want to turn, briefly, to another significant elaboration/ slippage from the core idea of connectivity. This is the idea that connectivity is globally encompassing and thus implies a certain 'unicity': a sense that the world is becoming, for the first time in history, a single social and cultural setting. Whereas it was in the past possible to understand social and cultural processes and practices as a set of local, relatively 'independent' phenomena, globalization makes the world a 'single place'. Obvious examples of this are the way in which the economic affairs of nation-states are locked into a global capitalist economy, or how the environmental effects of local industrial processes can rapidly become global problems.

In a strict sense, however, the idea of the world becoming one place is only contingently related to the idea of increasing connectivity. Although it is plausible to speculate that the rapid development of networks of interconnection will eventually encompass all of human society, this is by no means a logical entailment of the idea. Despite its reach, few would dare to claim that the complex connectivity of globalization currently extends in any profound way to every single person or place on the planet, and speculation on its spread must surely be tempered by the many countervailing trends towards social and cultural division that we see around us.

Nevertheless we also have to recognize a certain pull in the direction of the 'unitary' both in the concept of globalization and in the empirical processes it describes. The term 'global' itself has powerful connotations of wholeness and inclusiveness deriving both from its metaphorical usage (global as 'total') and from the sheer semantics of geometric form: for example in the connection of terms like 'encompassing' with the spherical form of the earth. Globalization as a concept, then, surely has a connotational force of 'tending towards unicity', and if the empirical state of connectivity we have identified has no such implications, then it simply looks as though, with 'globalization', we have all somehow got hold of the wrong word! What we require is a way of thinking through the implic-, ations of unicity that doesn't fetch up in more controversial slippages: unicity's shading into either 'uniformity' or 'unity'.

Roland Robertson's extensive work on globalization has centred on these problems and he offers a sophisticated formulation of the idea of 'the compression of the world into a "single place"' (1992: 6). Whilst maintaining that, 'the trends towards the unicity of the world are, when all is said and done, inexorable' (1992: 26), Robertson provides a model which disarms some of the immediate criticisms that such a view might attract. In essence Robertson's sense of global unicity is of a *context* which increasingly determines social relations and simultaneously of a *frame of reference* within which social agents increasingly figure their existence, identities and actions. For Robertson, then, global unicity does not imply a simplistic uniformity – something like a 'world culture'. Rather, it is a complex social and phenomenological condition – the 'global-human condition' – in which different orders of human life are brought into articulation with one another. He identifies four such orders: individual human beings, national societies, the 'world system of societies' and the overarching collectivity of 'humankind'. Globalization, for him, is the increasing interaction between these orders of human life, and so 'the world as a single place' implies the transformation of these forms of life as they are increasingly positioned against, and forced to take account of, each other. This is neither the unicity of homogenization nor a naive sense of emergent global (comm)unity. Indeed, far from suggesting an unproblematic process of integration, Robertson's model of unicity is one in which social and cultural difference may become accentuated precisely as it is identified in relation to the 'world as a whole'.

As an example, we can consider how Robertson's approach copes with the obvious objection to the broad idea of global unicity: the many counter-instances of fragmentation in the modern world – racial and ethnic hostilities, economic protectionism, religious fundamentalism and so on. Robertson's response is to point to a significant aspect of these counter-instances: the fact that they are 'reflexively monitored'. Taking the example of contemporary economic protectionism he argues that

> Compared to the older protectionisms and autarkies of the eighteenth
> and nineteenth centuries . . . the new ones are more self-consciously
> situated within a globewide system of global rules and regulations

concerning economic trade and a consciousness of the global economy
as a whole. This certainly does not mean that protectionism will be
overcome by such factors, but it does mean that relevant parties, including 'average citizens', are increasingly constrained to think in
terms, not necessarily favourable terms, of the world as a whole.
(Robertson 1992: 26)

For Robertson, then, the structures of global connectivity combine
with a pervasive *awareness* of this situation to raise any local events
inevitably to the horizon of a single world. A similar case might be
made for the 'cultural protectionism' implicit in religious fundamentalism, which may be read as a *self-conscious* defence of 'traditional'
beliefs, values and practices precisely defined by the undermining
of tradition threatened by global compression.

One of the great strengths of Robertson's approach is in providing
a conceptual framework which preserves the important sense of
globalization as involving wholeness and inclusiveness – as context
– whilst allowing it to cope with the empirical complexities of a world
which seems to display simultaneous processes of integration and
differentiation. The sort of world in which the technological connectivity of the internet can be used – as in the current proliferation of
'sectarian' websites – for the aggressive assertion of ethnic, religious
or racial differences. So I think Robertson is basically correct to see
globalization in terms of an underlying unicity. This is not just because of the sophistication of his model, but because there is also an
urgent political need to retain the idea. As connectivity reaches into
localities, it transforms local lived experience but it also confronts
people with a world in which their fates undeniably *are* bound together in a single global frame. This is clear in terms of the economic
integrations of the global market or of global environmental risk
which, as Ulrich Beck (1992: 47) puts it, 'makes the utopia of a world
society a little more real or at least more urgent'. Connectivity thus
supposes unicity as a cultural-political principle. Local experience
has to be raised to the horizon of a 'single world' if we are to understand it, and local practices and lifestyles increasingly need to be
examined and evaluated in terms of their global consequences.

Culture as a Dimension of Globalization

Most of the foregoing discussion has been within a broadly cultural
'register', distinguishable in its vocabulary and its stress from that

of, say, economics or politics. But how precisely should we think of culture as a concept and an entity in relation to globalization? One common answer is to see it as a 'dimension' of globalization. Globalization is now widely regarded as a 'multidimensional' phenomenon – on the surface an unproblematic description but, taken seriously enough, one with demanding implications for (not least, cultural) analysis.

The Multidimensionality of Globalization

Multidimensionality is closely related to the idea of complex connectivity. For the complexity of the linkages established by globalization extends to phenomena which social scientists have laboured to separate out into the categories into which we now, familiarly, break down human life: the economic, the political, the social, the interpersonal, the technological, the environmental, the cultural and so forth. Globalization arguably confounds such taxonomy.

Take the example of an environmental issue like ozone depletion caused by the use of chlorofluorocarbons (CFCs) in aerosol sprays or refrigerators. The recognition of the effects of these chemicals on the earth's protective ozone layer established a prime example of a global problem, one involving, as Steven Yearley says, the 'compression of the globe'. This in the sense that some of the main (if unknowing) culprits – deodorant users and furniture polish sprayers in the dense centres of population of the developed world – were producing pollution which could 'despoil the environment of [their] neighbours, thousands of kilometres away on the planet' – most intensely at the polar regions (Yearley 1996: 27). The CFC problem is certainly one of connectivity in this direct geographical sense. But it is also one which, in its complex ramifications, links together a number of interpretative discourses. It is obviously a technological matter for which a technical 'solution' in the form of alternative chemical propellants was quickly developed. But the adoption of this technical solution raised a whole raft of international political issues in the attempt to achieve a treaty on the regulation of CFC use: the 1987 'Montreal Protocol'. During these negotiations differences emerged between the economic interests of CFC-producing nations and those that were only consumers of the products. These problems were amplified in the case of 'First World' as opposed to 'Third World' interests,[3] where universal compliance raised the vexed question of economic assistance from the developed world as an incentive for poor countries such as India to make the transition to non-CFC technologies (Yearley 1996: 107ff). The CFC issue thus linked together political, legal, scientific, environmental-ethical and economic discourses. And there are several senses in which it was also a deeply cultural issue: for example the change in cultural sensibility ('green thinking') it involved as people began to link mundane aspects of their lifestyle with global consequences, or the change in cultural practices it produced as sunbathing suddenly became a matter of risk, linked with the danger of cancer, one of the great symbolic fears of the developed world.

Examples like this demonstrate that globalizing phenomena are, of their essence, complex and multidimensional, putting pressure on the conceptual frameworks by which we have traditionally grasped the social world. However, given both the difficulty of accounting simultaneously for all the aspects of such phenomena and the power of academic disciplines in the organization of knowledge, it is not surprising that attempts persist to account for globalization in 'one-dimensional' terms. People come to the issue from different traditions of thought and with different priorities and informing principles and these, understandably, tug back from complexity to the relative 'simplicity' of master concepts such as capitalism, the nation-state and so on. But if we take multidimensionality seriously, such accounts are bound to misrepresent globalization: lose the complexity and you have lost the phenomenon.

To illustrate this we can briefly consider two approaches, very different in their analysis and their politics, but twinned in terms of their conceptualization of globalization within the single domain of the economic – as a phenomenon of the capitalist market.

The first of these is drawn from the literature of corporate business strategy. One of the most prolific writers in this mould, the Japanese business strategist Kenichi Ohmae argues that the nation-state is becoming irrelevant seen from the point of view of the capitalist market. He claims that 'traditional nation states have become unnatural, even impossible, business units in a global economy.' Rather, he argues, we should think of a world of regional economies 'where the real work gets done and the real markets flourish': 'What defines [these] is not the location of their political borders but the fact that they are the right size and scale to be the true natural business units in today's global economy. Theirs are the borders – and the connections – that matter in a borderless world' (Ohmae 1995: 5).

The tendency to see the world simply as a business opportunity is unsurprising within this discourse. On this reading, people like Ohmae are just understanding the idea of globalization within their own discursive universe – a coherent, albeit a rather impoverished and instrumental one. But it is not quite so self-contained as this, for this discourse inevitably spills over into other realms. Not only does Ohmae obviously make claims about the political sphere of the nation-state system which are highly controversial (Anderson 1995; McGrew and Lewis 1992; Cerny 1996), he also intervenes in a cultural discourse. For example, he argues that the global market is producing, 'a cross-border civilization'. This is based in the (predictable) claim about 'convergence of consumer tastes and preferences': 'Global brands of blue jeans, colas, and stylish athletic shoes' (1995: 29). But he goes further than this simple consumption-convergence thesis, to argue that more profound cultural/generational cleavages are occurring, for instance in Japanese society, as the 'Nintendo kids' – Japanese teenagers of the 1990s – have learned a different set of perceptions and social values from those of their parents and grandparents. This generation he argues is much less accepting of traditional Japanese notions of authority and conformity, much more culturally open, questioning and creative: 'Everything can be explored, rearranged, reprogrammed ... Everything, finally, is open to considered choice, initiative, creativity – and daring' (p. 36). This shift derives, Ohmae claims, from the technological modality of connectivity: the use of computers, computer games and interactive multimedia: 'watching how a kid from another culture whom you've never seen before reveals character and mind-set through programming style' (p. 37).

The sort of cultural inferences Ohmae draws are deeply coloured by the unidimensionality of his framework. The emergent values he recognizes in Japanese kids are pretty plainly those of enterprise capitalism, and he paints a predictably Panglossian picture of 'the new melting pot of today's cross-border civilization' (p. 39). But the fault here is not just ideological: it involves sociological reductionism and mono-causal logics precisely characterizing a one-dimensional approach.

Some of the sharpest criticism of Ohmae and the position he represents comes in Hirst and Thompson's sceptical analysis of the thesis of economic globalization, *Globalization in Question* (1996). Hirst and Thompson specifically challenge the connected ideas of the transnationalization of the economy and the redundancy of the nation-state, as conceived in 'extreme globalization theorists like Ohmae' (1996: 185). Without examining the details of their critique, we can notice the self-consciously narrow terms within which it is constructed. Hirst and Thompson are *principled* one-dimensional analysts, deliberately defining globalization as a function of economics.

In arguing that the economic globalization which thinkers like Ohmae present 'is largely a myth' (1996: 2),[4] Hirst and Thompson are extremely careful to point out the limits of their critique. They recognize the 'vast and diverse' literature on globalization and the different understandings of the process in different disciplinary contexts. But despite this, they claim that a critique of the economic dimension is also fatal for all other understandings: '[W]e believe that without the notion of a truly globalized economy many of the other consequences adduced in the domains of culture and politics would either cease to be sustainable or become less threatening' (p. 3). But this is clearly to fall towards a reductionism in which the economy drives all else before it. Hirst and Thompson pay lip service to the idea that globalization is multiform, but then ignore any of the implications of this, on the assumption that the whole edifice of globalization theory is built upon the 'untenable assumptions' of the sort of economic position they criticize.

And, in fact, the failure to pursue the multidimensional nature of globalization has direct consequences for some of their claims about its 'mythical' nature. For they go on to argue, very properly, that accepting hyperbolic claims about global capitalist power can be politically disabling: 'One can only call the political impact of "globalization" the pathology of over-diminished expectations . . . we have a myth which exaggerates the degree of our helplessness in the face of contemporary economic forces' (1996: 6). Now such arguments have considerable force when directed at the rhetoric of globalization which views it simply as the untrammelled power of transnational capitalism. But to accept the *definition* of globalization in these narrow economic terms is to share the one-dimensionality of the positions they criticize. For if globalization is understood in terms of simultaneous, complexly related processes in the realms of economy, politics, culture, technology and so forth, we can see that it involves all sorts of contradictions, resistances and countervailing forces. Indeed the understanding of globalization as involving a 'dialectic' of opposed principles and tendencies – the local and the global, universalism and particularism – is now common, particularly in accounts which foreground cultural issues (Axford 1995; Featherstone 1995; Giddens 1990; Hall 1992; Lash and Urry 1994; Robertson 1995; Sreberny-Mohammadi 1991). None of this is to diminish the importance of the economic in the process of globalization. The dynamics of capitalism in each of its moments of the production, circulation and consumption of commodities is heavy with implications for our increasing interconnectedness. However this does not mean that the economic analysis of transnational capitalism is the royal road to grasping globalization.

But if we insist on the complexly related multidimensionality of globalization, what does this imply for a 'cultural approach' ?

The Cultural Dimension

Taking multidimensionality seriously can actually be *too* demanding. The sheer scale and complexity of the empirical reality of global connectivity is something which defies attempts to encompass it: it is something we can only grasp by cutting into it in various ways. What this suggests is that we are pretty much bound to lose *some* of the complexity of globalization in any feasible account of it, but it doesn't follow that an account of one dimension – one way of slicing into globalization – has to be a 'one-dimensional' account. For there are better and worse ways of doing this.

A bad way would be to start from the premise that the dimension under consideration is the master discourse, the domain that 'things really all boil down to', the logic that unlocks all else. A better way would be to identify the specific way of describing the world that is contained within an economic, a political or a cultural discourse, and to try to draw out an understanding of globalization within these terms, whilst always denying them conceptual priority: pursuing one dimension in the self-conscious recognition of multidimensionality. This sort of deliberately anti-reductionist analysis should also make us sensitive to the points at which different dimensions interconnect and interact.

So it must be for cultural analysis. Particularly so since the concept of culture is so 'encompassing' that it can easily be taken as the ultimate level of analysis – isn't everything in the end 'cultural'? Well, no. Or, at least it gets us nowhere to think of culture in this way, as simply a description of a 'total way of life'. For, as Clifford Geertz once memorably described it (Geertz 1973: 4), this leads to *'pot-au-feu'* theorizing – the throwing of anything and everything into the conceptual stew that is the 'complex whole' of human existence.

The dimension of culture has to be made more specific, and yet this has proved difficult to achieve, since culture is anyway such a complex and elusive idea (Williams 1981; Clifford 1988; Thompson 1990; Tomlinson 1991; McGuigan 1992). I do not, however, intend to dwell here on problems of definition. There are some fairly widely accepted features of 'the cultural' which we can build upon to get a reasonable sense of what properly belongs to the cultural dimension of globalization.

In the first place culture can be understood as the order of life in which human beings construct meaning through practices of symbolic representation. If this sounds a rather dry generalization, it nevertheless allows us to make some useful distinctions. Very broadly, if we are talking about the economic we are concerned with practices by which humans produce, exchange and consume material goods; if we are discussing the political we mean practices by which power is concentrated, distributed and deployed in societies; and if we are talking culture, we mean the ways in which people make their lives, individually and collectively, meaningful by communicating with each other.

The important thing is that to grasp these as 'dimensions' of social life is not to see them as entirely *discrete* spheres of activity: people don't turn from 'doing the economic' to 'doing the cultural' in the way that we might imagine them ending work for the day and turning to leisure activities. If this were so then we would have to suppose that no one ever derived any meaning from the activities by which they earned a living. And yet this way of thinking is quite deeply engrained in common-sense views of culture referring to the practices and products of art, literature, music, film and so on.[5] These are all important *forms* in which specific meanings are generated, but they will not do to define, exclusively, the cultural dimension.

Rather, we have to unravel from the complexly intertwined practices of the cultural, the economic and the political, a sense of the *purpose* of the cultural – that of making life meaningful. Now everything that is symbolizable is, in a broad sense, meaningful. There are, for example, vast amounts of symbolizations attaching to economic practices, for instance the technical language of the production process (such as the specifications of a car engine) or of the market-place (such as the daily announcement of share prices). But such symbolizations do not, for me, press to the heart of the 'cultural', and I am happy to cede most of this area of *instrumental symbolization* to the domains of the economic, the technical and so on.

On the other hand, many of the symbolic representations found in marketing, whilst having ultimately an instrumental (economic) end, are, for my purposes, very properly cultural. Advertising texts, for instance, though part of what Horkheimer and Adorno (1979) referred to disparagingly as the 'culture industry' linked to the instrumental purposes of capitalism, remain significant cultural texts. The way people make use of advertising texts may often be similar to the way they use novels or films. This is because they offer narratives (however ideologically suspect) of how life may be lived, references to shared notions of identity, appeals to self-image, pictures of 'ideal' human relations, versions of human fulfilment, happiness and so on.

This is the sense of the cultural dimension that I want to stress, with the emphasis on meanings as ends in themselves, as distinct from simply instrumental meanings. To use a slightly high-blown formulation we could think of culture in this sense as the realm of 'existentially significant' meaning. By this I don't mean to emphasize the 'problem of existence' as formulated either in the ontological anxieties of existentialist philosophy, or yet in the range of formal religious responses to the human condition. However important these may be for the way many people interpret their lives – and notwithstanding the significance of globalization for religious institutions (Beyer 1994) – these are, as it were, too specialized existential discourses to grasp what I am after in the idea of existentially significant meaning. We have to add to this Raymond Williams's famous dictum that 'culture is ordinary' (Williams 1989; McGuigan 1992). Williams first used this phrase of course in opposition to the elite sense of culture as a rarefied 'special' form of life available only to the few through the 'cultivation' of certain sensibilities. Culture is ordinary, then, in the 'democratic anthropological' sense that it describes 'a whole way of life': it is not the exclusive property of the privileged, but inclusive of all manner of everyday practices. But for Williams this sense coexisted, importantly, with a sense of culture as providing 'personal meanings': 'The questions I ask about our culture are questions about our general and common purposes, yet also questions about deep personal meanings. Culture is ordinary, in every society and in every mind' (Williams 1989: 4).

The principle that 'culture is ordinary' makes what I am calling questions of existential significance matters that every human being routinely addresses in their everyday practices and experiences. It is not a question of some symbolic practices being more 'edifying' than others, getting closer to the quick of the human situation, being more concerned with the big questions of life. Nor is it a question of cultural or aesthetic *value* in relation to particular cultural 'texts'. The Tao-te-Ching, the late quartets of Beethoven, Picasso's *Guernica*, or Robert Mapplethorpe's photographs are no more and no less 'cultural texts' than *NYPD Blue*, a Spice Girls album, the media coverage of the death of Princess Diana, football 'fanzines' and the latest Levis advert. All qualify to the extent that people draw upon them in making sense of their existence. And, indeed, we have to include on this reading of culture all sorts of practices which do not directly hinge on a relationship between a 'reader' and a 'text': the trip around the local supermarket aisles, or to the restaurant, the sports hall, the dance club or the garden centre, the conversation in the bar or on the street corner. Culture for my purposes refers to all these mundane practices that directly contribute to people's ongoing 'life-narratives': the stories by which we, chronically, interpret our existence in what Heidegger calls the 'thrownness' of the human situation.

When we slice into complex connectivity from this perspective, what we are concerned with is how globalization alters the context of meaning construction: how it affects people's sense of identity, the experience of place and of the self in relation to place, how it impacts on the shared understandings, values, desires, myths, hopes and fears that have developed around locally situated life. The cultural dimension therefore spans what Anthony Giddens has called both the 'out-thereness' and the 'in-hereness' of globalization: the connection between vast systemic transformations, and transformations in our most local and intimate 'worlds' of everyday experience (Giddens 1994b: 95).

Culture Distinguished from its Technologies

One particular reason for stressing this understanding of the cultural dimension is that discussions of globalization often take 'culture' to mean something rather different, eliding it with the globalizing communications and media *technologies* via which cultural representations are transmitted. This tendency is perhaps most evident in the widely distributed 'journalistic' discourse on globalization which often seems obsessed with the 'Gee-Whizzery' of new communications technologies: the internet, the global information superhighway and so on. Now though communication technologies are absolutely central to the globalization process, their development is clearly not *identical* with cultural globalization. In fact their impact has both broader and narrower implications. Broader because they have a significant role – as technology itself and, thus, in my sense, as transmitters of *instrumental* symbolizations – in *all* the dimensions in which globalization proceeds. An example of this is in the increasing integration of global news-gathering practices and the provision of market intelligence in global economic trading. But they are *narrower* because the media form only part of the total process by which symbolic meaning construction proceeds and only one of the forms in which globalization is experienced culturally. The mass media and other forms of mediated communication are increasingly significant in our daily lives, but they are not the only source of a globalized cultural experience. And, equally, not everything that can be said about the globalization of media and communications systems is directly relevant to discussions of culture.

An example of the conflation of culture and its technologies is, rather surprisingly, found in the otherwise sophisticated account of globalization provided by Anthony Giddens. Towards the end of a long discussion of the institutional dimensions of globalization, Giddens mentions, '... a further and quite fundamental aspect of globalization, which lies behind each of the various institutional dimensions ... and which might be referred to as cultural globalization' (1990: 77). But the reader looking for an account of culture as meaning construction will be disappointed: what Giddens discusses is how 'mechanized technologies of communication have dramatically influenced all aspects of globalization'. He stresses the importance of pooled information in the global extension of the institutions of modernity and, significantly, takes the 'instrumental' context of global money markets as his prime example. This, and the fact that his discussion of 'culture' (scarcely one page) is tucked away at the end of a long discussion of industrialism, suggests an interest in the 'disembedding' properties of technologies of communication rather than in culture in our sense of the social production of existentially significant meaning.

It is fair to say that Giddens has not paid all that much attention to the *concept* of culture in his work on globalization, and this may account for this rather offhand conflation of culture with communication technologies. And, to be fair, there are many other points in his discussion, which we shall come to in the following chapter, that suggest, albeit indirectly, a more nuanced view of the cultural. But what this example illustrates is the importance of tying down quite firmly the rather elastic and accommodating concept of 'culture' in relation to globalization. I certainly agree with Giddens that the cultural dimension is 'fundamental' to globalization, but I want to understand this in much broader terms than those available simply from the analysis of the impact of communications technologies – however significant these may be for the institutional and systemic connectivity of our world. And now I shall try to suggest how this may be done.

Why Culture Matters for Globalization

Culture matters for globalization in the obvious sense that it is an intrinsic aspect of the whole process of complex connectivity. But we can go further than this. We can try to understand the sense in which culture is actually *constitutive* of complex connectivity. Again there are better and worse ways of going about this.

One obvious hazard is to fall into arguments that assert a degree of causal priority to culture, privileging this dimension in just the same way we saw Hirst and Thompson do for the economy. An example of this is found in Malcolm Waters's account in which, having set up the standard economy/polity/culture distinction in terms, respectively, of sets of material, political and symbolic exchange relations, he goes on to claim, somewhat provocatively, that

> *material exchanges localize; political exchanges internationalize; and symbolic exchanges globalize.* It follows that the globalization of human society is contingent on the extent to which cultural relations are effective relative to economic and political arrangements. We can expect the economy and the polity to be globalized to the extent that they are culturalized, that is to the extent that the exchanges that take place within them are accomplished symbolically. We would also expect that the degree of globalization is greater in the cultural arena than either of the other two. (Waters 1995: 9–10 – emphasis in original)

Waters's justification for so privileging the cultural is, briefly, that the nature of symbolic exchanges means they are inherently less limited by the constraints of place than either material (economic) or political exchanges. He argues, for example, that material exchanges are 'rooted in localized markets, factories, offices and shops', simply because of the practical necessity or the cost advantage of physical proximity in the production and exchange of goods and services. In contrast to these constraints which 'tend to tie economic exchanges to localities', cultural symbols 'can be produced anywhere and at any time and there are relatively few resource constraints on their production and reproduction' (Waters 1995: 9). Culture is thus intrinsically more globalizing on account of the ease of the 'stretching' of the relations involved and the inherent mobility of cultural forms and products.

This is scarcely a convincing argument. For clearly there are all sorts of examples – the impact of multinational corporations, the international division of labour (involved for example in the production of automobiles or in the clothing industry), the increasing phenomenon of labour migration, financial and commodity trading, the significance of international trading regulatory agreements and bodies such as the GATT and now the World Trade Organization – that testify to the globalization of the 'material exchanges' involved in economic relations. Obviously there are lots of instances in which the production, exchange and consumption of commodities *do* remain relatively local activities, but a trip around the neighbourhood mall will quickly reveal how much is not local produce. It is of course true that all production has to be situated *somewhere* in the world. But as celebrated examples such as the intensive production of mange-tout peas in countries like Zimbabwe exclusively for the European market, or the journey of Australian parsnips 17,000 miles to the UK to provide year-round availability show, this is no real inhibitant to the globalization process. Equally the idea that symbolic exchanges float free of material constraints might suggest a strangely 'idealist' view – for don't symbolizations ultimately have to take material form – as books, CDs, celluloid, electron flows on to TV screens and VDUs and so forth? Although, obviously, electronically mediated 'products' are technically much more mobile, all the material production processes related to these various cultural forms surely suppose similar constraints to those involved in any other form of commodity production.

Such objections cast doubt on the plausibility of Waters's rather swashbuckling generalizations about the localizing and globalizing properties of various social spheres.[6] But on closer examination, what he turns out to be arguing is anyway something rather more modest: simply that those sectors of the economy that are most symbolically mediated or as he puts it 'tokenized' – for example financial markets – are the ones most amenable to globalization. This is a far more plausible claim, for clearly the movement of symbolic tokens like money by electronic means is far easier than the movement of large quantities of root vegetables.

But does this in any way support the claim of culture to predominance in the globalization process? I don't think so. Not, at least, in our preferred sense. For Waters is using culture here with the stress firmly on *instrumental symbolization* rather than on existentially significant meaning construction, and so trading on the elision warned against earlier. We can quite agree that some economic processes are becoming more 'tokenized' but this simply means they are more *informationalized* – the symbolizations employed are intrinsic to the economic process – not that they are 'culturalized'. To be more culturalized would mean that the processes and practices by which people furnish for themselves meaningful accounts of their social existence are becoming somehow more closely articulated with the economic sphere. This may in fact be so, but the argument needs to be based in something other than problematic claims about the 'dematerialized' nature of symbolic goods. Waters, then, may turn out to be right about the overall significance of culture in globalization, but for the wrong reasons.

The problem of understanding culture as constitutive of globalization turns on how we conceive of culture as having consequences. 'Culture is not a power, something to which social events can be causally attributed', says Clifford Geertz, and this is surely right to the extent that we should think of cultural processes as the construction of meanings, in Geertz's terms, as 'a context in which [events] can be intelligibly . . . described' (Geertz 1973: 14). To think in directly 'causal' terms pushes us towards the confusion of culture with its technologies. However this does not mean that culture is not *consequential*. It is certainly so in that meaning construction informs individual and collective actions which are *themselves* consequential. People do not produce meanings within some entirely separate interpretative channel which, as it were, runs parallel with other social practices but leaves them untouched. Cultural signification and interpretation constantly orientates people, individually and collectively, towards particular actions. Often our actions may be fairly instrumental ones, following a logic of practical or economic necessity, but even here they are undertaken within the 'context' of a broader cultural understanding. Even the most basic instrumental actions of satisfying bodily needs are not in this sense outside culture: in certain circumstances (slimming, religious fasting, hunger strikes) the decision to eat or to starve is a cultural decision.

One way to think about the consequentiality of culture for globalization, then, is to grasp how culturally informed 'local' actions can have globalizing consequences. Complex connectivity is not just the tighter integration of social institutions, but involves the integration of individual and collective actions into the way that institutions actually work. Thus cultural connectivity introduces the idea of the *reflexivity* of global-modern life.

The central insight of theories of reflexivity (Beck 1997; Beck, Giddens and Lash 1994; Giddens 1990) is the *recursive* nature of social activity: the various ways in which social entities may be said to act 'back upon' themselves, to adjust to incoming information about their behaviour or their workings. The idea builds upon the inherent reflexivity of human beings: the capacity we all have to be constantly aware of ourselves *as acting* in the process of acting, to 'routinely "keep in touch" with the grounds of what [we] do as an integral element of doing it '(Giddens 1990: 36). Social theories of reflexivity attempt to articulate how this sort of self-monitoring manifests itself at the level of social institutions, or rather the interface between social agents and institutions. In Giddens's account, this occurs in the phenomenon of 'institutional reflexivity': modern institutions are ones in which 'social practices are constantly examined and reformulated in the light of incoming information about those practices, thus constitutively altering their character' (Giddens 1990: 38). Modern institutions are thus increasingly, like human beings, 'learning entities'. It is this reflexive sensitivity of institutions in relation to inputs from human agents that marks the peculiar dynamism of modern social life and that defines the connectivity between a multiplicity of small individual local actions and the highest-level global structures and processes.

To illustrate this we can consider a claim that Giddens makes in relation to the 'local–global dialectic'. He writes that 'local lifestyle habits have become globally consequential. Thus my decision to buy a certain item of clothing has implications not only for the international division of labour but for the earth's ecosystems' (Giddens 1994a: 5). How might this be true ? Well, first, in the sense that the global clothing industry is a highly reflexive institution, attuned to the choices of a multiplicity of actors expressing themselves in the market-place though the cultural codes of fashion. Trace the consequences of the cultural choices made by a group of teenagers in a European shopping mall on a Saturday afternoon with their eyes on how they will look that evening in the local club: this uncovers a level of connectivity leading to the employment prospects of a sweatshop worker in the Philippines. And second, the connectivity implied is in the fact that clothing choices, like all consumption choices, have global ecological consequences in terms of the natural resources they consume and the industrial production processes they entail.

A world of complex connectivity (a global market-place, international fashion codes, an international division of labour, a shared eco-system) thus links the myriad small everyday actions of millions with the fates of distant, unknown others and even with the possible fate of the planet. All these individual actions are undertaken within the culturally meaningful context of local mundane lifeworlds in which dress codes and the subtle differentiations of fashion establish personal and cultural identity. The way in which these 'cultural actions' become globally consequential is the prime sense in which culture matters for globalization. To be sure, the complexity of this chain of consequences simultaneously entails the political, economic and technological dimensions of globalization. But the point is that the 'moment of the cultural' is indispensable in interpreting complex connectivity.

Thinking about globalization in its cultural dimension also discloses its essentially *dialectical* character in a particularly vivid way. The fact that individual actions are intimately connected with large structural-institutional features of the social world via reflexivity means globalization is not a 'one-way' process of the determination of events by massive global structures, but involves at least the possibility for local intervention in global processes. There exists a cultural politics of the global which we can grasp by continuing the example of the ecological consequences of local actions.

Though the consequentiality of routine lifestyle choices may not always be recognized – most of us surely don't shop habitually as 'ecoaware' consumers – there is nevertheless a trend in certain sections of all societies towards deliberate eco-friendly consumption practices, which is itself a manifestation of connectivity. The famous Green movement slogan 'Think globally, act locally' suggests a political strategy motivated by a very clear collective cultural narrative of what the 'good life' entails. This strategy involves the mobilization of agents – increasingly via sophisticated media campaigns – to achieve institutional changes at a global level (Lash 1994: 211). And if such a strategy is (sometimes) successful, it is because it draws on and appeals to very general cultural dispositions more than engagement with scientific-technical arguments over environmental problems.

For instance, Greenpeace's spectacular defeat of Shell UK over the deep-sea dumping of the Brent Spar oil platform in June 1995 was achieved by mobilizing public opinion – particularly in Germany, Denmark and The Netherlands – which directly threatened Shell's 'customer relations' at the filling stations. From the perspective of the Green movement this could be seen as a conspicuous success story of social reflexivity. But if we ask what lay behind the mobilization of public opinion, it seems likely that it was something other than the precise issues of the campaign itself – over which there was considerable confusion. For example, many of those boycotting Shell's filling stations apparently thought that the plan was to dump the platform in the North Sea – their 'locality' – rather than the Atlantic. Furthermore, Greenpeace later admitted to having been themselves misled about the actual composition of the chemicals on board the platform. There were in fact claims following the campaign that the media had been 'bounced' into providing favourable coverage of Greenpeace, along with emotive footage of the activists under siege by Shell's security staff, at the expense of the full complex scientific argument. The senior commissioning editor for the UK's Channel 4 claimed, 'The pictures provided to us [by Greenpeace] showed plucky helicopters riding into a fusillade of water canons. Try and write the analytical science into that.'[7]

However, we can understand all this differently if we see the Brent Spar campaign as appealing to people's ongoing life-narratives, rather than to specific environmental arguments whose technicalities few can anyway grasp. So what was, perhaps, most significant was the *symbolic* value of the occupation of the platform: a particular dramatization of a 'battle' against a generalized threat of environmental degradation that people experience as part of their everyday 'lifeworld'. Understood in this way, the strategy of Greenpeace is (at least in part) a cultural one. Even the issue of scientific accuracy could be seen as having cultural significance in the maintenance of general trust relations between Greenpeace (or Shell), the media and the public – as much as in terms of information or misinformation. As Scott Lash puts it, environmental politics now involve 'the social construction of reality' – 'a struggle in the media between environmental protest actors, business actors and policy-makers around a set of meanings to be disseminated among the lay public [and framing] their reality' (1994: 208). Environmental politics are thus *cultural* politics, dependent for their success on the degree to which they can tap into the horizon of relevance of local lifeworlds. So culture also matters for globalization in this sense: that it marks out a symbolic terrain of meaning-construction as the arena for global political interventions.

Why Globalization Matters for Culture

Globalization disturbs the way we conceptualize 'culture'. For culture has long had connotations tying it to the idea of a fixed locality. The idea of 'a culture' implicitly connects meaning construction with particularity and location. As Eade (1997: 25) notes, 'an emphasis on boundedness and coherence traditionally dominated the sociological treatment of the idea of culture', particularly in the functionalist tradition where collective meaning construction was dealt with largely as serving the purposes of social integration. So 'a culture' parallels the problematic notion of 'a society' as a bounded entity (Mann 1986) occupying a physical territory mapped as a political territory (predominantly the nation-state) and binding individual meaning constructions into this circumscribed social, political space. The connectivity of globalization is clearly threatening to such conceptualizations, not only because the multiform penetration of localities breaks into this binding of meanings to place, but because it undermines the thinking through which culture and fixity of location are originally paired.

In anthropology, James Clifford's work on 'travelling cultures' (Clifford 1992, 1997) has focused on prising culture apart from location. Writing of the 'practices of crossing and interaction that troubled the localism of many common assumptions about culture' he argues: 'In these assumptions authentic social existence is, or should be, centred in circumscribed places – like the gardens where the word "culture" derived its European meanings. Dwelling was understood to be the local ground of collective life, travel a supplement; roots always precede routes' (1997: 3). Clifford demonstrates how the practices of anthropological fieldwork have contributed to the localizing of the concept of culture: 'centering the *culture* around a particular locus, the *village*, and around a certain spatial practice of dwelling/research which itself depended on a complementary localization – that of the *field*' (1997: 20). So the traditional research methods of anthropology – the village taken as a 'manageable unit' for cultural analysis, the practice of ethnography as 'dwelling' with the community – have contributed to a synecdoche in which location (village) is taken for culture. And, Clifford argues, this has endured into contemporary ethnographic fieldwork practices where the locations may be, 'hospitals, labs, urban neighbourhoods, tourist hotels' rather than remote villages, but the informing assumption for the researcher and subject is one of 'localized dwelling'.

Clifford goes against the grain of this inheritance to think of culture as essentially *mobile* rather than static, to treat 'practices of displacement . . . as constitutive of cultural meanings'. And in this he raises something very close to the conceptual challenge globalization makes to culture. Culture cannot be thought of as having these inevitable *conceptual* ties to location, for meanings are equally generated by people 'on the move' and in the flows and connections between 'cultures'.

Yet the notion of 'travelling culture' can also be tendentious. It's not that we have to *reverse* the priority between 'roots and routes', insisting on the essence of culture as restless nomadic movement. Rather we need to see 'roots and routes' as always coexistent in culture, and both as subject to transformation in global modernity. To return to the earlier discussion of travel, we have to remember that a huge proportion of cultural experience is still for the majority the day-to-day experience of physical location, rather than of constant movement. In fact Clifford admits this point in describing an objection to the trope of 'travel', made by another anthropologist, Christina Turner. Turner pointed to the obvious limitations on movement that vast numbers are subject to – being 'kept in their place' by their class and gender position. Her ethnographic work with female Japanese factory workers, 'women who have not "travelled" by any standard definition', led her to question Clifford's stress on 'literal travel'. But these women's 'local' cultural experience and practice also disturbed the culture–locality connection: 'They do watch TV; they do have a global/local sense; they do contradict the anthropologist's typifications; and they don't simply enact a culture' (Clifford 1997: 28). In accepting this, Clifford concedes that the notion of travelling culture 'can involve forces that pass powerfully through – television, radio, tourists, commodities, armies' (ibid.).

This is precisely the point I want to stress: globalization promotes much more physical mobility than ever before, but the key to its cultural impact is in the transformation of localities themselves. It is important to keep to the fore the material conditions of physical embodiment and of political-economic necessity that 'keep people in their place', and so for me the transformation of culture is not grasped in the trope of travel but in the idea of *deterritorialization*. What I shall understand by this – as I explore it in chapter 4 – is that complex connectivity weakens the ties of culture to place. This is in many ways a troubling phenomenon, involving the simultaneous penetration of local worlds by distant forces, and the dislodging of everyday meanings from their 'anchors' in the local environment. Embodiment and the forces of material circumstance keep most of us, most of the time, situated, but in places that are changing around us and gradually, subtly, losing their power to define the terms of our existence. This is undoubtedly an uneven and often contradictory business, felt more forcibly in some places than others, and sometimes met by countervailing tendencies to re-establish the power of locality. Nevertheless deterritorialization is, I believe, the major cultural impact of global connectivity. And it's not all bad news.

For the final point to make is that connectivity also furnishes people with a *cultural resource* that they lacked before its expansion: a cultural awareness which is, in various senses, 'global'. Roland Robertson has always stressed that globalization intrinsically involves 'the intensification of consciousness of the world as a whole'(1992: 8) and Giddens (1991: 187) also argues that people's 'phenomenal worlds', though situated locally, 'for the most part are truly global'. This doesn't mean that we all experience the world as cultural cosmopolitans, much less that a 'global culture' is emerging. But it does imply that 'the global' increasingly exists as a cultural horizon within which we (to varying degrees) frame our existence. The penetration of localities which connectivity brings is thus double-edged: as it dissolves the securities of locality, it offers new understandings of experience in wider – ultimately global – terms.

Grasping the nature and significance of this global consciousness constitutes an important agenda in the cultural analysis of globalization. The Japanese women Christina Turner describes are surely not unusual in having a 'global/local sense' as part of their everyday life, and one obvious source of this is the images and information that flows to them – as to millions of us – through the routine use of globalizing media technologies like television. One task for cultural analysis is therefore to understand the 'phenomenology' of this global consciousness, particularly in the mediated form in which it mostly appears to us. And it is not difficult to see that the horizon of significance made available by the connectivity of media technologies suggests possibilities not only for the reconstitution of the cultural meanings and identities depleted by deterritorialization, but also for associated forms of global cultural politics. A sense of our mutual interdependency combined with the means for communicating across distance is producing new forms of cultural/political alliance and solidarity. These are undoubtedly weakly developed at present in comparison with the concentrations of power within, for instance, transnational capitalism. But as some argue (Castells 1997), the global perspective of the 'new social movements' may prove to be embryonic forms of a wider, more powerful order of social resistance to the repressive aspects of globalization. However this turns out, it is clear that the reconfiguration of cultural experience that connectivity produces will be crucial to the possibilities of a cosmopolitan politics. Globalization therefore matters for culture in the sense that it brings the negotiation of cultural experience into the

centre of strategies for intervention in the other realms of connectivity: the political, the environmental, the economic.

This concludes the broad discussion of the scope of cultural
globalization. The chapters which follow pursue the cultural implications of complex connectivity along a number of different traject-
ories: pursuing the theme of unicity into ideas of a global culture
(chapter 3); examining the 'lifting off' of cultural experience
from locality (chapter 4); interrogating the significance of mediated
experience in globalized culture (chapter 5) and finally discussing
the role of culture in an emergent 'cosmopolitan' politics (chapter 6).
But before this, we turn in the following chapter to arguments that
locate globalization within the historical and theoretical context of
social modernity, and try to draw out the cultural implications of
this way of thinking about the complex connectivity which defines
our times.

2

Global Modernity

Globalization refers us to an empirical condition: the complex connectivity evident everywhere in the world today. But this condition does not appear to us in the pristine terms of direct, naive observation, but always through mediating categories and theories by which we already understand the social and cultural world. Perhaps the most powerful of these is the category of *modernity*, an idea so all-embracing and deeply embedded in our cultural self-understanding as to provide the implicit context against which other analytic descriptions must apparently situate themselves: 'western modernity', 'capitalist modernity', 'postmodernity' – and so 'global modernity'. To discuss globalization, then, is inevitably to engage with the discourse of modernity, even for those who try to escape its theoretical spell.

'Forget modernity', urges Martin Albrow. 'Escape the stifling hold of the modern on our imagination. We live in our own time and the Global Age opens worlds up to us in unprecedented ways' (Albrow 1997: 6). Albrow wants us to think of globalization on its own terms and in its own time – the 'Global Age'– which he argues has replaced the modern age. But it is not so easy to make such heroic leaps of intellectual imagination. We need to ask what it is about the 'thoughtworld of modernity' (Albrow 1997: 2) that is so *attractive* in framing our reception of the empirical realities of complex connectivity.

This chapter explores these attractions whilst at the same time retaining a degree of scepticism towards the 'grand narrative' of modernity that Albrow wants to overthrow. But my scepticism does not approach Albrow's bold refusal of the category of modernity:

rather I ask how useful the cluster of ideas that constitute 'modernity' are for making sense of cultural experience in a globalizing world. Or whether, on the contrary, they obscure this experience. I approach this in three ways.

First I address globalization in the historical context of modernity, exploring the argument that complex connectivity is peculiar to the 'modern period': that the social-institutional conditions, and the resources of cultural imagination enabling connectivity are simply not in place before this period. Here I also engage more fully with Albrow's escape attempt, assessing his argument that we have indeed surpassed the age of modernity, that our cultural time is the time of the global.

Secondly I explore the sociological argument that globalization is not simply situated within the historical period of modernity but is actually a 'consequence of modernity', and I pursue this argument into the realm of cultural experience. The focus here is on the work of Anthony Giddens, who has provided one of the most sophisticated analyses of modernity and the most robust claim as to its 'inherently globalizing' properties.

Finally I address some of the ideological objections that have been raised to the 'hegemony' of modernity as an analytic category. Here the focus is not so much on modernity's broad intellectual enchantment (Albrow) but on suspicions about its strategic role in the maintenance of western cultural dominance, its universalizing tendencies, or its deployment as a sort of diversionary discourse masking the aggressive advance of global capitalism . The final part of the chapter assesses the degree to which these suspicions compromise the potential of the idea of modernity to illuminate the cultural condition of complex connectivity.

Global Modernity as Historical Period

The most basic argument linking complex connectivity with modernity is one that simply situates these phenomena within the modern historical period. This argument generally focuses on the historical appearance of key modern institutions: claiming that only within the institutions of capitalism, industrialism, urbanism, a developed nation-state system, mass communications and so on can the complex network of social relationships characteristic of globalization arise. For example, it may be argued that the interconnections of the global economy arise from the peculiarly expansionist nature of the modern capitalist system, driving it beyond the confines of any locality in the search for ever-wider markets. But, equally, it is only within the context of modern industrial production that the technological developments which allow distance to be 'swallowed up' – mechanized transport, telecommunications, information technology – become possible. In a simple, but none the less important sense, modernity, understood as the nexus of these institutions, is the essential historical 'context' of globalization.

But this way of reasoning has its problems. In the first place, defining modernity simply in terms of a set of institutions deemed 'modern' may be seen as tautological: more argument is required to explain why these *particular* institutions describe the modern social condition and how each qualifies for the description. This objection uncovers the fundamental *ambiguity* of modernity – a category which refers at the same time to a particular type of social formation (in part defined by its institutions), to a form of cultural imagination (involving distinct forms of rationality, cosmology, values and beliefs, conceptualizations of time and space and so on), to a definite historical period, and to notions of novelty, contemporaneity, the present, the 'up-to-date'. Given this ambiguity it is not surprising that the theoretical discourse surrounding modernity is so complex and often confused, and this of course adds to the difficulties of assessing the relationship between globalization and modernity. But we can continue for the present with the relatively simple approach via institutions, to raise the obvious question of when in history these institutions actually *do* arise.

The emergence of the modern period is controversial: it may be dated anywhere from the early sixteenth to the mid-nineteenth century, dependent upon how it is conceived. Wagner for instance points out that typically 'modern' social processes such as urbanization, industrialization and the democratization of the political process all 'extend over long periods of time . . . do not always occur simultaneously and some of them can be traced to regions and times quite distant from the so-called modern world and era' (Wagner 1994: 3). The crucial difficulty of periodizing modernity via its typical institutions, then, is that they all have their own distinct 'times'. Take capitalism as an obvious example and one might easily be persuaded by Immanuel Wallerstein's claims that the 'modern world system' emerges 'around 1500' (1987: 318). Wallerstein's dating of modernity makes sense if we see it as concerned primarily with economic responses to the 'crisis in feudalism' – as the emergence of the time of *capitalist* modernity. But then how to reconcile this with a view that takes another institution as paradigmatic? The emergence of degrees of political democracy – political modernity – may point us towards events in the seventeenth century (the English Civil War) or the eighteenth century (the French and American revolutions). Industrialism, on the other hand, moves the inception of modernity even further forward, pushing, with the industrial revolution, from the eighteenth into the nineteenth century.

So, if the institutions of modernity each have their own different 'histories', conditions of emergence, preconditions and so on, as Stuart Hall argues, 'it does not make much sense to say modern societies started at the same moment and developed uniformly within a single historical 'time' (1992: 9).

However, as Zygmunt Bauman implies, the difficulty of dating modernity is not in itself the main issue, but points towards a deeper problem: 'How old is modernity? is a contentious question. There is no agreement on dating. There is no consensus on what is to be dated. And once the effort of dating starts in earnest, the object itself begins to disappear' (Bauman 1991: 3). What Bauman means is that in the attempt to apply precise periodization we soon confront the essential ambiguity of modernity. This doesn't merely frustrate efforts at historical dating, it tells us something about the nature of modernity: that it isn't something we can easily 'prise off from the continuous flow of being' in a neat and tidy way, that to approach it this way is to discover that its 'referent is opaque at the core and frayed at the edges' (1991: 4).

So how should modernity be approached historically? Bauman admits to a pragmatic choice of dating which 'seems unavoidable in order to ward off an intrinsically barren debate' and opts, like Giddens, for beginnings in seventeenth-century Europe (Bauman 1991: 4; Giddens 1990: 1). This may be as precise as we need to be from the point of view of *contemporary* cultural analysis. We could simply conclude that tracing processes further back than the seventeenth century is not really helpful in understanding 'our time' of contemporary globalizing modernity. Periodization thus becomes a pragmatic issue of drawing the plausible historical line designating the modern era as it has relevance for us.

Discontinuities and Epochs

However this approach to the modern period may be given a more principled articulation. Giddens for instance argues that modernity marks a historical *discontinuity*. That is to say, although modern societies develop out of pre-modern societies and contain various remnants and traces of these earlier forms, they are, none the less, quite different *types* of society from 'pre-modern' ones:

> Rather than seeing the modern world as a further accentuation of conditions that existed in . . . [pre-modern] societies, it is much more illuminating to see it as placing a caesura upon the traditional world, which it seems irretrievably to corrode and destroy. The modern world is born out of discontinuity with what went before rather than continuity with it. (Giddens 1984: 239)

Stressing the discontinuities of modernity means insisting on understanding it on its own distinct terms rather than as part of a long, steady process of social 'evolution' – a 'world growth story' (Gellner 1964). Giddens's principle of historical discontinuity is precisely opposed to evolutionary theories which construct a 'grand narrative' – a 'story line' in which 'History "begins" with small, isolated cultures of hunters and gatherers, moves through the development of crop-growing and pastoral communities and from there to the formation of agrarian states, culminating in the emergence of modern societies in the West' (Giddens 1990: 5). This narrative – suggesting some inevitable uniform direction or even 'goal' to human history – is clearly misleading as a general social theory[1] but Giddens's particular point here is that this way of thinking obscures the understanding of modernity. For example, it invites specious connections between modern phenomena like urbanism and the pre-modern cities which urban locales have incorporated. Cities obviously existed before the modern period, but Giddens argues that modern urbanism is organized around quite different social principles from those which governed the relationship between the pre-modern city and countryside (1990: 6). So looking for continuities here means missing the important differences that really matter in understanding our sort of societies.

A similar case could be constructed for the inherent discontinuities of globalization. On this basis we might doubt Roland Robertson's claim that globalization is 'at least as old as the rise of the so-called world religions two thousand years ago' (1992: 6). And whereas Robertson merely *implies* a 'continuist' view in this extended time scale, Stephen Mennell's view of globalization as 'a very long-term social process' seems to fall clearly into evolutionary thinking. Mennell uses the work of Norbert Elias to argue for globalization as 'an overall trend in world history towards bigger survival units incorporating more people and more territory' (Mennell 1990: 362). By employing Elias's concept of the 'survival unit', he is able to draw a historical-evolutionary sweep between the very earliest and most primitive social groups, through the emergence of the nation-state in Europe to speculations about the future 'pacification of global society'.

But connecting globalization with a discontinuous modernity rules out such evolutionary thought. Whatever forms of 'global inter-connection' occurred before modernity did so in a context which makes them, in a sense, *incomparable* with globalization. There are many impressive examples of spatially spread systems of political-economic dominion in the pre-modern world: the ancient empires of the Chinese, the Persians, Alexander or the Romans; the 'Holy Roman Empire' of Charlemagne in Europe in the ninth century, the medieval Mongol empires of Ghengis Khan ('ruler of all') and his grandson Kublai. But these forms of dominion – what Wallerstein refers to as 'world empires' to distinguish them from a 'world sys-tem' – in fact had none of the features which characterize today's global complex connectivity. They lacked the extensional character-istics of modern societies, having neither the capacity for political and cultural integration over distance, nor the surveillance capaci-ties to establish, monitor and police political-territorial borders in the routine way we associate with the modern nation-state system.

The issue is not just one of the level of technological development. Rather, the point is that these were different *kinds* of societies, with-out, as Giddens would argue, the peculiar dynamic properties of modernity which make possible not only technological develop-ments, but also the social capacity to handle time and space as we routinely do in the modern world. Thus, as we shall see in the following section, we may have to understand the break between modernity and pre-modernity in terms of very different ways of handling basic ontological categories.

Stressing the discontinuous nature of modernity is important in avoiding the mistakes of evolutionary thinking. However the dis-continuity argument has its own problems and the main one is that it may simply be overstated, presenting too rigidly compart-mentalized a view of history. As Giddens himself recognizes (1990: 4-5), it is simply implausible to argue that there are no continuities at all between the pre-modern and the modern. We can see plenty of cultural 'survivals' in modern societies, particularly in religious practices: for example the cultural influence of Catholicism in southern European countries like Spain or Italy, of Islam in Iran or

Malaysia or of Buddhism in Sri Lanka or South Korea. The
'discontinuist' answer to this might be that Spain and Italy, Iran,
Malaysia, Sri Lanka and South Korea are, none the less, ineluctably
modern societies, different in nature from the 'traditional' societies
in which religious observance played a more intrinsically structuring role. It may be argued that there simply are no nation-states in
the world today that are 'traditional', in the sense that they lack the
institutional features of modernity and the profound influence on
social and cultural experience that this entails.

But this is not entirely satisfying. The term 'discontinuist' tries
to grasp an overarchingly significant change in social organization
and cultural imagination which renders all the 'survivals' of earlier
practices – the manifest *continuities* across periods – more or less in-
significant. But though it correctly identifies the changed totality
within which we have to understand 'continuities', it signals too complete and categorical a break to grasp the much less *orderly* process
of historical change, at least in the realm of culture. For the continuities of, for example, 'traditional' religious belief, may have more
cultural significance than can be grasped by seeing them as mere
survivals. The robust assertion of Islamic culture evident today, for
example, quite clearly coexists – in various degrees of tension – with
'modern' values deriving from the European Enlightenment. This is
evident in a country like Iran in which the constitution recognizes
'sovereignty' but believes it to belong with Allah rather than with
either the state or the people, and respects democratic rights but
nevertheless subordinates these to the propagation of Islamic culture (Mowlana 1996). Islamic states certainly have to cope with the
global context of modern institutions, but it would be wrong to see
them as either marginalized by or absorbed within a modern cultural totality. 'Discontinuity' simply seems the wrong word to grasp
this sort of complex coexistence. We need a concept that can register
the significant transformations of modernity in a more fluid, less
categorical way.

One possibility is the revival of the idea of the historical 'epoch',
as it is deployed in Albrow's discussion of the 'Global Age' or in
Therborn's analysis of European modernity (1995a). Often used rather
loosely and interchangeably with other periodizing terms – 'era' or
'age' – the idea of an epoch is of a period marked by a major shift in
social organization or cultural imagination, expressing itself in distinctive formative events. So for example the term has been used in
the West in relation to the period dating from the birth of Christ –
the 'Christian epoch'. But the identification of significant events with

major social-cultural shifts is also applied to the consequences of scientific discoveries – the 'Steam Age', the 'Atom Age', the 'Computer Age' – or to shifts in ideas and intellectual outlook – the 'Age of Enlightenment' or indeed to amalgams of the two: the 'Digital Age'.

Tending towards the broad brush, the impressionistic, epochs are hopeless concepts for providing analytic precision. Their focus on 'significant events' or cultural principles leaves far too much room for disagreement on the criteria of significance. So Therborn (1995a: 4) describes modernity, culturally, as an epoch 'turned to the future'; Albrow (1997: 26) as one in which 'the new, the up-to-date, is associated with rationality.' Both are plausible characterizations but each identifies a different central principle and neither could pretend to be analytically exhaustive. However, in favour of the idea of the epoch is precisely its imprecision – its flexibility – with respect to beginnings and endings. The discourse of epochs is not dominated by the 'banality of dating' and does not insist on the rigid cut-off points that seem to go along with ideas of discontinuity. As Therborn argues, epochs bracket time with permeable limits: 'epochs are not fortresses of time in which people can be shut up. They are expanses open at all ends. But even moving across the prairie you may notice the moving time of dawn and dusk. Epochal concepts are heuristic devices, like time zones' (Therborn 1995a: 3). I think Therborn is exactly right to highlight the *heuristic* nature of epochal thinking: the point is not exhaustively to analyse everything that could count as a description of 'the modern', nor to pin down all these to precise points of emergence. It is, rather, to discover something about the nature of our time of global modernity by understanding both its historical contingency and the way it differs from previous eras in respect of its informing social-cultural principles. These principles may remain matters of theoretical dispute, but this does not prevent us from engaging in some heuristic comparison.

The Cultural Imaginary of Pre-modern 'Globality'

So an alternative way of grasping the distinctive nature of contemporary connectivity is to compare the 'cultural imagining' it involves with that of spatially spread 'communities' in pre-modernity. This is to look for an 'epochal shift' in cultural outlook differentiating the global-modern from any earlier form of social-cultural distanciation.

What Benedict Anderson describes as 'the great transcontinental sodalities of Christendom, the Islamic Ummah and the rest' (1991:

36) provide good examples of 'communities' of faith existing over huge distances and incorporating vast numbers in the pre-modern world . How do these 'imagined communities' compare with the sense we may have of global relatedness today?

Well, though these were remarkable examples of a *kind* of distanciated relationship, they were quite different from those that become possible in modernity. As Anderson says, pre-modern communities of Christendom and Islam were ones in which a *universal* belonging was always imagined in *particular*, local contexts:

> The humble parish priest, whose forebears and frailties everyone who heard his celebrations knew, was still the direct intermediary between his parishioners and the divine. This juxtaposition between the cosmic-universal and the mundane-particular meant that however vast Christendom might be, and was sensed to be, it manifested itself *variously* to particular Swabian or Andalusian communities as replications of themselves. (Anderson 1991: 23 – emphasis in original)

One interpretation of this argument is simply in terms of the relative isolation and immobility of social life before the modern era. For example, communities in Europe in the Middle Ages were in the vast majority small local rural communities – villages, parishes – in which the inhabitants were relatively immobile and isolated from other communities (Sumption 1975: 11; Manchester 1992: 11). Although long-distance travel and population movement were not at all uncommon, the normal expectation for the average peasant must have been to be born, live and die within the same few square miles and to 'know' only those they were physically in contact with from day to day. The sense of belonging to a wider transcontinental religious communion must therefore have been, as Anderson suggests, a peculiarly local and particular one for the majority of believers. People probably thought of other distantly located Christians or Muslims or Buddhists – if they thought of them at all – as 'replications of themselves'. Without much expectation of ever encountering – either directly or in representation – any one from foreign lands, the belief for most communicants in a wider communion must have been pretty much the same order of faith as belief in the Holy Trinity, in the deeds of the Prophet, or in reincarnation.

Indeed religious observance – as repeated familiar local practices – probably served to reinforce people in the security of a local lifeworld, rather than to introduce much sense of a wider world. It seems unlikely that 'belonging' to these religious communities gave any comparable sense of 'the global' that people today can routinely derive from switching on the television. Indeed what seems most interesting about the cultural spread of pre-modern Christendom is how it 'assumed its universal form through a myriad of specificities and particularities' (Anderson 1991: 23).

This argument about the relative social immobility and isolation of communities is, however, historically controversial. Against images of a majority of location-bound, illiterate rural parishioners we must recognize the existence of a small but much more mobile, elite literate clerisy united by the 'sacred script languages' of Latin or Arabic. Against the multitude of isolated villages we must place the cities and cosmopolitan centres of pilgrimage – Rome, Mecca, Jerusalem, Walsingham, Benares, Santiago de Compostela. In contrast with the relative immobility of the peasantry[2] we must reckon, from at least the ninth century, the systems of long-distance trading linking the Christian and the Muslim world and establishing the cosmopolitan prosperity of great mercantile cities like Venice, Genoa or Constantinople (Morris 1988). Finally, we have to contrast the particularities of local parish worship with phenomena such as the pan-European expansion in ecclesiastical architecture of the late Middle Ages – the remarkable spread of the Gothic style from its invention in twelfth-century France to virtually every part of Europe (Holmes 1988).

So it would be foolish to underestimate either the degree of mobility (at least for certain classes) or of cultural influence across distance occurring in pre-modern societies. But, granted all this, it would be implausible to describe pre-modern societies, as Lash and Urry (1994: 252) describe modern ones, as societies 'on the move'. Travel over any distance was difficult, arduous and often perilous. A traveller in medieval Europe had to reckon with roads which were at best like the country lanes and tracks used by farmers or ramblers today. These were frequently impassable in winter, and simple matters like the crossing of rivers posed major obstacles, as bridges and causeways were routinely damaged or even washed away in winter floods (Bennett 1990: 18ff). Add to these the ever-present danger of attack by thieves in the wild places between towns and villages and the risks and discomforts of overnight lodgings (Manchester 1992: 63ff) and it is clear that travel was not something to be undertaken lightly. For pre-modern people the etymological connection between travel and 'travail' – painful or laborious effort – must have been all too evident.

In all these ways distinctions arise between whatever mobility and consequent connectivity existed in pre-modern times, and the taken-for-granted integration of organized travel into the daily life of people in modernity. The 'epochal shift' we need to understand lies in the axial principles that put communication, mobility and connectivity at the centre of our lives.

And we can glimpse in the historical record something suggestive of this cultural shift – something more significant than technological advances overcoming physical inhibitants on mobility. Take, for instance, Bennett's discussion of the apparently common practice in fifteenth-century England of digging up the highway: 'At Aylesbury a pit was dug in the highway, of such a size that an unfortunate itinerant glove seller fell into it and was drowned. The local miller who dug the pit was acquitted by the jury, who said there was nowhere else he could get the clay he needed' (Bennett 1990: 134). What is interesting about this is not just the hazards of travel that it illustrates, but how it suggests a set of social priorities and a communal outlook utterly different from those of our own time. The example makes sense when seen in the context of a time in which, as Brooke, commenting on the twists and turns of medieval roads around estate boundaries, puts it, 'the field counted for more than the road' (Brooke 1975: 74). The immediate concerns of the locality took general precedence over those of connectivity. If we can't imagine a modern jury reasoning in the way of this late medieval one, this reveals one order of epochal shift: from a time in which the imperatives of communication – the need above all to keep connected – had not yet come to govern all other concerns.

Moreover the modern axial principle of connectivity clearly applies to more than simple physical mobility. Indeed the very fact that 'connectivity' for the pre-modern world was inevitably centred on the physical mobility of people – individual travellers (merchants, journeymen, pilgrims, mendicant priests) as the embodied carriers of trade, information and cultural influence – was surely a major limitation on the degree and complexity of that connectivity. The simple movement of people from place to place surely had limited impact on the cultural composition of these places, when compared with the deep penetration of place achieved by modern media and communications technologies.

Thus, even as people managed in relatively large numbers to make perilous journeys to the sites of pilgrimage that were the centres of the imaginative geographies of Christendom or Islam, they assembled, as Anderson says, as strangely juxtaposed figures: 'from remote and *otherwise unrelated* localities . . . The Berber encountering the Malay before the Kaaba must, as it were, ask himself: "Why is this man doing what I am doing, uttering the same words that I am uttering, even though we can not talk to one another?"' (Anderson 1991: 54 – emphasis in original).

What separates the pilgrims of pre-modernity from those of today – apart from all the ways in which religious conviction is now compromised with secular rationality – is the fact that twentieth-century pilgrims in some senses 'know' each other before they arrive. Complex connectivity thus involves (at least a basic) overcoming of cultural distance through the routine integration into daily 'local' life of all the locality-penetrating experiences of cultural difference provided through education, employment, consumer culture and globalizing mass media.

To summarize: we can reasonably talk of an axial shift between pre-modern and modern connectivity. This does not mark a rigid historical 'break' and there are surely plenty of examples of continuities across the permeable boundaries of these epochs. None the less this shift is crucial in understanding our condition of 'global modernity', and supports Giddens's contention that we should not depend on long historical continuities for clues to our own time and cultural condition. Despite superficial similarities, globalization does not have deep roots in the pre-modern world. On the contrary, the comparison with earlier forms of ostensible 'global connectivity' serves better to throw into relief the distinct but taken-for-granted nature of our own mundane globalized experience.

The 'Global Age': The End of Modernity?

But there is another difficulty to be addressed before we use the term 'global modernity' with confidence, and this arises from the openness of the modern epoch at, as it were, our end of history. For the logic of epochal thinking implies that modernity too will be superseded by a new time with its own axial principles and specific cultural imaginary. So shouldn't we take seriously the idea that globalization, far from being the working through of the axial principles of modernity, is in fact the central indication of its passing?

This, as we glimpsed at the beginning of this chapter, is in essence Martin Albrow's claim: the modern age has in fact been supplanted by the 'Global Age'. Albrow's argument is premised on an important insight into the ambiguities of the concept of modernity: the fact that it is a description that seems to arrogate to itself the quality of being 'ever new' and therefore beyond historical supersession:[3]

> Can there ever be another epoch when the modern claims to be the ever new? Does it make sense to think of ourselves as anything other than modern? On the face of it, it ought to be easy. If the Modern Age is a period in history, surely like any other it can end. But to counter that, if the modern is the new, it seems to have the secret of perpetual self-renewal. (Albrow 1997: 13)

This is more than a formal semantic point, for Albrow argues that this embedded assumption of modernity as being both 'our time' and, as it were, at the 'end of time', has mesmerized theorists to the extent that they have been unable to discern the signs of a new age struggling to make itself evident. Ironically then, the 'disenchantment of the world' that Max Weber saw as characteristic of modernity (Weber 1977) has turned into its own form of 'enchantment', holding social and cultural analysis under the spell of the modern. On this reading, even those theoretical discourses that suggest a surpassing of modernity remain under its spell: postmodernity is seen as no more than 'the expression, however self-destructive of modernity'; Francis Fukuyama's (1992) claims about the 'end of history' really amount to an acceptance of the eternal condition of modernity. Thus 'modernity cannot imagine the future except as its own continuation or else chaos' (Albrow 1997: 9).

Albrow's argument registers our uncertainties about our *precise* time: the last decade(s) of the twentieth century. The 'modern era' has not seemed sufficient to grasp this time without some sort of qualification. The extraordinarily historically evasive discourse of postmodernity is emblematic of this uncertainty – but so equally is the idea of 'late modernity' favoured by modernist thinkers like Giddens. How can we use the term 'late modernity' without some sense of an imminent ending – of being at the final part of a period? And this worry is intimately connected with how we understand the condition of globalization, since, despite its roots in earlier phases of the modern epoch, few would deny that complex connectivity is a more salient feature of very recent history – forcing itself on our attention in the last few decades of the twentieth century.

In the light of this, Albrow takes what might be considered the next logical step – abandoning the axial principle of modernity altogether in favour of 'globality': 'Fundamentally the global age involves the supplanting of modernity with globality and this means an overall change in the basis of action and social organization' (Albrow 1997: 4).

A bold claim, and a difficult one to redeem. For it is one thing to reveal, as Albrow elegantly does, the conceptual grip that modernity continues to exert. It is another to provide compelling reasons to abandon this way of thought. What must be shown is not simply that modernity like all things must pass away, but that the portents of the global age he detects have sufficient force to displace it from its dominant conceptual-discursive position.

Albrow argues along two basic lines. First he outlines a number of empirical features of our time which have 'taken us beyond the assumptions of modernity': '[T]he global environmental consequences of aggregate human activities; the loss of security where weaponry has global destructiveness; the globality of communication systems; the rise of a global economy; and the reflexivity of globalism, where people and groups of all kinds refer to the globe as the frame of their beliefs' (Albrow 1997: 4). Albrow returns to these themes at various points in his book (for example pp. 114–15). Though he very reasonably argues that it is perhaps too early in the new epoch to identify what may become its most significant features (p. 114), he clearly counts these themes as marking the shift to the global age. This is plausible enough – it amounts to saying, 'Think of these phenomena in a new way, as emblematic of a new age'. But this does not provide the compelling reason to abandon modernity – which would mean saying, 'These things *cannot* be thought of in the conceptual terms of modernity.' And this is the stronger claim he wants to convince us of.

But to do this requires additional arguments. For all the globalizing phenomena he cites can easily be accommodated within modernity's 'thought-world', simply by connecting them with conventional 'modern' institutions: environmental threats with industrialism and mass consumption; the global threat of weapons with the modern military-scientific-industrial complex; the global economy with modern capitalism and so forth. Albrow in fact tends to read these features most basically as challenges to the *nation-state* (pp. 4–5) which he takes above all to be emblematic of modernity itself. These challenges are well known and widely and contentiously discussed within the political discourse of globalization (McGrew 1992; Horsman and Marshall 1994; Axford 1995; Held 1995). But even if globality *does* threaten the nation-state, this threat is surely not something incomprehensible or unaccountable within the discourse of modernity. There is something missing here, and to discover it we must move on to Albrow's second line of argument.

This shifts the challenge of globalizing phenomena from threats to the viability of modern institutions to threats to the underlying sense of order and process of the modern intellectual outlook. Multiplying environmental risks, threats of nuclear Armageddon, the anarchy of the global capitalist market, the sheer unruly expansiveness of cultural practices across national cultural 'boundaries' that global communication affords – all these escape the sort of grand plan that may be associated with modernity as a 'project'. Thus it is the axial principles of order, planning, project, control, development and so on that are challenged by a globality which is precisely disordered, unsystematic, 'non-directed': 'Globalization . . . has no inherent or necessary end point . . . the end point of modernity is when it arrives at the exhaustion of the Modern Project; but globality is not a project. The difference is profound. Not only is globalization not just a continuation of modernization: it isn't a law-like process either' (Albrow 1997: 95). This amounts to saying that globalization is an epochal shift marked by an 'aggregate of historical changes' but not driven by a developmental logic. This is fine. There is every reason to avoid narrating global connectivity in terms of some unfolding inner logic of history. However, it has the effect of casting modernity, both as period and as discourse, as inescapably dominated by this sort of 'Grand Narrative '(Lyotard 1984) of teleology, law-governed development and so forth. Albrow, indeed, seems to think that accounts which associate globalization with modernity are *necessarily* caught up in the Grand Narrative (Albrow 1997: 101).

But this is not so. Modernity as a broad category has plenty of room for looser, non-normative models of change, for indeterminacy, the critique of teleology and of Enlightenment rationality within it. Moreover, to argue compellingly for the exhaustion of the modern analytical account, Albrow has to engage with arguments connecting globalization with modernity at a quite different level of analysis. Such arguments locate the sources of globalization in deep structural transitions set in train by modernity – changes in the social organization of time and space – which can account for the expanding connectivity we witness in today's world . These are not teleological or evolutionary claims and cannot be dismissed along with the Grand Narrative version of history.

In moving on to consider them now, I don't want to lose sight of Albrow's significant problematizing of the *general* dominance of 'the modern' in social and cultural analysis. Modernity undoubtedly has its problems as an analytic – as well as an ideological – category. But, on the other hand, it can provide a powerful way of illuminating our current condition of global connectivity and before we rush to dismiss it we need to give attention to this level of analysis.

Globalization as a 'Consequence of Modernity'

Some of the most powerful arguments for the globalizing properties of modernity are found in Anthony Giddens's work, beginning with his influential essay *The Consequences of Modernity* (1990). Here Giddens introduces the concept of globalization into his social theory defining it as 'the intensification of worldwide social relations which link distant localities in such a way that local happenings are shaped by events occurring many miles away and vice versa' (1990: 64). This definition – clearly a version of complex connectivity – is introduced simultaneously with the claim that modernity is 'inherently globalizing' (1990: 63). And in a later work the definition is elaborated so as to tie globalization even more closely to the expansion of modernity: 'Globalization concerns the intersection of presence and absence, the interlacing of social events and social relations "at distance" with local contextualities. We should grasp the global spread of modernity in terms of an ongoing relation between distanciation and the chronic mutability of local circumstances and local engagements' (1991: 21–2). But in what sense is modernity 'inherently globalizing'? There is a weak and a strong version of the claim detectable in Giddens's overall analysis.

The weak version derives from Giddens's discussion of four core institutional dimensions of modernity: capitalism, industrialism, surveillance (particularly the political control of the nation-state) and military power (1990: 55-78). Giddens in turn relates these to four 'dimensions of globalization': the world capitalist economy, the international division of labour, the nation-state system and the world military order. Superficially these are simply versions of the four dimensions of modernity writ large – writ globally. Giddens briefly discusses the nature of these institutional dimensions, stressing their complex interdependence but also their independent features and the irreducibility of each one to any single globalizing principle – for example to the Wallersteinian story of a world system of capitalist expansion. But he does not provide at this point any real account of the dynamic that drives the expansion of these institutions. The weak version is thus simply the implicit claim that the global spread of these modern institutions from their origins in seventeenth-century Europe is accountable in terms of their

inherently expansive characteristics: capitalism restlessly searching
for new spheres of operation and new markets; the nation-state rapidly expanding to a reflexively ordered political system occupying
almost all areas of the earth's surface; industrialism following a logic
of the division of labour leading to 'regional specialization in terms
of type of industry, skill and production of raw materials' across the
globe (1990: 76); military power unconfinable to individual nation-
states, becoming globally organized via international alliances, the
flow of weaponry and so on.

This weak account is vulnerable to the charge that it simply constitutes globalization as, in Robertson's words, *'an enlargement* of
modernity, from society to the world. It is modernity on a global
scale' (1992: 142). With no demonstration of any inherent logic,
modernity and 'globality' are, Robertson argues, simply conflated.
But on the other hand Martin Albrow attacks Giddens precisely for
supposing an inner logic: 'The notion "modernity is inherently globalizing" treats an outcome as a necessary product of a process, as if it
had inner laws of development. It suggests an end state as the point
at which the earlier episodes are all directed. The analysis is then
teleological' (Albrow 1997: 99). Given Giddens's own critique of teleological and evolutionary theories there is a sharp irony in this charge.
But in the absence of other explanations one can see how this weak
version of the inherently expansionist character of modern institutions might be taken as supposing some intrinsic developmental logic.

There is however another story in Giddens that Albrow fails to
engage with. This is a much more compelling argument, tracing the
institutional manifestations of modernity to deeper transformations
in the way that basic social-ontological categories – time, space, place,
distance and proximity – are perceived and organized. This strong
version of the globalizing properties of modernity not only avoids
teleology, it also provides a richer theoretical framework for the interpretation of the experience of complex connectivity.

Modernity as Time-Space Transformation

One of the striking things about Giddens's definitions of globalization is their 'abstract' character. Ideas like 'the intersection of presence and absence' or the even sparer 'action at distance' (1994a: 4)
seem deliberately to avoid conventional social science terminology
(societies, the nation-state, multinational capitalism) to establish
a discourse 'that concentrates upon analysing how social life is

ordered across time and space – the problematic of time-space distanciation' (1990: 64).

And it is within this problematic that the globalizing dynamic of modernity is to be found. Giddens claims that modern social institutions possess peculiar dynamic properties lacking in those of the pre-modern world, and these derive in large part from a transformation in the relationship between the fundamental ontological categories of time and space.

In pre-modern societies, Giddens argues, the reckoning of time was limited, for the majority, by its reliance on a connection with *place*. Of course pre-modern societies all possessed their own culturally mediated perceptions of time and some methods of time calculation. But before the invention and mass diffusion of the mechanical clock,[4] it was impossible to tell the time of day without referring to the context of a locality and, especially, natural time-space markers. Thus, for example, 'dawn', 'dusk' and 'noon' or the indications on a sundial, were not only imprecise markers of time, they were intrinsically tied to the locality in which they were used. The same could be said of a statement like 'when we finish work in the fields and go back to the village.' Though a social rather than a 'natural' measure of time, this is still dependent for its meaning on the 'presence availability' of local communities. The limitations of pre-modern time reckoning can thus be seen in the difficulty in making statements like 'at three o'clock' or 'in half an hour' – not merely difficulties in terms of *precision* before mechanical clocking but, more significantly, in terms of *abstraction* – independence from place. Thrift (1990: 113–14) gives a nice literary example of this: 'Thomas Hardy, in *The Mayor of Casterbridge* . . . lets a farm labourer explain that the death of Henchard took place "about half an hour ago, by the sun; for I've got no watch to my name."' This gives a glimpse of the historical intersection – in early nineteenth-century England – of two quite different worlds, the modern one engulfing the 'traditional' in its social demands for accuracy and abstraction-from-context represented by clocked time.

The uniform abstract – 'empty' – nature of clocked time thus freed time reckoning, and therefore the co-ordination of social activity, from the particularities of place. The implications of this change were of course bound up, as Thrift's example shows, with the transition from an agricultural economy to a (capitalist) industrial one. Barbara Adam, for example, discusses the commodification of time (cf. Thompson 1967; Giddens 1981) made possible by clocking in modern industrial societies. She compares (1990: 112) the modern calculation of 'man hours' necessary to complete a task with an earlier concept used to link time and work with the particularities of place:

> In industrial societies time has become the measure of work where work was the measure of time in earlier periods. The German *Tagwerk* (day[s]work) used to be such a measure: variable and context dependent. It entailed the knowledge that a prime piece of land is easier to work than one on a stony hill. . . . The calculation of 'man-hours', on the other hand, like the clock time units on which it is based is an invariable, standardised measure that can be applied universally regardless of context.

To shift the social orientation from 'task to time', Adam implies, is to lose some of the local knowledge which served previous ages well and had advantages in terms of the quality of experience and autonomy of labour. The 'emptying out' of the particular contents of time, then, is by no means an unambiguous social and cultural gain.

On the other hand, it cannot be denied that clocked time is also in certain respects genuinely emancipatory in its consequences. To say it 'freed time from the particularities of place' does not imply its place in some benign pattern of gradual ('evolutionary') human emancipation. However we have to acknowledge gains in mobility and the consequent raising of people's cultural horizons made possible by the co-ordination of clocked time. Thrift (1990: 115ff) refers to the ubiquity of clocks and timetables in factories, offices and schools by the late nineteenth century, pointing to their role in the imposition of time-discipline on industrial labour. But he also discusses the indispensability of co-ordination of various local times for the successful development of the railways. Greenwich Mean Time was adopted by all British railway companies by 1848, thirty years before it became the legal standard in Great Britain. And it was the railways – as organizations for the co-ordination of time-space via their *timetables*, as much as a transport technology – that first made possible modern mass travel. Thomas Cook's first famous railway excursion from Leicester to Loughborough in 1841 can genuinely be seen – as Cook himself saw it – as the beginning of the democratization of travel: 'Railway travelling is travelling for the Million; the humble may travel, the rich may travel . . .' (quoted in Lash and Urry 1994: 261).

So, like the condition of modernity itself, the separation of time from place is an ambiguous development, bringing a mixture of emancipations and new forms of domination. However the implications of time-space distanciation extend, for Giddens at least, far beyond issues of commodification.

One direct implication is the extension of the standardization of clock times from a national to a global context. The International Meridian Conference held in Washington in 1884 adopted Greenwich Mean Time as the standard for the system of international time zones. Thus 'the specifically western temporal regime which had emerged with the invention of the clock in medieval Europe became the universal standard of time measurement. Indeed its hegemonic development signified the irreversible destruction of all other temporal regimes in the world . . .' (Nguyen 1992: 33, quoted in Lash and Urry 1994: 229). We can add to this the worldwide standardization of calendars: 'Everyone now follows the same dating system: the approach of the "year 2000" for example, is a global event' (Giddens 1990: 18).[5]

So, in some quite obvious ways the separation of time from local particularities has led to forms of co-ordination that rapidly became global: GMT became the legal standard time in Britain in 1880, and just four years later was adopted as the international standard. However Giddens warns against interpreting all this too superficially. He does not want to suggest that clock time is, in some technologically determinist way, a *source* of modernity. Rather it is the broader social process involved in the separation of time and space that is significant: '[T]he widespread use of mechanical timing devices facilitated, but also presumed, deeply structured changes in the tissue of everyday life' (1991: 17).

For example, the year 2000 as a global event signifies more than the global adoption of a standard calendar. It suggests a context in which (nearly) everyone relates to 'history' in a particular way, universalizing what Giddens calls 'historicity' – 'the use of history to make history' (1991: 243). Historicity implies the capacity to appropriate knowledge of the past to shape the future – something which can only arise in societies which have the ability systematically to store and retrieve knowledge of the past. So the fact that all societies can relate to the idea of the 'year 2000' also presupposes a fundamental transformation in their conceptualization and social use of historical time – in turn presupposing transformations in the recording and 'storage' of information, and in communications. It is this sort of broad transformation that Giddens wants to grasp in the idea that time-space distanciation marks a 'discontinuity' with the pre-modern world and simultaneously globalizes this epochal shift.

Giddens develops his discussion by considering the implications that 'the emptying of time' has for 'the emptying of space' and it is here that the force of his argument in relation to globalization is greatest. 'Empty space' refers to 'the separation of space from place' which abstract time reckoning makes possible. In everyday language, he observes, space and place are often used synonymously. But we can distinguish them by thinking of place as 'locale' – a term coined in Giddens's earliest work on time and space (1979: 206ff) which 'refers to the physical settings of social activity as situated geographically' (1990: 18). A locale can be anything from 'a room in a house, a street corner, the shop floor of a factory, towns and cities, to the territorially demarcated areas occupied by nation-states' (1984: 118). The point is that locales are not merely physical-geographical points or environments but, crucially, *physical settings of interaction*. Giddens argues that in pre-modern societies, space and place (locale) largely coincide. This is because relations of presence – local face-to-face interactions – dominate social life for most people. Thus pre-modern locales – the fields, the homestead, the village green, the church, the market-place, the manor – are the geographically-situated 'local' contexts for nearly all social interactions. And clearly the dominance of relations of presence in such settings derives, largely, from limitations imposed on social co-ordination across distance by pre-modern time reckoning.

Modernity, Giddens argues, 'tears space away from place' in that it allows, indeed 'fosters', relations at distance – between people who are not united in the face-to-face presence of a locale. It is this, above all, that makes modernity inherently globalizing. To understand this better we can consider Giddens's rather striking description (1990: 19) of locales in modernity as increasingly 'phantasmagoric': 'that is to say, locales are thoroughly penetrated by and shaped in terms of social influences quite distant from them. What structures the locale is not simply that which is present on the scene; the "visible form" of the locale conceals the distanciated relations which determine its nature.' Why 'phantasmagoric'? The term has its most general sense as a derivation from 'phantasm' – an illusion or a deceptive appearance. But it has an interesting subsidiary usage as 'a supposed vision of an absent (living or dead) person' (Hawkins and Allen 1991: 1087). Giddens's use of the term seems to trade more on this subsidiary sense, suggesting a situation in which locales are not so much 'illusory' as peopled by the 'absent' as much as the 'present'. This recalls Walter Benjamin's description of the nineteenth-century domestic interior as a 'phantasmagoria' in which the bourgeois citizen 'assembled the distant in space and in time. His drawing room was a box in the world-theatre' (Benjamin 1973: 168). For Giddens, however, the sense is broader than that of commodity aesthetics: the influences of distant social forces and processes are the phantasms – the 'ghostly presences' – in locales.

We can understand this by comparing a mundane modern locale with its equivalent in pre-modernity. Pre-modern houses were almost exclusively settings for intimate interactions of presence. Le Roy Ladurie (1978: 24), in his description of life in the fourteenth-century French village of Montaillou, stresses the close *conceptual* identification between the 'house' and the family that inhabited it:

> This basic cell [of the village society] was none other than the peasant family, embodied in the permanence of a house and in the daily life of a group co-resident under the same roof. In the local language this entity was called an *ostal*; and in the Latin of the Inquisition files it was called a *hospicium* or, more often, a *domus*. It should be noted that the words *ostal*, *domus* and *hospicium* all and inextricably mean both family and house. The term *familia* is practically never used. . . . It never crossed the lips of the inhabitants of Montaillou themselves, for whom the family of flesh and blood and the house of wood, stone or daub were one and the same thing.

Le Roy Ladurie presents the houses of Montaillou as locales which are, as it were, 'enclosing' of social relations as much as of physical space. Thus the religious heresies which flourished in the village were 'preserved to the utmost when whispered beneath the door of the *domus* . . . or, preferably when shut up in the damp fug of the *ostal's* four walls' (1978: 27). This was a locale which was *socially*, as much as due to the low level of communicational technology, 'inward looking'.

A present-day (western) family house is still, of course, a locale in which intimate face-to-face relations are the norm. But, in sharp contrast with its pre-modern equivalent, there are several ways in which it is also the setting for distanciated interaction and is thus 'opened out to the world' from the family. For example it is typically furnished with a number of taken-for-granted communication technologies: the letter box to receive both mail and newspapers,[6] the telephone (often now connected to an answering machine which allows communication in distanciated time as well as space), the radio(s), the television (increasingly connected to a satellite dish, cable system and VCR). In more affluent homes you might also find fax machines, computers linked via modems to a distant workplace, the internet and the worldwide web, or cellphones and paging machines resting in coat pockets and briefcases. These communication technologies are the most striking ways in which modern houses become settings for distanciated relations. Though relations of presence may still dominate here, increasingly homes are open to the world: our sitting rooms places 'where the global meets the local' (Morley: 1992).

Moreover the impacts of communications and media technologies are not the only way in which domestic locales are determined by distanciated relations. The utilities connected to our houses – for example our electricity supplies – 'connect' us with wider grids and systems in more than a physical sense: our routine lives are tied into a relation of dependence on the 'expert systems' which maintain them. As Giddens points out (1991: 135) electricity in the home has profoundly transformed the experience of domestic life – making possible 'the colonisation of the night'.[7] But our routine expectations of being fully active during the hours of darkness also reveal our dependence on the modern expert systems of electricity generation and distribution, as is quickly shown in the extraordinary incapacitation caused by power cuts – particularly for users of word processors.

Finally, the very way we commonly 'own' our houses – via loans and mortgages – connects us to a global system of finance, the effects of which can be felt acutely in our day-to-day lives, for example in the – sometimes dramatic – fluctuations in mortgage interest rates. We can appreciate the 'phantasmagoric' nature of modern locales in these economic forms of distanciated relations: for our relations with the global market system – via the 'local' bank branch which arranges our mortgage loan – is certainly not visible in the intimate domestic setting of the home. Yet its influence is surely felt there, as for example in the UK in the 1980s, when dramatic movements in the housing market caused houses to be perceived more sharply as lucrative tradable assets for some – or as 'traps' of negative equity inhibiting mobility for others – than as simply dwellings.

The sense in which our own homes are settings in which globalization makes itself felt is important. But there are, of course, other examples of modern locales which have no precise equivalents in pre-modernity: think of the airports we considered in chapter 1, or of television studios, petrol stations, leisure centres or shopping malls. All such modern locales are, as a result of the separation of space from place, thoroughly penetrated by distanciated relations. Familiar aspects of our lived environment, often parts of our experienced 'locality', they are however no longer unambiguously 'local'. What these modern locales express is the *disembedding* of social activity from contexts of presence.

Disembedding

Giddens describes 'disembedding' as, 'the "lifting out" of social relations from local contexts of interaction and their restructuring across indefinite spans of time-space' (1990: 21). This is an important idea for understanding the inherently globalizing nature of modernity and more broadly for grasping the cultural experience of globalization. Giddens discusses two types of 'mechanism' which lift out social relations from their embeddedness in locales: 'symbolic tokens ' and 'expert systems'. I shall briefly summarize these and then go on to discuss how, taken together as what he refers to as 'abstract systems', they suggest a distinctive way into grasping the cultural condition and the phenomenology of global modernity.

'Symbolic tokens' are 'media of exchange which have standard value, and thus are interchangeable across a plurality of contexts' (1991: 18). Money is Giddens's obvious example: money is a means of 'lifting out' social (economic) relationships from the time-space determination of physical locales. It is, as Wagner (1994: 26) observes, 'the proto-typical means of lengthening interaction chains': as an abstract system of exchange of standard value it allows exchange relations to exist beyond the particularities of locale; and as a means of credit, it represents a mode of temporal deferral, thus allowing exchange relations to span time. Of course Giddens recognizes that money existed in pre-modern societies, but in the fairly undeveloped form of material coinage.[8] It is only with the development of 'money proper' that it becomes a genuine abstract token, in today's economies, 'independent of the means whereby it is represented, taking the form of pure information lodged as figures in a computer printout' (1990: 25).

A sense of the difference between modern and pre-modern money economies can be gained from accounts of the problems experienced by medieval travellers in exchanging local currencies. Although bills of exchange were in use from at least the thirteenth century in Europe, there was no guarantee that they would be accepted in any particular town even within the same country. Even as late as 1458, William Wey, a pilgrim to Jerusalem, advised others to take with them 'a supply of "coins of Tours, Candi and Modena", as well as the ubiquitous Venetian coins which came nearest to being the international currency of the Mediterranean' (Sumption 1975: 206). The comparative simplicity and immediacy of modern currency exchange for international travel – particularly the use of internationally accepted charge cards – is striking. And this is attributable not only to the development of the international capitalist market, but, as Giddens notes (1990: 24), crucially to the role of the state in banking, acting as the guarantor of value. 'Money proper' thus emerges with the modern nation-state system, and this money simultaneously becomes 'international'. The implications for the argument that modernity is inherently globalizing are clear.

'Expert systems' also bracket time and space,'through deploying modes of technical knowledge which have validity independent of the practitioners and clients who make use of them' (Giddens 1991: 18). Here the 'lifting out' of social relations from local contexts is achieved by the systematic mediation of everyday life by institution-alized expertise. Giddens argues that routine activities like driving a car imply a distanciated relationship of 'trust' in a range of expert systems – the technologies of car design and manufacture, traffic control systems and so on. Modern people's routine interaction with these expert systems represents a 'stretching' of social relations, since we relate to the abstract system embodying technical knowledge, rather than to the specific personnel who might have constructed our car, or who wrote the computerized traffic flow programme.

Expert systems 'penetrate virtually all aspects of social life in con-ditions of modernity – in respect of the food we eat, the medicines we take, the buildings we inhabit . . .' (1991: 18). Indeed it is a con-dition of modernity that none of us has specialized knowledge across the whole range of contexts which order our daily lives: 'all experts are themselves lay people most of the time' (1991: 138). This routine requirement for trust in institutionalized expertise is another way of understanding the disembedding of modernity. For Giddens (1991: 137–8) also argues that expert systems, in comparison with pre-modern patterns of local daily life, are 'deskilling':

> In the much more strongly localized life of most of pre-modern societies, all individuals developed many skills and types of 'local knowledge' in Geertz's sense, relevant to their day-to-day lives . . . With the expansion of abstract systems, however, the conditions of daily life become transformed and recombined across much larger time-space tracts; such disembedding processes are processes of loss.

However Giddens does not want us to see this 'loss' in the familiar terms of 'left' cultural critique of modernity.[9] He admits that deskilling is 'an alienating and fragmenting phenomenon as far as the self is concerned'. But he maintains that this is not due, primarily, to a transfer of power from one social group to another; rather the loss of control is seen as a 'sieving off' of knowledge and skills once widely distributed amongst lay people into abstract systems, 'which no one directly controls'.[10]

It will by now be clear that the disembedding of 'abstract systems' is, for Giddens, a main means whereby the (global) stretching of social relations across time-space occurs. If we wanted to construct an axial principle of the global-modern epoch out of this, it might be tempting to choose the principle of *abstraction* itself – abstraction, that is, from the particularities of context. This would be supported by Giddens's linking of disembedding mechanisms with the formation of rationalized *organizations* – for him the quintessential expression of the dynamism of modernity – which, 'are able to connect the local and the global in ways which would have been unthinkable in more traditional societies '(1990: 20). This presents global modernity as the increasing structuring of social existence in relation to webs of rationalized organizations, inevitably opening our local lifeworlds up to distant – ultimately global – influences.

The principle of abstraction introduces another important Giddensian theme: the significance of 'trust' in modernity. Trust is here *conceptually* related to time-space distanciation and disembedding since, as Giddens argues, 'there would be no need to trust anyone whose activities were continually visible . . . or to trust systems whose workings were wholly known and understood' (1990: 33). Trust is 'a *medium of interaction* with the abstract systems which both empty day-to-day life of its traditional content and set up globalizing influences' (1991: 3 – emphasis added). Giddens means that modern people, though they may not trust every aspect of the systems they live amongst (and indeed may be very suspicious of scientific expertise in its application to some human problems) nevertheless *have* to adopt a routine attitude of trust – almost as a 'default position' – in their daily lives. He puts this rather nicely (1990: 90) by saying that many people make a 'bargain with modernity' in terms of the trust they vest in abstract systems. This 'bargain' – 'governed by specific admixtures of deference and scepticism, comfort and fear' – is a way of coping with our forced reliance on abstract systems. We are only able to operate socially, to 'take things for granted' without apprehension about the most routine activity – driving our cars, paying in a cheque at the bank, eating food from the supermarket, posting a letter – by taking the 'leap into faith' implied in the routine, continuous trust in abstract systems. So abstract systems work 'by providing "guarantees" of expectations across distanciated time-space' (1990: 28). They assure us that – barring the catastrophic failure of the systems themselves which is the risk which haunts modernity – the food will always be there in the store, the money in our bank accounts will not disappear, lose its value or its connection to us as it floats around the computerized cyber-world of information systems, the plane will not – at least not usually – fall out of the sky.

With these principles of abstraction and trust, we can see how Giddens's claims about the globalizing properties of modernity are tied closely into his broader social analysis. It is difficult to separate out these specific globalizing implications without losing some of the theoretical complexity of Giddens's work. However it will be useful to concentrate on what we can take as the central thrust of disembedding for understanding complex connectivity. This is the idea of the transformation of localities.

Cultural Disembedding: The Globalizing of Local Experience

As I argued in chapter 1, complex connectivity cannot be understood simply in terms of an increase in mobility or even in the 'quasi-mobility' of electronic networks (the mobility of cyber-space). However dramatic these developments are, they still concern only a relatively small dimension of cultural experience: 'local life', in contrast with the 'global life' strung out between air or computer terminals, actually occupies most of time-space. The implications of Giddens's approach are clearly attractive for this view.

It is interesting, first, to note how Giddens's argument leads us away from a more obvious sense of disembedding as the literal removal of people from their localities. This is the sense we get, for example, from Wagner's use of the term (1994: 56) to imply 'processes through which people are ejected from identity-providing social contexts . . . such as in forced migration after wars . . .' Of course, modernity *does* 'displace' people in this way, bringing about, in Marshall Berman's vivid description, 'immense demographic upheavals, severing millions of people from their ancestral habitats, hurtling them halfway across the world into new lives' (1983: 16). But, though obviously recognizing this order of displacement, when Giddens says that modernity 'dis-places' (1990: 140) he is referring to the process whereby place becomes 'phantasmagoric', penetrated by the ghostly presences of distant influences. Notwithstanding the massive population movements in the modern world, we all, as

Giddens says (1991: 187), continue to lead local lives – in the sense that 'the constraints of the body ensure that all individuals, at every moment, are contextually situated in time and space'. But – and this seems to me to be a distinctive feature of Giddens's grasp of globalization – this 'locality' is fundamentally transformed in modernity from the self-contained localities of pre-modernity. The predominant experience of everyday life in the global-modern world becomes one of the penetration of our locally situated lifeworlds by distant events, relations and processes.

It is fair to say, however, that Giddens's formulations remain primarily in the realm of social rather than cultural analysis. As I pointed out in chapter 1, his reference to the 'cultural dimension' of globalization is in effect merely to cultural technologies. This apparent neglect – or at least underemphasis – of the significance of culture is something for which Giddens has been widely criticized (Featherstone 1995: 145; Robertson 1992: 145; Thrift 1996: 55). This is curious, since, as Nigel Thrift admits, 'after all Giddens refers constantly to symbolic resources, texts, selves, and the like which are the very stuff of culture.' Despite this, Thrift claims that Giddens 'has little sense of culture' and what sense he has is 'curiously anaemic' (1996: 55). What Thrift seems to be getting at is a reluctance to pursue his analyses of the social-institutional *contexts* of cultural experience very far into depth-hermeneutic or psychoanalytic understanding of that experience – a point also stressed by Ian Craib (1992: 178ff).

However true this may be, it is clear that a concept like 'disembedding' can be put to work in the cultural domain in ways that Giddens does not take full advantage of. For example, as Graham Murdock (1993: 529) points out, media and communications systems seem obvious examples of disembedding mechanisms, and yet Giddens does not discuss them here at all. It is in fact rather difficult to fit something like television into his formal analysis – would it count as a symbolic token on account of the generalizable 'currency' of its formal representations, or as an expert system on account of its technology and institutional organization? Neither really seems to grasp the essence of television as a globalizing cultural form. Yet the more general idea that television lifts experience out of local contexts is rather obvious and compelling.

It is not that Giddens fails to recognize the significance of mediated experience in relation to globalization: indeed at one point he goes so far as to claim (perhaps rashly) the point of origin of contemporary globalization as 'the first successful broadcast transmission made via satellite' (1994a: 80). Furthermore, as we shall see in chapter 5, he provides some incisive analysis of the nature of mediated experience in modernity. But despite all this, his analysis as a whole remains rather programmatic (Silverstone 1994: 7) and does not pursue in 'thick description' the complex ways in which such mediated experience reaches into and transforms daily local life.

Given the scope of Giddens's analytic project however, this can scarcely be judged a severe criticism. What he provides in his analysis of the deep structures of globalizing modernity is not directly cultural analysis,[11] but a conceptual framework that is certainly 'culture-friendly' and that can be built upon and adapted to the interpretation of cultural experience.

Suspicion of Global Modernity

Giddens is probably the most powerful advocate of the view of globalization as the global extension of modernity, hence the attention he has been given here. His work illustrates that, despite any hesitations one may have about historical periodization, distinctive features of the social and cultural forms of modernity – the dynamism of time-space distanciation and disembedding – offer compelling explanations for the contemporary phenomena of complex connectivity. None the less there remain deep wells of suspicion of the category of global modernity, and I want to address some of these in this final section, beginning with those that surface in direct criticism of Giddens's version.

Some of the problems and vulnerabilities in Giddens's overall account of modernity have already been mentioned: his tendency to cast the passage from pre-modernity to modernity as too sharp a rupture; his rather cursory, 'thin' treatment – despite its acknowledged centrality – of culture. To these may be added the criticism of his rather programmatic approach and the theoretical gaps this leaves in his account: most significantly the failure to spell out the precise connections between his meta-analysis of time-space distanciation (the 'facilitating conditions' of modernity (1990: 63)) and his rather more conventional analysis of the social institutions of modernity (Robertson 1992: 144). However we can distinguish these particular criticisms of Giddens's approach from the more general problems with modernity that he might be said in certain ways to typify.

The broad drift of this criticism is that the category of modernity is in one way or another ideologically / politically suspicious on account of either (a) its blindness to global relations of domination and the inherent 'unevenness' of the globalization process, (b) its western-centric bias, or (c) its universalizing tendencies. All these criticisms are closely connected and all contain important elements of truth. However none of them, it seems to me, poses problems that cannot be answered from within the general 'thought-world' of modernity – none is therefore disastrous for the conceptualization of complex connectivity as global modernity.

The Unbalanced Dialectic of Modernity

The first set of issues can be illustrated directly in relation to Giddens's account. Giddens can hardly be accused of ignoring power relations in his work as a whole. And yet, despite several references to the unevenness of the globalization process (1990: 175; 1994a: 81) there remains a suspicion that he has a comparatively undeveloped view of this as a problem. This is not a matter of the rather crude charge that used to be made in some Marxist criticism, that to speak of modernity is *inevitably* to obscure the more significant reality of class relations (or this argument's correlate in terms of First World–Third World relations). Rather, the question is of how the dynamics of 'global' as opposed to 'local' power *in general* is theorized in relation to global modernity. Giddens is insistent that this has to be seen as a *dialectic* process in which 'the global spread of modernity [involves] an ongoing relation between . . . the chronic mutability of local circumstances and local engagements' (1991: 21–2). There is therefore always a 'push-and-pull' between the 'disembedding forces' of globalization and countervailing 're-embedding forces' coming from localities.

There are two points of principle in Giddens's stance here. First, as mentioned earlier, he argues, *contra* neo-Marxist 'alienation theorists' or 'mass society' critics, that modernity does not inevitably increase real or perceived powerlessness. Indeed he holds that, phenomena like 'deskilling' notwithstanding, we have overall substantially *more* power over our lives in general than people in pre-modern societies (1991: 192). Second, his dialectical formulation of power relations goes to the root of his understanding of the reflexivity of the 'agency-structure' relationship – what he more generally calls the 'dialectic of control in social systems' (1984: 16). Thus he constantly stresses the reassertion of local agency in relation to the expropriating nature of global modernity. Where there is deskilling there is reskilling, where there is disembedding there is also re-embedding. Giddens offers an example from the built environment:

> The self-same processes that lead to the destruction of older city neigh-bourhoods and their replacement by towering office blocks and sky-scrapers often permit the gentrification of other areas and a recreation of locality. Although the picture of tall, impersonal clusters of city cen-tre buildings is often presented as the epitome of the landscape of modernity, this is a mistake. Equally characteristic is the recreation of places of relative smallness and informality. (1990: 142)

The crux of the problem of power in Giddens's account lies, it seems to me, in reconciling this dialectical principle with what might be regarded as an *uneven balance of forces* involved.

On the one hand, thinking culturally, Giddens is surely right to argue against viewing modernity as simply a force for massification and depersonalization. For the very idea of cultural practices im-plies the capacity for the active appropriation of meaning and identity within circumstances that are, to paraphrase Marx, 'not of our own choosing'. In this Giddens aligns with Marshall Berman's cultural dialectic of modernity, where 're-embedding' represents the constant attempt by human beings to 'make themselves at home in the modern world' (Berman 1983). Nor is this merely a gesture towards the resilience of the human spirit but, much more funda-mentally, a recognition that human reflexive agency is intrinsic to what the modern cultural condition *actually is*. It is because people in modernity constantly assert their claims on their own biographies – projecting towards and 'taking hold of' the future – that there is a constant dynamic tension between the conditions people find them-selves in, and those they both desire and recognize as possibilities.

But on the other hand, there is, arguably, much more unevenness in the balance of the dialectical forces than Giddens manages to imply. Where he finds sources of local reassertiveness – as in his example (perhaps rather unfortunate in its class connotations) of the 'gentrification' of inner-city areas – others find a more total expropriation by globalizing forces. Lash and Urry (1994: 18), for example, instance the 'hollowing out of the black ghetto' in the large cities of the United States:

> the institutions empty out of the ghetto. Many institutions of economic governance migrate away. Markets of all sorts, including labour markets, the small corner shop, the pizza parlour, the sports shop, the

bank branch vanish. So do hierarchies as the large plants relocate beyond the suburbs. State governance declines [and its] physical presence, in drug abuse clinics, libraries, funded schools and social workers distributing supplementary benefits, disappears.

It might be argued that Giddens and Lash and Urry are simply look-ing in different directions here. Both processes may be occurring and the bleak picture of disorganized capitalism hollowing out inner-city neighbourhoods, or the more optimistic one of urban renewal are simply discrete instances conjured by slicing into the overall pro-cess at different points in time-space. But even so, it is difficult to escape the impression that Giddens paints too rosy a picture. Global modernity may be essentially dialectical, but it distributes both its goods and its 'bads' along some pretty familiar lines of entrenched social division (Massey 1994) and the resources for resistance at the local level in the face of these forces cannot be conjured into existence simply by articles of theoretical faith.

Recognizing the uneven character of globalization is fundamental to any sort of critical approach. But does this recognition seriously compromise the theory of global modernity? Not so far as I can see. We surely must understand the dynamics of time-space distanciation in the *context* of complex power relations which are sometimes rein-forced, sometimes refigured in the process of globalization (Robins 1997; Tomlinson 1997a) – this is indeed part of what is meant by '*complex* connectivity'. But nothing in this recognition undermines the central argument that complex connectivity is a consequence of modernity. Persistence in suspicion of the category of modernity probably occurs where this sort of criticism shades into the next one.

Occidental Bias, Theoretical Dualisms and Multiple Modernities

The most frequent accusation against modernity is that it is applic-able to the western social and cultural experience, and therefore only claims global relevance by its audacious assertion of this particular story as a general phase in human history. This criticism is quite a complex one. It includes the claim that modernity has its historical roots in the West, that this provenance explains the West's rise to global political-economic dominance, and that this dominance in turn established a discursive position from which the West has claimed its particular cultural development and current way of life as universally valid. One popular way of expressing this is that globalization theory amounts to 'a theory of westernization by another name' (Nederveen Pieterse 1995: 47). I shall discuss 'westernization' as a form of cultural imperialism in some detail in the next chapter. But for now I want to raise a couple of broader points linking the concept of 'the West' with the category of modernity.

The first is the idea that the western experience is discursively privileged by erecting a simple dualism between modernity and 'tradition'. Modernity is said to replace tradition historically and to occur first in Europe and in significant points of European colonial expansion, most obviously the United States. The tradition–modernity dualism thus becomes the single, universal story of human development, thereby placing the West in the van of history. Not only does this dualism obliterate different non-western histories, it may be subtly transposed from a historical description to one of current cultural distinctions: modernity seen as the cultural property of the West, and tradition as the defining cultural deficit of the 'rest'. The *locus classicus* of this sort of ideological play is 'modernization theory' developed in North American sociology of development during the 1950s and 1960s, casting the 'problem' of underdeveloped societies as an endogenous one: either of innate deficit (McClelland 1961) or of obstacles to the 'stages of development' towards 'the era of high mass consumption' (Rostow 1960). Although comprehensively critiqued (Frank 1969; Webster 1984), the suspicion is that the ideological drift of modernization theory is re-emerging in globalization theory (Nederveen Pieterse 1995).

Another way of formulating this is to compare the tradition–modernity pair with the 'oriental–occidental' dualism in Edward Said's celebrated critique of Orientalism (Said 1985). The same suspicion that falls on the category of 'the oriental' – that it is the negative pair, the 'bad other' of the West – falls upon 'tradition'. The category of 'traditional societies' bundles together a whole array of historically constituted cultural difference in a simple binarism that simultaneously homogenizes, denigrates and silences it by counterpoising it to the single, equally homogenized, master category of (western) modernity.

These criticisms are well founded. The susceptibility of the simple idea of 'traditional society' to discursive manipulation makes it a term best avoided, and the neutral category of 'pre-modernity' preferred – as I have tried to here – to refer to the variety of social and cultural forms that precede the modern epoch. However, behind the critique of the modernity–tradition dualism there exists a more generalized theoretical distrust of dualistic thinking.

This is articulated, for example, by Barbara Adam: 'With dualisms
... we cannot handle complexity, implication, simultaneity, and
temporality. Dualisms are static and linear; they fix and generalize
into atemporal, decontextualized form, processes and relationships
that are specific, embodied and embedded' (Adam 1996: 141).
Specifically Adam argues that 'theories in the binary code' are
'fundamentally unsuitable to grasping a globalized reality where
everything is linked to everything else ... a world enmeshed in
networks of information, transport, finance capital and industrial
technology '– in short, for grasping complex connectivity. Few would
argue with this as a general theoretical observation, and yet we have
to go further to understand how the criticism bites into the category
of modernity.

In fact it bites *only* where modernity *is* constructed on a binary
opposition to some single defining 'other'. This is clearly the case
with 'tradition–modernity', but does it apply to the sort of epochal
shift that we have been describing in this chapter? Well, not necessarily. For the axial principles of time-space distanciation and so forth,
even admitting their western provenance, have no necessary implications of binarism. It is perfectly possible to think of this central
historical shift without obliterating the different pre-histories, the
different 'routes to and through modernity' (Therborn 1995a, b;
García Canclini 1995) taken by different cultures and, consequently,
the different, *multiple* forms of modernity that presently exist.

This implies that there are always, in Mike Featherstone's phrase,
'Global Modernities'. Featherstone argues this in a cogent critique of
western-centric theories of modernity (1995: 145ff), stressing the need
to understand modernity as a spatial as much as a temporal category.
He criticizes Giddens (along with Habermas) for the failure to recognize this, and the necessary pluralism it implies, pointing not only
to the ideological problems discussed above, but to the distinct forms
of non-western modernity to be found in countries like Japan. Again,
this is justified criticism of the occidental bias of most versions of
modernity. But does it threaten the category of global modernity
itself? Do plural versions of modernity undermine the idea of a
central epochal shift? I don't think so. For surely the preservation of
the root 'modern' in its plural formulation – modernities – implies
that particular histories none the less all refer to a common context.
If not, then why preserve the term 'modern' at all? Why not follow
Miyoshi and Harootunian's more radical suggestion that 'the signifier
"modern" should be regarded as a regional term peculiar to the West'
(Miyoshi and Harootunian 1989, quoted in Featherstone 1995: 147)?

The answer I think is simply that the weight of sociological and historical evidence is against this sort of table-turning *élan*. The central deep-structural transformation that Giddens describes as occurring first in Europe plainly has been felt in all other societies today. To recognize different histories, contexts and responses to this transformation is quite different from denying its common occurrence. The (preferred) term 'global modernities' therefore correctly preserves an element of the 'universal' category of the 'modern'.

Global Modernity and the Distrust of Universalism

This brings me to the last area of suspicion of modernity, its general association with universalizing discourse. Universal categories have been widely looked upon with scepticism – particularly in the wake of postmodernism – for their assumed alignment with the sort of historical 'grand narratives' that we saw Martin Albrow objecting to. This debate is complex and I propose to simplify it somewhat by focusing on one particular critical intervention.

The political philosopher John Gray is a severe critic of globalization, largely on account of the way in which he connects it with the universalizing properties of modernity. Gray grasps globalization in a distinctly narrow way, defining it almost exclusively as an *economic* phenomenon: 'a perverse and atavistic form of modernity – that, roughly, of nineteenth-century English and twentieth-century American economic individualism – projected worldwide' (Gray 1997: 183). But what is curious about this position is that Gray is not articulating a standard leftist critique of global capitalism. He indeed comes from a conservative tradition in political thought, albeit one opposed to the neo-liberal turn in conservative politics. So what stands behind Gray's critique of globalization is not a simple opposition to the global spread of capitalism, but a wide-ranging critique of the universalizing power of Enlightenment modernity. This critique bundles together global free-market capitalism and neo-liberalism with a whole range of Enlightenment principles: humanism, the belief in open-ended progress, the conquest and control of the natural world and, indeed, 'the left project of universal emancipation in a cosmopolitan civilization' (Gray 1997: 160). So one curious outcome of this broad critique is that Gray can criticize both neo-liberal capitalism and the Marxian tradition – that is, the major tradition of opposition to capitalism – in the same breath. He believes that 'all contemporary political thinking is a variation on the

Enlightenment project' and that all such projects 'have now become dead ends' (p. 161).

For Gray, then, the narrow articulation of globalization as the spread of neo-liberal economic principles is actually part of a much wider implicit critique of global modernity focused on its universalizing of Enlightenment principles. He describes universalism as 'one of the least useful and indeed most dangerous aspects of the western intellectual tradition . . . the metaphysical faith that local western values are authoritative for all cultures and peoples'. This 'foundational' cultural principle of universalism, he argues, is to be seen in 'the Socratic project of the examined life, in the Christian commitment to a redemption for all humankind and in the Enlightenment project of progress towards a universal human civilization' (p. 158).

Gray has two reasons to object to universalism. The first – implicit in his definition – is that he sees universalism as the illegitimate projection of western values on to all other global cultures. The universalism he objects to here is actually a case of the particular disguising itself – *masquerading* – as the universal. This is a familiar – albeit powerful – critical strategy. We see it not only in critiques of cultural imperialism and westernization, but, for instance, in Marx's ideology-critique, where he exposes the mystification involved in the particular interests of the bourgeoisie pretending to be universal interests. In Gray's version, he points out, for example, that the capitalist free market, as opposed to the general, ubiquitous notion of market exchange, is a product of the recent history of the West and that its global spread is therefore a case of the particular passing off as the universal. This reminds us that the free market system is not an inevitable destiny for all economies but a contingent historical development. Things – *contra* the neo-Hegelianism of a Francis Fukuyama – could be otherwise.

This objection to universalism – as masquerade – is perfectly valid, but it does not pose any real problems for the theory of global modernity that cannot be handled by the pluralist formulations discussed in the previous section. However Gray has another, deeper, reason for objecting to universalism. He sees the 'modern notion of a universal civilization' as in inherent tension with the sustenance of human *cultural* life. This is how he puts it:

> The disposition to constitute for itself different cultures or ways of life appears to be universal and primordial in the human animal. Yet the idea of a human universal civilization, as we find it in Condorcet, J. S. Mill, Marx and Rorty, is compelled to treat cultural difference as

transitory or epiphenomenal, a passing stage in the history of the species. (Gray, 1997: 177)

So universalism as a wide-ranging cultural-political *project* is deplored because of its supposed opposition to 'culture' itself – which is understood here as centred on *difference*. Culture as a 'way of life' is therefore understood – essentially in the plural – as local, particular, tied to and expressive of place and so forth, and universalism is bad to the extent that it threatens to undermine this 'natural' plurality of different ways of life.

Well, there are some obvious problems with this way of arguing – not least the apparent contradiction involved in invoking a 'universal disposition' to constitute cultural difference in the attack upon universalizing thought. But I want to focus on Gray's key claim against the universalism of modernity that it is *as a principle* in tension with the sustenance of culture. This is *only* true if culture is intrinsically and essentially about difference.

But is it? I don't believe so. Indeed the arguments of the previous chapter suggest that culture is associated with difference only contingently and not necessarily. The business of culture is not primarily the establishment and maintenance of difference; rather it is the *constitution of meaning* which speaks to the existential condition of human beings. *This* is what all human beings have a common disposition towards: cultural practices provide resources of meaning through collective symbolization woven into a set of material practices that sustain a viable way of life. So how does the idea of culture get connected with the idea of difference? Well, setting aside for the moment structuralist anthropological notions of binary opposition, it seems to me that, for the most part, the connection is simply in the work of history. That is to say, collectivities pursue cultural practices with the aim of making their lives meaningful, and different local circumstances, combined with the sedimenting of particular practices as 'traditions' (not 'tradition'!) over time, result in the rich array of cultural difference that we see in the world. But the important point is that this difference does not arise as the *telos* of cultural practices, but simply as its consequence. Cultural work may produce difference but this is not the same as saying that culture is founded in difference.

This is not to deny that, once established and institutionalized, cultural distinctions *themselves* can have an important role as a resource for individual and collective meaning construction – as in the obvious case of the 'us–them' binarism of national identity. But I think it is a mistake to take the very special case of in-group/out-group identification as typical of the whole of cultural practice and experience. People are chronically, constantly engaged in culture, but they are only periodically, or in particular circumstances of cultural oppression, preoccupied with cultural difference.[12]

So if culture is not wedded essentially to difference, it also follows that it is not antithetical to universals *as such*. Recognizing this allows us to discriminate between the 'bad universalism' of cultural imperialism, imposed westernization, cultural homogenization and so forth, and more benign forms of universalism. By benign universalism I mean the recognition that there may be *some* common underlying conditions of existence that hold true for all human beings on the planet, irrespective of cultural particularities, and that there may be consensual values to be constructed in respect of this commonality. The pursuit of such consensual values – for instance in the politico-legal discourse of universal human rights or in a global politics in relation to common environmental problems – is certainly virtuous[13] and does not, so far as I can see, have to entail a suppression of difference. It may even be the case that some sense of the universal human interest is intrinsic in the re-embedding of local identity in global modernity. I think here, for example, of what Roland Robertson (1995: 37) calls 'the "international" organization and promotion of locality'. What he refers to here – under the general category of 'glocalization' – is the tendency for the promotion of the legal rights and cultural identities of indigenous peoples to be co-ordinated in political movements at a global level.

To summarize: global modernity does indeed imply various forms of universalism. But universalism is not *in principle* a bad thing. In recognizing its noxious forms, we have to avoid throwing away the baby with the bathwater. For, as I shall argue further in chapter 6, the complex connectivity of globalization is making some sort of benign universalizing perspective – in the form of cosmopolitan cultural politics – increasingly relevant.

Conclusion

'Together globalization and modernity make up a ready made package.' So argues Nederveen Pieterse (1995: 46) and he sees this as an affinity that needs to be prised apart. Global modernity certainly emerges from the scrutiny of the arguments we have considered in this chapter as an ambiguous category, prone to various problematic articulations. Furthermore it is always important to avoid fetishizing theoretical categories – and in particular modernity, as Albrow warns, must not preoccupy us to the exclusion of other ways of thinking about our world as it moves into the future. But despite all this, the core idea of global modernity as the social and cultural condition that proceeds from an epochal shift in the social organization of time-space remains a highly compelling way of understanding our present complex connectivity, and this surely justifies its retention at least as a theoretical backdrop to the discussion of the relationship between globalization and culture.

3

Global Culture: Dreams, Nightmares and Scepticism

Does global modernity promise to deliver a 'global culture'? In one sense it might be argued that one has already arrived. As Ulf Hannerz puts it,

> There is now a world culture, but we had better make sure we understand what this means ... No total homogenization of systems of meaning and expression has occurred, nor does it appear likely that there will be one for some time soon. But the world has become one network of social relationships, and between its different regions there is a flow of meanings as well as a flow of people and goods. (Hannerz 1990: 237)

What Hannerz means, of course, is that there is now a *globalization* of culture in our preferred sense of complex connectivity. This *context* of the integration – the networking – of cultural practices and experiences across the world can be understood very broadly as a 'world culture'. We saw a theoretically sophisticated version of this sort of underlying global context of 'unicity' in our discussion of Roland Robertson's ideas of 'the world as a single place' in chapter 1. But Hannerz rightly implies that this sense has to be distinguished from the stronger, and more commonly held, understanding of a global culture as a single 'homogenized' system of meaning. A global culture in this stronger sense means the emergence of one single culture embracing everyone on earth and replacing the diversity of cultural systems that have flourished up to now.

Well, pretty obviously such a culture has not yet arrived. But though Hannerz is understandably sceptical about its emergence in the near future, it is interesting to note that – wisely – he does not entirely rule the possibility out. For in discussing the emergence of a global culture in this more robust sense, we enter an essentially *speculative* discourse. The questions we are dealing with are ones of possibility, likelihood and the reading of trends and indications. But they are also questions that have been driven by, on the one hand, hopes and aspirations for a better world in which all human existence may be united, improved and pacified, or on the other, fears of a dystopia in which global cultural diversity will be squeezed into one dominant, impoverished homogenized version. The discourse of an emergent global culture has thus, historically, been largely one articulated around threat and promise, dream and nightmare.

In this chapter we explore this speculative discourse not so much in the spirit of weighing the balance of probabilities, but as an attempt to understand the hopes, fears and assumptions that have ordered these speculations, and the implications of these for a critical stance towards the complex connectivity of global modernity. First we will look at some aspects of the historical tradition of thinking about a global culture in the modern period, and at the utopian cast of these speculations. Next we shall consider, in slightly more detail, the ways in which a global culture has been regarded rather as a threat than as a promise – the dystopian visions of cultural imperialism and homogenization. Finally we will review some of the contemporary sources of scepticism over the whole idea of an emergent global culture. In particular we will try to understand how a stress on the resilience of national identities feeds this sort of sceptical position. But while agreeing with some aspects of this scepticism, in the final part of the chapter we will introduce some criticism of a 'nation-state-centric' approach. This will point us towards the more nuanced views which we will go on to develop in the rest of the book, of what the emergent features of *globalized* culture if not a *global* culture might be.

Dreams: Historical Imaginings of a Global Culture

The idea of a global culture is not, of course, something that only becomes imaginable in the present accelerated phase of global modernity. Various sorts of dreams and speculations about the emergence of a 'global culture' have existed throughout the modern epoch and these can, I think, both be interpreted in relation to the emergence of the globalization process, and cast some light on the issue as it poses itself for us today.

If we were to take a very broad view, we would have to include amongst these all the cultural imaginings by which a particular culture simply placed itself at the centre of things and declared itself to be, to all intents and purposes, 'the world'. There are different versions of this sort of ethnocentrism, beginning with the simple case of the isolation of some pre-modern cultures – such examples as the Inuit people of the polar region or the various isolated tribal societies in the Amazon region or in New Guinea – until relatively recently in remote parts of the world. For such peoples, their world was, naturally, *the* world and their cultural identity, presumably, untroubled by rivals. What we can call this 'naive ethnocentrism' also persists, for example, in early contacts between native peoples of the 'New World' and Europeans. Native Americans commonly referred to themselves as 'Human Beings' (the literal translation of several of the names of native American tribes) to distinguish themselves from the foreigners. Thus the Onandaga orator Sadekanaktie said in 1694, 'We Human Beings are the first, and we are the eldest and the greatest. These parts and countries were inhabited and trod upon by the Human Beings before there were any Axe-Makers [Europeans]' (quoted in Calloway 1994: 20).

However, the most interesting cases are those in which ethnocentrism exists as a more developed ideology in the face of evidence of other cultures with rival claims. Something of a watershed between these cases can be glimpsed in the example of the early attempt at diplomatic and commercial contact between King George III of Great Britain and the Chinese Emperor Ch'ien Lung in 1793. To the Middle Kingdom Emperor and 'Son of Heaven' it was inconceivable that George's envoy, Lord McCartney, could be admitted to the Celestial Court, since

> Our ceremonies and code of laws differ so completely from your own that, even if your envoy were able to acquire the rudiments of our civilization, *you could not possibly transplant our manners and customs to your alien soil.* . . . Swaying the wide world, I have but one aim in view, namely to maintain a perfect governance and to fulfil the duties of the state . . . I set no value on objects strange or ingenious, and have no use for your country's manufactures.
> (quoted, Toynbee 1948: 72 – emphasis added)

Ch'ien's attitude might be said to occupy a sort of transitional place between the self-assured ethnocentrism of pre-modern 'world empires' existing in relative isolation from and ignorance of one another, and a world of global modernity in which the assertion of claims to cultural superiority take on a different, more self-conscious and deliberate ideological form. Ch'ien of course misjudged the military and technological power of the British (to him, the 'South Sea Barbarians') to impose their presence – as they were to do fifty years later in the Opium wars. But his cultural attitude as heir to a 2,000-year-old, 'self-sufficient' civilization is perfectly intelligible. And it is one, of course, mirrored in the assumptions of cultural superiority of Europeans at the same time. Hegel, for example, writing not much later than Ch'ien's speech, regarded Chinese civilization as having 'a natural vegetative existence' and believed it to be the 'necessary fate of Asiatic Empires . . . to be subjected to Europeans' (Hegel, *The Philosophy of History*, quoted in Shohat and Stam 1994: 90).

It is not, then, as though ethnocentrism disappears with the European Enlightenment,[1] but rather that it becomes more self-conscious and dependent on the cultural 'other' to sustain the myths of cultural superiority. It is clear, for instance, from Edward Said's analysis of orientalist discourse that the myths of the Orient that sustained nineteenth-century European imperialism were based not simply on cultural self-assurance and bluff ignorance of the non-European Other, but on the deliberate discursive construction – in an 'imaginary geography' – of the Orient as the binary opposite of core European cultural values and practices (Said 1985). Thus ethnocentrism, paradoxically, may itself be described as *reflexive* in the modern period. This is because the ethnocentric imagination – and the projects of cultural dominance this licensed – is only possible via a deliberate construction in relationship to other cultures which are taken as the enhancing mirror of the dominant one. In this respect, the myths of modern European civilization and the associated 'cultural imperialism' of the West from the eighteenth century onwards can be seen as concomitant features of an emerging global, reflexive modernity. These particular cultural projections on to a universal screen are not, for the most part, survivals from pre-modernity. Nor can they be seen simply as reactions to the emergent globalization process – stubborn or complacent assertions of the superiority of 'our culture' as a bulwark against threatening cultural plurality. Rather, they need to be seen as of a piece with the emergence of a reflexively ordered nation-state system (the reflexive awareness built into political conceptualizations of 'borders', of sovereignty and so on), and even with ideas of the plurality and incommensurability of cultures beginning to emerge more widely in late eighteenth-century critics of ethnocentrism like Johann Gottfried Herder.[2]

So it is within the same broad context of the dawning cultural awareness of unicity and proximity, that the various eighteenth- and nineteenth-century utopian speculations about a world culture emerge. Though these cannot, of course, be entirely disentangled from the ideological threads of universalizing cultural histories narrated from the position of the West, they do proceed from a rather different standpoint: the aspiration towards a unified and, importantly, *pacified* realm based in the Enlightenment theme of the 'higher unity of mankind'. The 'cosmopolitanism' in political thought that emerges in the eighteenth century, for instance in the thought of Kant,[3] Hume, Voltaire, Leibniz or Benjamin Franklin for all that it is, in the main, a European 'worlding', none the less articulates a sense of genuinely global interdependency and common interests. As Thomas Schlereth (1977: xii–xiii) says, these thinkers 'usually maintained a belief in human solidarity and uniformity throughout the world. As such the [cosmopolitan] ideal usually allied with humanism, pacifism, and a developing (though ambivalent) sense of universal human equality [which] provided the rationale behind the philosophe's involvement in the numerous humanitarian reform movements of the eighteenth century.' Now these ideals were, as Schlereth says, often articulated in rather ambiguous and even contradictory relation to other less progressive ideas – 'in the form of a compromise with nationalism, race consciousness' and so on. But the point is that they do express a clear sense of both the perceived possibility and desirability of a common global society and culture. This is perhaps most clearly expressed in a thinker like Leibniz, enthusiastic for a single world society, polity, religion, language and culture: 'I am indifferent to that which constitutes a German or a Frenchman, because I will only the good of all mankind' (quoted in Schlereth 1977: xxv).

It is within this complex and often contradictory mixture of ethnocentric cultural projection, increasing awareness of, and interchange with, other cultures, 'cosmopolitan humanism', and, importantly, the promise of the social impact of technological developments, that we can view the 'utopian' globalism of nineteenth-century radical thinkers such as Marx. Standing in a tradition of socialist internationalism stretching back to Saint-Simon, Marx presents a particularly bold picture of a global culture in his depiction of a future communist society. This is a world in which the divisions of nations have disappeared, along with all other particular, 'local' attachments, including religious beliefs; a world with a universal language, a world literature and cosmopolitan cultural tastes.[4] There are a number of interesting features of Marx's vision, the first being the strikingly modern sense of the impact of economic globalization – transnational capitalism – on culture. Thus, for example, in the *Communist Manifesto* he projects from the impact of the bourgeoisie in producing, 'a cosmopolitan character to production and consumption in every country':

> In the place of the old wants satisfied by the productions of the country, we find new wants, requiring for their satisfaction the products of distant lands and climes. In the place of the old local and national seclusion and self-sufficiency we have intercourse in every direction, universal interdependence of nations. And as in material, so also in intellectual production. The intellectual creations of individual nations become common property. National one-sidedness and narrow-mindedness become more and more impossible and from the numerous national and local literatures there arises a world literature. (Marx and Engels 1969: 52–3)

But Marx – here the theorist of globalization *avant la lettre* – combines a sharp analysis of the power of transnational capitalism, which 'must nestle everywhere, settle everywhere, establish connections everywhere', with a marked ambivalence towards its cultural effects. Of course he recognizes all the immiseration that capitalism brings in its wake (the main rallying cry, after all, of the *Manifesto*), and the shallow pseudo-satisfactions of the commodity form. But he nevertheless welcomes the way in which the bourgeois era sweeps away pre-modern 'civilizations' on the way towards the coming revolution and the communist era which, he insists, 'can only have a "world-historical" existence' (Marx and Engels 1970: 56). Towards this end Marx is quite happy to see the destruction of non-European cultures. The *Manifesto* continues:

> The bourgeoisie, by the rapid improvement of all instruments of production, by the immensely facilitated means of communication, draws all, even the most barbarian, nations into civilization. The cheap prices of its commodities are the heavy artillery with which it batters down all Chinese walls, with which it forces the barbarians' intensely obstinate hatred of foreigners to capitulate. (1969: 53)

The way this presents itself to us today is in the form of an almost gross Eurocentrism, echoing Hegel's attitude to Asia. And indeed, though Marx condemns the cruelty and stupidity of British imperialist actions in India and China, he none the less believes that 'whatever the crimes of England she was the unconscious tool of history in bringing about . . . a fundamental revolution in the social state of

Asia'[5] – that is in rescuing Asian societies from their 'ancient despot-ism', their 'self-sufficiency' and 'stagnation', so that they may progress towards the world-historical communist revolution.

The fact is that Marx is a convinced cosmopolitan humanist who despises nationalism and patriotism as reactionary forces in all societies, set against the true cosmopolitan interests of the proletariat – the 'workers of the world'. Reading him, you also get the sense of a generalized impatience with the particularity and narrowness of all 'local culture' which he seems to associate with what he refers to as the 'idiocy of rural life' (1969: 53), 'restraining the human mind within the smallest possible compass, making it the unresisting tool of superstition, enslaving it beneath traditional rules, depriving it of all grandeur . . .' (Marx 1973b: 306). This is not only impatience with the 'backwardness' of Asia, but with all manifestations of the traditional, the pre-modern, insofar as they represent the constraining local.

From our perspective at the end of the twentieth century, it is easy to recognize the Eurocentric cast of Marx's thought, and also the flaws in his historical and revolutionary thinking that led him to under-estimate the enduring power of ethnic and religious attachments (or their transformation into nationalism) in modernity. We might thus be both suspicious of the implicit 'cultural imperialism'of his global vision and sceptical of the chances for its realization. However we can also recognize both the genuine humanistic ideals that inform his universalizing stance and the sense of the *imminent possibility* of a harmonious global order arising out of revolutionary change signalled, for him, by the tumult of global modernity he sees in the bourgeois era (Berman 1983).

Marx's position on a global culture thus exemplifies something of the ambiguity of the idea. Like nationalism, the idea of globality comes down to us today as distinctly 'Janus-faced'. On the one hand there are the manifest attractions of creating 'one-world' in the inter-ests of peace, of concerted action on global environmental problems, of the recognition of our 'common humanity' and even, perhaps, of the emancipation from the cultural narrowness of the local that Marx desired. But on the other there is the fear of the 'homogenization' of culture and the suspicion that any sort of specification for a global culture is bound to reproduce one particular dominant version as *the* version of how life should be lived.

To some extent, contemporary visions of global culture simply exist within different ideological discourses, having greater or lesser sen-sitivity towards the issues of ethnocentrism and cultural domin-ation. Thus the 'one-worldism' of the peace movement (e.g. Boulding

1988) is easily distinguishable from the corporate global rhetoric of CNN, self-styled 'town crier to the global village'.[6] However something of the essential ideological ambiguity of the concept of a global culture can be seen if we take an issue that might be considered central to the idea of a global culture – that of a global language. In imagining this, Marx may well have been influenced by the increasing interest in the construction of artificial universal languages current in the nineteenth century (see Crystal 1987: 354ff). The most well-known and enduring of these – Esperanto – was propagated by Ludwik Zamenhof in 1887, four years after Marx's death. The enthusiasts for such artificial languages of course stressed their potential for overcoming communicational problems in the interests of international peace and understanding. Today the teaching of Esperanto is endorsed by UNESCO, and its institutional body, the Universal Esperanto Association, enjoys consultative status with UNESCO and other UN agencies. The principle behind an artificial language is that it should not displace ethnic languages but act as a *lingua franca* which, being artificial, is not biased towards any particular 'natural' national language. But of course this is only true within very narrow limits. Esperanto, for example, derives its lexicon and its script from classical and modern western European languages – Latin, Greek, the Romance and Germanic languages – and so in this sense is entirely Eurocentric.

Though it continues to have its adherents, it is clear that Esperanto is not going to become the global language and that the real candidates for this are the most successful – in the sense of most widely spoken – natural languages such as (in descending order) Mandarin Chinese, English, Spanish, Arabic or Hindustani. However, amongst these, there is clearly another hierarchy of dominance established around the status of certain languages as *international* ones – *de facto* lingua franca – that is, as the most commonly spoken *second* language, the international business, media, scientific, academic language and so forth. On pretty well all available indices, English is incontestably at the top of this hierarchy. For example, 'over two thirds of the world's scientists write in English, three quarters of the world's mail is written in English [and] of all the information in the world's electronic retrieval systems, 80% is stored in English' (Crystal 1987: 358). An ideological division thus arises between those who celebrate this linguistic concentration as the potential overcoming of Babel and those who argue the need to defend other languages, and in particular minority languages, against the threat posed by the advance of English.

So, for example, the American philosopher Roy Weatherford is perfectly happy to see English displacing all other languages as a result of 'the dominance of the United States as a military, economic and entertainment superpower' in the (perhaps premature) belief that this will secure world peace – that, 'the worst fears of patriots and jingoists everywhere are about to be realised: we are finally about to become One World, One Government, One Culture' (Weatherford 1993: 117).[7]

Pretty much at the other end of this particular ideological spectrum we find a thinker like George Monbiot, an advocate of environmental and cultural 'localism'. Monbiot argues for the defence of threatened minority languages (the rather startling contemporary phenomenon of accelerating 'language death'), not simply because of their centrality to the cultural identity and integrity of local communities, but precisely on the grounds that linguistic and hence cultural diversity promotes *peace*: 'As languages die, the concomitant loss of meaning compromises everyone's ability to sustain both a peaceful and purposeful life. . . . Without pluralism there can be no peace. In society as in ecosystems, diversity affords stability' (Monbiot 1995).[8] One person's utopian dream can be another's dystopian nightmare.

Nightmares: Global Culture as Cultural Imperialism

The issue of language dominance and the threat to linguistic diversity opens out to the broader issue of cultural imperialism: the idea that a global culture is in one way or another liable to be a hegemonic culture. This pessimistic construction of the idea of a global culture has been, if anything, the more prominent one in the late twentieth century. Indeed there is a case for seeing the theory of cultural imperialism as one of the earliest theories of cultural globalization. As Jonathan Friedman says, the discourse of cultural imperialism from around the late 1960s tended to set the scene for the initial critical reception of globalization in the cultural sphere, casting the process as 'an aspect of the hierarchical nature of imperialism, that is the increasing hegemony of particular central cultures, the diffusion of American values, consumer goods and lifestyles' (Friedman 1994: 195).

The idea of cultural imperialism has been heavily criticized and, as a result, is far less fashionable a critical position in academic circles in the 1990s than it was during the 1970s and 1980s. However, it retains a continuing relevance in that it has become part of the general cultural vocabulary of modern societies, invoked in all sorts of contexts beyond those of academic debates. For instance, the idea frequently emerges in the journalistic treatments of globalization issues. To give just one example, the merger of the Disney corporation with ABC in 1995 prompted a piece in the *Guardian* by Martin Woolacott which reflects on the implications of the creation of a media conglomerate 'as big as the entire media sector of a large European country'. But from this question, Woolacott goes on to discuss the dominance of global culture by American culture: 'What will it be like when all the globe is Disneyland?' (1995: 12). Although he does not simply reproduce the standard arguments of 'Americanization', his article provides a good example of how 'ready to hand' the discourse of cultural imperialism is as a response to globalization issues. For despite its sensitivities to changing contexts produced by recent globalizing tendencies, the article preserves intact certain assumptions about American cultural dominance – and even references to its standard icons – hamburgers, Mickey Mouse, Coca-Cola. This sort of argument, together with the readiness with which the threat of cultural imperialism is invoked in cultural policy debates conducted at the level of the nation-state,[9] attests to an abiding sensitivity towards these issues in the cultural discourses of late twentieth-century societies (see, for example, Hall 1991: 27ff).

Although its central proposition is quite simple – the idea that certain dominant cultures threaten to overwhelm other more vulnerable ones – what has become known as the 'cultural imperialism thesis' actually contains a rather complicated, ambiguous and contradictory set of ideas. In fact 'cultural imperialism' gathers in a number of fairly discrete discourses of domination: of America over Europe, of the 'West over the rest' of the world, of the core over the periphery, of the modern world over the fast-disappearing traditional one, of capitalism over more or less everything and everyone. I have discussed these discourses at length elsewhere (Tomlinson 1991) and also their relationship to the idea of cultural globalization (Tomlinson 1997a). Rather than recapitulating all these discussions here, I want to focus instead on two specific dystopian visions of a global culture that have emerged from this set of critical discourses. The first is the idea of a global culture dominated by the commodifying practices of global capitalism – the cultural 'heavy artillery' that Marx so percipiently describes. And the second is the threat, which as we have seen escapes Marx's critical vision, of the global dominance of western culture.

Global Capitalist Monoculture

In the first scenario, the power of transnational capitalism to dis-
tribute its cultural goods around the world is projected towards the
distribution of a capitalist monoculture. Out of the 'incorporation' of
all national cultures into the global capitalist economic system is
arising an overarching culture of capitalism.

One of the most consistent and powerful proponents of this view
has been the American Marxist media theorist Herbert Schiller. Over
many years, Schiller has pressed the case that the capitalist world
system, through its main agents the transnational corporations, is
relentlessly incorporating all societies into its ambit. In his original
formulation Schiller tended to stress the predominant power of
American capitalism, though he subsequently recognized the increasingly international nature of capital and directed his critique more
generally towards the transnational corporate sector. However he
has continued to elide – in a manner typical of the cultural imperialism perspective as a whole – capitalist culture with *American* culture
or as he puts it in typically robust fashion, 'homogenised North
Atlantic cultural slop' (Schiller 1985: 19). This sort of elision, coupled
with a rather loose empirical base, the tendency towards functionalist logic and even hints of conspiracy theory, has made Schiller's work
subject to a wide range of criticism (Boyd-Barrett 1982; Fejes 1981;
Lull 1995; Thompson 1995; Tomlinson 1991). I shall not be concerned
with these specific problems with Schiller's work here. Rather I want
to use his approach as a general way into the idea of a global culture
as a global *capitalist* culture. For despite its problems, Schiller's
perspective, as John Thompson has argued (1995: 173), has been
highly significant in establishing a critical perspective on the power-
structuring of cultural globalization – if only in its tenacious head-
on engagement with some of the most powerful institutional forces
in the world today.

The political-economic power of the transnationals and their
global reach is, according to Schiller, accompanied by an ideological
power to define global cultural reality. Thus he interprets transnational media corporations as thoroughly integrated into the
capitalist world system and having a functional role in its expansion: 'They provide in their imagery and messagery, the beliefs and
perspectives that create and reinforce their audiences' attachments
to the way things are in the system overall' (Schiller 1979: 30). So
what is argued here is not just that capitalism defines and structures

the global political economy, but that in the process it determines global culture: in the distribution of commercialized media products containing the ethos and values of corporate capitalism and consumerism. This is conceived in terms of a cultural totality – a 'way of life' and a 'developmental path' for developing nations to follow (1979: 31).

This sort of political-economy approach to cultural hegemony remains a strong strand in the critical analysis of international media systems. For example Herman and McChesney writing in 1997 stand squarely in the tradition of Schiller's work. Their book *The Global Media* signals this in its subtitle, *The new missionaries of global capitalism*. In it they offer convincing evidence of the accelerating concentration and integration of the ownership and control of global media systems in the hands of a few main transnational corporate players: Time Warner, Disney, News Corporation, Viacom, Bertelsmann and so on. Herman and McChesney's work is interesting in that it combines very up-to-date empirical research from the mid-1990s with a 'totalizing' critical theory that has hardly changed since Schiller first articulated it in the early 1970s. They claim, for example, that the power of media transnationals, 'is not only economic and political but extends to basic assumptions and modes of thought . . . To no small extent the stability of the system rests upon the widespread acceptance of a global corporate ideology' (Herman and McChesney 1997: 35). Later they develop this ideological incorporation thesis in a way that exactly parallels Schiller's thesis of the establishment of a capitalist 'developmental path' for developing societies:

> The crucial incursion [of transnational media systems] is the implementation of the model . . . [This] primary incursion defines the path that will be taken and brings the country in question into the orbit of interests of the dominant powers. This is the 'neo-imperialist' form that has replaced the older, cruder, and obsolete methods of colonialism. (1997: 154)

The persistence of this sort of totalizing analysis surely derives from the sheer inescapable evidence of the steady advance of the power and influence of transnational capitalism in the contemporary world. Writers like Schiller, Herman and McChesney and others in this broad neo-Marxist tradition (Golding and Harris 1997) extrapolate a cultural theory from strong empirical evidence in political economy: there is no denying the deep structures of capitalism within global modernity nor its incorporative power – its manifest 'success' – as an economic system. Moreover Schiller is right, I think, to stress the way this economic system has organized and structured much of modern cultural life within certain rather narrow commercial parameters. There is no doubt that the tendency towards commodification of cultural experience in modern societies is a highly significant one. But the question for us is, does this amount to a plausible claim that a single hegemonic 'homogenized' global culture is emerging?

The most obvious evidence for this claim is the 'convergence' and the standardization that is evident in cultural goods around the world. Take any index, from clothes to food to music to film and television to architecture (the list is only limited by what one wants to include as 'cultural') and there is no ignoring the fact that certain styles, brands, tastes and practices now have global currency and can be encountered virtually anywhere in the world. As we saw in chapter 1, international airports – those supposed gateways to cultural diversity – are prime (if rather particular) examples of this sort of 'cultural synchronization' (Hamelink 1983): almost identical worldwide, offering uniform styles of furnishing, 'international cuisine' and a whole range of familiar international brands in the duty-free shops. Examples of global brands and mass-cultural icons have indeed become clichés – Coke, McDonalds, Calvin Klein, Microsoft, Levis, Dallas, IBM, Michael Jackson, Nike, CNN, Marlboro, Schartzenegger – some even becoming synonyms for western cultural hegemony itself: 'McWorld' (Barber 1995), 'Coca-colonization' (Howes 1996), 'McDonaldization' (Ritzer 1993) and even 'McDisneyization '(Ritzer and Liska 1997).

But what does this distribution of uniform cultural goods actually signify, other than the power of some capitalist firms (and to give credit to Schiller, they are regularly American ones!) to command wide markets around the world? Well, if we assume that the sheer global presence of these goods is *in itself* token of a convergence towards a capitalist monoculture, we are probably utilizing a rather impoverished concept of culture – one that reduces culture to its material goods. As we argued in chapter 1, culture should (at least) be seen as existentially meaningful symbolization and experience. On this view, the thesis of global cultural convergence must contain the idea that our (that is everyone's) interaction with these goods penetrates deeply into the way in which we construct our 'phenomenal worlds' and make sense of our lives.

The problem with the cultural imperialism argument is that it merely assumes such a penetration: it makes a leap of inference from the simple presence of cultural goods to the attribution of deeper cultural or ideological effects. This tendency – involving what John Thompson has termed 'the fallacy of internalism'– is very tempting for totalizing critical accounts of capitalism like Herbert Schiller's, for it constructs what appears to be a seamless connection between the functional requirements of an expanding capitalist system – the need for people to act as good consumers, to be thoroughly 'bought into' the system – and the ideological representations of cultural texts like TV programmes and advertisements. The reason why it has to be treated with scepticism is, as Thompson says, that 'it ignores the hermeneutic appropriation which is an essential part of the circulation of symbolic forms' (Thompson 1995: 171). Culture simply does not transfer in this unilinear way. Movement between cultural/geographical areas always involves interpretation, translation, mutation, adaptation, and 'indigenization' as the receiving culture brings its own cultural resources to bear, in dialectical fashion, upon 'cultural imports' (Appadurai 1990; Lull 1995; Robins 1991; Tomlinson 1991). This argument about active adaptive cultural appropriation is most usually made in relation to media texts and is associated with the broader thesis of the 'active audience' (Morley 1992) . However it has the same force when applied to any commodity form, as Howes (following Prendergrast 1993) demonstrates in relation to Coca-Cola:

> No imported object, Coca-Cola included, is completely immune from creolization. Indeed, one finds that Coke is often attributed with meanings and uses within particular cultures that are different from those imagined by the manufacturer. These include that it can smooth wrinkles (Russia), that it can revive a person from the dead (Haiti), and that it can turn copper into silver (Barbados) . . . Coke is also indigenised through being mixed with other drinks, such as rum in the Caribbean to make *Cuba Libre* or *aguadiente* in Bolivia to produce *Ponche Negro*. Finally it seems that Coke is perceived as a 'native product' in many different places – that is you will often find people who believe the drink originated in their country not in the United States. (Howes 1996: 6)

Recognition of this sort of complexity in cultural appropriation is now fairly general amongst cultural and media theorists, even those who maintain a strong political-economy critique (see, for instance, Golding and Harris 1997: 6), and relatively few today would cling unwaveringly to the idea that 'hegemony is prepackaged in Los Angeles, shipped out to the global village, and unwrapped in innocent minds' (Liebes and Katz 1993: xi) . But while we are discussing the issue of cultural reception, we should also note a tradition of cultural analysis emerging from the third world experience – from Latin America – which insists on the dynamic interaction between external cultural influence and local cultural practice. A key aspect of this tradition (in the work of cultural and media theorists such as Néstor García Canclini 1992, 1995 and Jesus Martin-Barbero 1993) is the concern with the nature of cultural mixing and hybridization rather than with the notion of direct cultural imposition from the developed world. In Martin-Barbero's words (1993: 149), what is central to the experience of cultural modernity in Latin America is the way in which 'the steady, predictable tempo of homogenizing development [is] upset by the counter-tempo of profound differences and cultural discontinuities.' The idea that global culture may turn out to involve complexly shifting forms of cultural hybridity is something we will examine further in the following chapter. But clearly it suggests another reason to doubt the plausibility of the homogenization thesis.

What all this suggests, then, is that arguments which extrapolate from the global ubiquity of capitalist consumer goods and media texts towards the vision of a uniform capitalist monoculture are to be doubted precisely because they trade on a flawed concept of culture.

This does not mean, however, that capitalism is innocent in the shaping of a global culture. For Schiller's notion of capitalism as a 'way of life' may be construed in a broader way to grasp the sense in which the actual *commodification* of culture – rather than the ideologically incorporative influence of particular cultural goods or texts – structures and orders cultural experience. This, I believe, is a much more plausible version of the capitalist monoculture argument, for there can be little doubt that a large proportion of cultural practices in modernity have become commodified – turned into things which are bought and sold. Indeed the activity of shopping itself is now undoubtedly one of the most popular cultural practices in western societies and the 'shopping element' is present – structured into – almost any contemporary leisure activity. Thus the internal layouts of museums, galleries, stately homes, heritage sites and even parks and gardens now invariably route visitors through to a terminus (the ultimate goal?) in a shop where the (already commodified) experience can be more concretely re-purchased in the form of souvenirs, toys, tea-towels, posters, videos, postcards and so on. Football clubs are now also significant retailers of clothing for their supporters, changing the team strip regularly in order to keep up demand. Even a simple leisure activity like walking has become a commodifiable practice – experienced as connected with the purchase of special equipment, guidebooks, magazines and so on.

One of the most prominent examples of the conflation of broader cultural/leisure practices with consumption practices is found in the area of tourism. As Ritzer and Liska argue in relation to North America and Canada, 'a large proportion of time and money devoted to vacations is spent on shopping while on vacation. And some . . . have taken this to its logical extreme – shopping has become the vacation.' Thus, 'more Canadian package tours now go to the West Edmonton Mall than to Niagara Falls' (Ritzer and Liska 1997: 103).

The West Edmonton Mall that they refer to – along with other 'mega-malls' like the Mall of America in Minneapolis – can be seen as the apotheosis of this process of cultural commodification, combining as it does the conventional features of a shopping mall with features of the theme park – hence Ritzer and Liska's hybrid description of 'McDisneyfication'. John Urry (1995: 123) describes this 'ultimate temple of depthless consumerism, playfulness and hedonism':

> It is a mile long with over 800 shops, a 2.5-acre indoor lake with four deep-sea mini submarines, a reproduction Spanish galleon, dolphins, an eighteen-hole mini golf course, 40 restaurants, a 10-acre water park, a nineteenth century imitation Parisian boulevard (Haussman will no doubt be turning in his grave), a New Orleans street with nightclubs, and a hotel offering a variety of theme rooms in such styles as Hollywood, Roman and Polynesian!

Examples like this raise a wide range of issues for cultural analysis: for instance, the postmodern fascination with the cultural bricolage they represent, or the evidence they offer of the 'aestheticization of everyday life' (Featherstone 1991) implied in the 'visual consumption' of the sights and signs of such places, as much as in the consumption of actual goods within them (Urry 1995: 148). But for our present purposes the most significant argument is that they represent a high point of homogenization of cultural experience via commodification. This sort of argument is rather different from the simple one about the global ubiquity of certain commodities – 'world brands' – commonly found within the cultural-imperialism perspective. It also pushes the idea of capitalist culture further than the thesis of ideological incorporation – towards a vision of a world dominated entirely by the single, systematic principle of consumerism. Thus Baudrillard extrapolates from the experience of the mall to the overcoming of all manner of social differentiations:

> Here we are at the heart of consumption as the total organization of everyday life, as a complete homogenization. Everything is appropriated and simplified into the translucence of abstract 'happiness' ... Work, leisure, nature and culture, all previously dispersed, separate, and more or less irreducible activities that produce anxiety and complexity in our real life and in our 'anarchic and archaic' cities have finally become mixed, massaged, climate controlled, and domesticated into the simple activity of perpetual shopping. (Baudrillard 1988: 34)

And this vision of culture as entirely mediated through the pure principle of commodification is further developed into a potentially all-embracing global culture by Benjamin Barber in his idea of 'McWorld': 'McWorld is an entertainment shopping experience that brings together malls, multiplex movie theatres, theme parks, spectator sports arenas, fast-food chains (with their endless movie tie-ins) and television (with its burgeoning shopping networks) into a single vast enterprise that, on the way to maximising its profits, transforms human beings' (Barber 1995: 97). No doubt such views tend towards the hyperbolic, and to this extent they are easy to criticize. They obviously extrapolate a general global case from a relatively small sample of experience restricted to the more affluent sectors of the developed world. Even within the developed world it could be argued that routine consumer experience remains for many people a much less seductive, aestheticized, more mundane and instrumental business, involving the daily and weekly struggle with necessity – 'making ends meet' on a tight family budget (Lunt and Livingstone 1992: 89ff). If we turn to the vast populations of the Third World, this struggle is so materially and culturally dominant that we might suppose anxieties over commodification to be scarcely significant.

None the less I do believe this sort of argument about global capitalist monoculture needs to be taken seriously (remembering the speculative and extrapolative discourse within which all talk of global culture is lodged). For despite the obvious questions of material inequality, commodification is now deeply structured into modern cultural life in the developed world, and this undeniably represents a distinct narrowing and convergence of cultural experience: a marshalling of 'what we do' into one particular form of doing it. Moreover, the spread of this commodification to the Third World is frequently seen as a threat to the richness and diversity of cultural practices (Blackwell and Seabrook 1993; Classen 1996; Latouche 1996). However, extrapolation towards the bleaker sorts of dystopia clearly risks exaggerating the one-dimensionality of capitalist influence. Baudrillard's well-known dictum that in post-modern societies 'there is nowhere to go but to the shops' tells only part of the story. What it does register well are the signs of a broad cultural shift, in the West, away from a dominance of production over our everyday lives to a dominance of consumption: the mega-malls representing, as Urry puts it 'cities of consumption as opposed to previously dominant industrial cities' (1995: 123). But what it neglects are the many aspects of people's cultural experience and practices – their personal relationships, their religious or political affiliations, their sexual orientation, their sense of national or ethnic identity, their attachments to 'local' practices and contexts, and so on – which have not been colonized by a commodifying logic.

And indeed these aspects of individual 'lived cultures' as they are enacted and experienced within different local contexts and traditions produce the 'thickening' of cultures (Geertz 1973) that in various ways preserves cultural distinctions and chafes against the smooth advance of a uniform capitalist culture. In a huge range of particular customs and predilections – from religious traditions to the attachment to local types of bread or beer – people demonstrate the countervailing cultural force of the local situation. So ultimately the existence of a dialectical 'localizing' resistance to the 'globalizing' moment of capitalism does need to be recognized here. This resistance can be seen in deliberate counter-cultural movements – from new-age ecological 'tribes', to ethical consumerism and fair-trade movements based in local (often church-based) communities, to alternative economic systems such as the recent rise of 'local exchange and trading schemes' (LETS) aimed at circumventing or subverting mainstream consumerist patterns. Underdeveloped though these are, they none the less represent a focusing of what might be seen as a more general, though dim, dissatisfaction with commodified experience in developed societies. It remains an open question whether and to what degree the balance of this particular dialectic will shift away from the present heavy weighting towards consumerist culture. But whilst recognizing the power of the cultural logic of global capitalism, it would surely be foolish to assume that all cultural diversity is likely to collapse – like Marx's Chinese walls – entirely before it.

The 'Westernization of the World'

I want to turn now to the other vision of global uniformity that I mentioned: the spectre of a malign 'westernization' of world culture. We have already considered, in chapter 2, some objections to the idea of global modernity which focus on the theory's supposed occidental bias – its tendency to stress the particular experience of the West and to ignore, obscure or repress the rich diversity of non-western cultures. One way of thinking about a global culture, then, might be to stress the need for a historical retrieval of these non-western cultural traditions. Indeed, a recent reference book, *A Dictionary of Global Culture*, does just this. Its authors, Kwame Anthony Appiah and Henry Lewis Gates (1998), simply provide entries which redress the balance in the representation of world culture from the dominance of western figures and themes. Martin Luther appears alongside Toussaint L'Ouverture; the Zulu king Shaka alongside Shakespeare. But, valid and necessary though this sort of reconstruction is, it does not raise the more radical suspicions of western cultural dominance that I want to explore here.

These are encapsulated in the title of a book by the French political economist Serge Latouche, *The Westernization of the World*. Latouche presents a particularly forceful indictment of westernization as the 'drive towards planetary uniformity' and the 'world-wide standardization of lifestyles'(Latouche 1996: xii, 3) and so his position represents a good example of this style of global cultural critique.

What do people mean when they talk about 'westernization'? A whole range of things including, obviously, the spread of European languages (particularly English) and the consumer culture of 'western' capitalism that we have already discussed. But also styles of dress, eating habits, architectural and musical form, the adoption of an urban lifestyle based around industrial production, a pattern of cultural experience dominated by the mass media, a set of philosophical ideas, and a range of cultural values and attitudes – about personal liberty, gender and sexuality, human rights, the political process, religion, scientific and technological rationality and so on. We can see from this how easily the idea of the global domination of western culture can get conflated in the discourse of cultural imperialism with the ideas of the domination of capitalist culture, or even with the domination by individual nation-states – most obviously the United States.

We can, nevertheless, distinguish in Serge Latouche's work, a specific set of claims about and fears of westernization. In the space available here, I want to focus on what I believe is a key aspect. Latouche thinks of westernization as the global spread of a social and cultural totality. He discusses a range of aspects of 'the West' – its technology, its industrial economic base, its tendency towards urbanization, its ethical, philosophical and religious systems, its relation to capitalism and so on. But none of these alone, he insists, contains the 'essence' of the West, which must be considered as 'a synthetic unity of these diverse manifestations [as] a "cultural" entity, a phenomenon of civilization' (Latouche 1996: 38). His argument for seeing westernization as essentially a *cultural* phenomenon rests on a broadly existential view of culture close to the one I articulated in chapter 1, as 'a response to the problem of being' (1996: 41). To speak of western 'civilization' is thus a way of describing one particularly powerful *version* of such a response that has managed to establish itself everywhere. (Latouche stresses the connection of the term 'civilization' with ideas of the 'civic' – of cities and urbanization – and he takes this to be (partly) emblematic of the western response to the question of 'how we are to live'.) So, for Latouche, the historical 'success' of this model is bound to result in a cultural uniformity that he deplores, since its success involves the destruction of all other 'versions', all other ways in which life may be lived. Western civilization is thus for him, paradoxically, 'anti-cultural' (p. 43) in that it is opposed in its 'universalizing' drive to the survival of a diverse set of local particular cultures.

So far these are fairly familiar arguments. For example, the parallels here with John Gray's view of Enlightenment universalism as a threat to 'culture as difference' (chapter 2) will be evident. But now I want to come to what I think is a crucial point in Latouche's argument for understanding the idea of westernization in relation to global modernity. This is the idea that the West has lost its specific moorings in any cultural-geographical location and has become something of an abstract generator of cultural practices. As he puts it,

> I analyse [the West] as a sort of Megamachine that has now become anonymous, deterritorialized and uprooted from its historical and geographical origins . . . The West no longer means Europe, either geographically or historically; it is no longer even a collection of beliefs shared by a group of people scattered over the earth. I see it as a *machine*, impersonal, soulless, and nowadays masterless, which has impressed mankind into its service. (Latouche 1996: xii, 3)

The determinism of the machine analogy is obviously problematic from any sort of reflexive theoretical position, as is Latouche's general tendency to overplay the alienating character of modern social life without recognizing its emancipatory moments or even its ambiguities. However the more significant point seems to me to be the way in which 'the West' as something like an abstract cultural principle is prised apart from 'the West' as a specific geo-cultural entity, a set of particular cultural practices identifiable with a territorial base, a set of nation-states, real places like Spain, Switzerland, Canada, Denmark or New Zealand. Latouche expresses this difference in a (slightly strained) borrowing from Sartre by distinguishing between the West-in-itself (the 'deterritorialized' cultural principle) from the West-for-itself (the geo-cultural entity, the real places).This allows him to account for the cultural-territorial retreat that occurred with the contraction of European empires and the process of decolonization in the twentieth century, whilst maintaining the idea of western cultural hegemony.

But if we ask what it is that distinguishes these two senses it soon becomes clear that what Latouche is really describing in the deterritorialized cultural principle is in fact *social and cultural modernity itself*. This is particularly clear where he describes the 'three principal vectors of . . . the Western steamroller':

> The first is the process of mimetic industrialization prompted by the worldwide spread of a transnational economy. The second concerns the process of urbanization, connected . . . with the destruction of peasant communities. The third . . . could be called 'nationalitarianism' meaning the process of constructing rootless, mimetic states intended to create an artificial nation and manage its economy. (1996: xii)

His citing of these key institutions – industrialism, urbanism, the nation-state system – shows that Latouche's critique of the West could equally be taken as a critique of modernity. But he seems to want to hang on to the idea that there is something *essentially* western about this institutional–cultural complex, even as it is lifted off its territorial connection with actual western states and cultures. I'm not at all convinced that this can be demonstrated. It seems to me that it is simply confusing to talk of western domination as something separate from the actual practices and *interests* of western societies. We can readily agree that a certain cultural response to 'the question of being' has become globally ubiquitous and in a certain sense 'deterritorialized' – but it is better I believe to think of this as the response of *modernity*. The questions that can then be posed are of whether social and cultural modernity is necessarily 'western modernity' – of whether to become modern is in any sense necessarily to become western – or, what we may call the *cui bono* question of modernity: do western nations stand to benefit exclusively or particularly from its spread?

For a rather different set of answers to these questions we can turn once more to Giddens's account. Put at its simplest, his argument is that, though the process of 'globalizing modernity' may have *begun* in the extension of western institutions, the very fact of the current global ubiquity of these institutions (capitalism, industrialism, the nation-state system and so on) represents 'the declining grip of the West over the rest of the world' (1990: 52), as the institutions of modernity that first arose there now become ubiquitous. In a sense the West's very 'success' in disseminating its institutional forms represents a loss of its once unique social/cultural 'edge'. As he puts the point:

> The first phase of globalization was plainly governed, primarily, by the expansion of the West, and institutions which originated in the West. No other civilization made anything like as pervasive an impact on the world, or shaped it so much in its own image. . . . Although still dominated by Western power, globalization today can no longer be spoken of only as a matter of one-way imperialism . . . increasingly there is no obvious 'direction' to globalization at all and its ramifications are more or less ever present. The current phase of globalization, then, should not be confused with the preceding one, whose structures it acts increasingly to subvert. (1994b: 96)

Now we *could* read Giddens here as simply proposing an ironical 'winner loses' situation: the very success of the West resulting in the loss of its socio-cultural advantage. However we can put a little more flesh on the argument by asking whether the West might in some ways be *substantially* losing its socio-cultural grip. There are various possible ways in which this claim may be understood.

For example, it might be pointed out that certain parts of what we were used to calling the 'Third World' are now actually more 'advanced' – technologically, industrially, economically – than some parts of the West. A comparison might be made between, for example, some booming urban regions of Latin America – São Paulo, Mexico City – and depressed areas of Europe – say parts of southern Italy. The most tempting comparison here of course has been (at least until very recently) that between the so-called 'Asian Tiger' economies – South Korea, Taiwan, Hong Kong, Singapore and Malaysia – and some of the economically depressed heavy-industrial regions of Europe or the US. Singapore, for example, during the mid-1990s had a GDP per capita 'comparable with that in the poorest regions of the advanced countries (like West Glamorgan in the U.K.)' (Hirst and Thompson 1996: 114). Giddens (1990: 65; 1994a: 65) suggests that there might be a complex causal relationship between the rise and decline of such regions connected by a globalized capitalist market. At the very least, such rapid development has presented a challenge to the conventional wisdom on western political-economic dominance. Summarizing a penetrating and detailed analysis of the rise of the Asian Tigers within the context of the Pacific Rim region, Manuel Castells concludes:

> They are integrated on an equal level with OECD countries, and are substantially increasing their competitive edge vis à vis the United States and Western Europe. For the first time in the two centuries of Western-dominated industrialization, West and East ... are deeply interrelated in a pattern that does not reflect overwhelming Western domination. (Castells 1998: 309)

Well, signs of the economic instability of the Asian Tigers – for instance the crisis in the South Korean economy at the end of 1997 – are clearly troubling for the more enthusiastic long-term global projections from this compressed pattern of regional growth. Hirst and Thompson's (1996: 99ff) caution on extrapolating from these cases to a more general pattern of levelling out of economic relations between the developed and developing world is probably justified by these recent events. But on the other hand it might be argued that the thesis of the deep interrelation between the Asian Tiger economies and western economies that Castells stresses is not really compromised by any checks in the advance of the former. The rapidity with which the Korean crisis was addressed by the provision of reconstruction loans from the IMF attests to the intimacy of the interconnection between these economies and western ones. The threat of economic collapse throughout the Pacific region – to the huge potential markets and production centres of China, to Japan (economically, if not culturally, part of the West) and beyond, triggering recessions in the western European and US economies – now seems one of the major anxieties of the end of the millennium. And this can hardly be read as a return to the status quo of assured western economic dominance.

Putting the case of economic uncertainty slightly differently, it might be argued that just as globalized capitalism demonstrates its fickle affinities in the case of the newly industrialized countries, so it has no 'loyalty' to its birthplace in the West, and so provides no guarantees that the geographical patterns of dominance established in early modernity – the elective affinity between the interests of capitalism and of the West – will continue. There are signs of this, for example, in the increasingly uneasy relation between the international capitalist markets and the governments of western nation-states: the periodic currency crises besetting the western industrial nations – the so-called 'black days' on the international currency markets. And a rather spectacular instance of the global capitalist system's unsentimental attitude to western institutions could be seen in the debacle of Britain's oldest merchant bank, Baring Brothers, in February 1995. Barings – founded in 1762 and bankers to the Queen – was destroyed within a few days' trading as a result of the high-risk globalizing speculations on the 'derivatives' market carried out by one of its comparatively junior employees, Nick Leeson, via high-speed electronically mediated (distanciated) dealings. And, appropriately enough, this occurred in Singapore on one of the world's 'youngest' markets, that of South-East Asia. It is hard to resist seeing this as emblematic of the old (complacent?) world of (western) European imperial power being overtaken by the new world of decentred global capitalism in which events can be unpredictable, indiscriminate, instantaneous and catastrophic.

It is of course important not to exaggerate the implications of this political-economic 'decentring' of the West. Though it clearly suggests that complex economic connectivity does not mean a smooth, untroubled expansion of western power in the post-colonial era, neither does it argue away the manifest 'unevenness' of the globalization process in either economic or cultural terms. We shall return to these inequalities in the following chapter. But for the present we can connect the more complex, uncertain and shifting power relations that globalization brings with what we might loosely call the lived experience of 'western cultural identity'. The issue for us here is whether the cultural hegemony of the West proposed by theorists like Latouche is actually experienced as such within real western societies.

Zygmunt Bauman makes an interesting distinction in this regard between the 'universalizing' pretensions of western modernity (as the emancipatory project of the Enlightenment) at the height of its cultural self-confidence, and what he calls the mere 'globality' of the present cultural condition of the West. In contrast with 'universality', 'the rule of reason – the order of things that would replace the slavery to passions with the autonomy of rationality': '"Globality" ... means merely that everyone everywhere may feed on McDonald's hamburgers and watch the latest made-for-TV docudrama. Universality was a proud project, a Herculean mission to perform. Globality in contrast, is a meek acquiescence to what is happening "out there"' (Bauman 1995: 24).

Now Bauman's distinction between the 'high cultural' project of Enlightenment rationality and some rather specific popular cultural practices may be a little overdrawn, but it does grasp something of the spirit in which ordinary people in the West probably experience the global spread of their 'own' culture. Indeed a lot probably hangs on the extent to which westerners actually feel 'ownership' of the sorts of cultural practices that, typically, get globalized. Although this is a complicated issue, my guess is that there is only a very low level of correspondence between people's routine interaction with the contemporary global 'culture industry' and their sense of having a distinctive *western* cultural identity, let alone feeling proud or proprietorial about it. It seems more likely to me that things like McDonalds restaurants or multiplex cinemas showing Hollywood blockbusters are experienced as simply 'there' in our cultural environments: things which we use and have become familiar and perhaps comfortable with, but which we do not – either literally or culturally – 'own'.

In this sense a *decline* of western cultural self-confidence may align with the structural properties of globalizing modernity – the 'disembedding' of practices and institutions from contexts of local to global control. In a world in which, increasingly, our mundane 'local' experience is governed by events and processes at a distance, it may become difficult to maintain a sharp sense of everyday culture as distinctively 'the way we do things' in the West – to understand these practices as having any particular connection with our specific histories and traditions. Thus, far from grasping globalized culture in the self-assured, 'centred', proprietorial way that may have been associated with, say, the *Pax Britannica* of the nineteenth century, modern-day westerners may experience it as a more ambiguous 'decentred', 'placeless' modernity to which they relate effortlessly, but without much sense of 'local' cultural control. This general sense of cultural deterritorialization[10] will be the main focus of the following chapter.

But now, to summarize these responses to the thesis of the

'westernization of the world' proposed by Latouche, we can make two general observations.

The first is that the installation of global modernity does not necessarily represent a continuing cultural domination of 'the West' – as a set of real nation-states rather than an abstract cultural principle – over the rest. Western nation-states clearly do for the present enjoy considerable political-economic dominance in the world – though, as we have observed, there is no reason to consider that this is indefinitely guaranteed. But the point is that the cultural experience of the West that accompanies this is not unambiguously one of a rugged, unquestioning conviction of its own cultural superiority, destiny or mission. It is indeed rather more likely to be one of uncertainty about once unquestioned cultural values, this being directly related to the pluralizing cultural properties of globalization – a growing awareness (through travel or popular cultural representation) of different lifestyles, beliefs and customs. This undermining of certainties is also liable to be accompanied by apprehension about the future – for example about the sustainability (in economic or environmental terms) of high-consumption western lifestyles. Given this, it seems unconvincing to speak of the present or future global cultural condition as the 'triumph of the West' (Latouche 1996: 2).[11]

The second point to make is that recognition of this more ambiguous cultural position of actual western societies also suggests some reasons to doubt the homogenizing thrust of Latouche's argument – his assumption of the swamping of all other particular cultures under the advance of the West. We can agree that modernity does involve the installation of a set of institutions which are in a very broad sense 'uniform' across the world and which establish a sort of general cultural agenda. However, as we suggested in chapter 2, there may be quite a wide range of cultural responses to this agenda – a range of 'routes to and through' or 'strategies for entering and leaving modernity' (García Canclini 1995) – that non-western cultures can and do adopt. To give just one obvious example of this, an acceptance of the technological-scientific culture of the West, of its economic rationality and even of some aspects of its consumerism may well coexist with a vigorous rejection of its secular outlook, along with its sexual permissiveness, attitudes towards gender and family relations, social use of alcohol and so on – as is common in different mixes in many Islamic societies (Sreberny-Mohammadi and Mohammadi 1994; Mowlana 1996). This particular 'route through' modernity is well put in a statement by the Tunisian Islamist intellectual Rached Gannouchi, quoted by Manuel Castells: 'The only way to accede to modernity is by our own path, that which has been traced for us by our religion, our history and our civilization' (Castells 1997: 13). Contemporary Islam, then, lived today as a central feature of cultural identity by about a billion people in a wide variety of social articulations, is by no means a capitulation to the inexorable logic of westernization. But neither is it, in most instances, simply a 'fundamentalist' rejection of all things modern. Such divergent cultural responses moreover, as they become more and more forced together through the globalization process, are likely to result in all sorts of complex admixtures – and these are liable to act back upon western versions of modernity, perhaps further destabilizing its hegemony.

But enough has now been said to indicate that there must be serious doubts that globalization issues in a uniform westernized culture. It is worth repeating that this conclusion, along with scepticism about the emergence of a global capitalist monoculture, does not mean that globalization proceeds in a benign way, sensitive to the maintenance of cultural differences and entirely free of domination. Of course this is not the case. Globalization is an uneven process in which there are, as it were, winners and losers. But the point is that it is a far more complex process than can be grasped in the simple story of the unilinear advance of the West. And, more importantly for the concerns of this particular chapter, for all the superficial signs of cultural convergence that might be identified, the threat of a more profound homogenization of culture can only be deduced by ignoring the complexity, reflexivity and sheer recalcitrance of actual, particular cultural responses to modernity.

Global Culture: The Sceptical Viewpoint

In contrast with both the utopian and the dystopian visions of a global culture, there is a marked scepticism in many quarters about *any* sort of emergent global culture. This scepticism can be distinguished from the more specific criticisms I have made of the homogenization scenario. One of its sources lies simply in a cool 'realist' assessment of the rather obviously divided world we see about us at the end of the twentieth century. After all, none of the nineteenth-century enthusiasts came anywhere near to seeing their vision of global unity realized and the historical record of the twentieth century as a whole has not been encouraging. If we discount the possibilities of the sort of 'world-historical' revolution that Marx looked to, the sudden punctual transformation of all things, then we may seem forced back on to sober reflection on, and projection from, the far-from-unified world we see around us. The almost instantaneously fading promise of the 'new international order' following the end of the Cold War is a significant source of current global-cultural scepticism. Not only do we see a proliferation in ethnic, religious and nationalist hostilities in many parts of the world, but the resumption of testing of nuclear weapons by France and China in 1995 seems emblematic of a wider perception that we have not moved significantly closer to a more secure world, let alone a unified one. The United Nations celebrated its fiftieth anniversary in September 1995 against a background of criticism of its lack of effect in intervention in the wars in, for example, Somalia or Bosnia, and of talk of a crisis in its institutional and financial management. None of this encourages political or cultural optimism.

Yet, on the other hand, the world of the 1990s is also characterized by a set of technological 'revolutions' comparable to those that inspired the visions of nineteenth-century thinkers. Indeed the popular *expectation* of ever-new technological wonders, particularly in the areas of communications, computing and information technology, now seems a significant aspect of the texture of modern culture. Such modern 'techno-utopianism' exists most evidently in the discourse surrounding the 'global information superhighway' promised by politicians like US Vice-President Al Gore: 'We now have at hand the technological breakthroughs and economic means to bring all the communities of the world together' (quoted in Schiller 1995: 17). And this is not simply the familiar vote-directed 'vision thing' of politicians, nor the ever-upbeat futurology of corporate advertising: 'The future's bright; The future's Orange.' There is clearly something else going on. Information technology entrepreneurs like Bill Gates of Microsoft, now have syndicated columns in daily newspapers, write 'visionary' books about the transformative potential of their technologies (Gates 1995) and buy up the 'virtual' rights to whole national art collections. However cynical one may be about all this, it can't be entirely grasped as simply the familiar grandiosity of corporate capitalism. Neither can the almost frantic techno-enthusiasm of magazines like *Wired* which famously launched its first UK edition with a quote from Thomas Paine: 'We have it in our power to begin the world over again.' What is interesting about such texts is the extraordinary sense of 'virtual' cultural optimism they manage to generate in the face of some bleak global 'realities'. *Wired UK's* first editorial stated:

It's finally time to embrace the future with optimism again in the realization that this peaceful, inevitable revolution isn't a problem, but
an opportunity to build a new and better civilization for ourselves
and our children. Our first instruction to our writers: Amaze us. Our
second: Report back from the future about what's coming – about work
outside workplaces, markets without masters, entertainment beyond
mass media, civic mindedness beyond government, community beyond neighbourhoods, consciousness that spans the globe. (*Wired*, 1
January 1995: 13)

It is of course tempting to dismiss this enthusiasm as naive and un-
critical – which in some senses it quite obviously is. And it is also
probably true that the centre of gravity of popular cultural aspiration – the expectations that most ordinary people have about the
transformative impact of such technologies – lies far away from the
visionary or the utopian, seeing in them sources of increasing social
convenience or new forms of entertainment. However it is equally
clear that we cannot ignore the huge transformative potential of these
globalizing technologies – the way they are already dramatically
changing our lives.

How can we make sense of these contradictory tendencies? One
tempting way of framing the issue of global culture at the end of the
twentieth century might be to say that it is a case of very bad timing:
the intersection of manifest technical possibility with a low point in
cultural-political confidence. But this is obviously too glib. Instead
we need to see such contradictions as going to the heart of global
modernity. It has been argued, for instance by Marshall Berman, that
we are simply not very good in the twentieth century at dealing with
such contradictions and ambiguities. Compared with nineteenth-
century thinkers – 'simultaneously enthusiasts and enemies of modern life, wrestling with its ambiguities and contradictions' (Berman
1983: 24) – our responses tend towards flat polarities of the celebratory or the apocalyptic. On this reading, the distance between Karl
Marx and Bill Gates is (amongst other things!) their respective capacity to grasp the dialectic involved in the social and cultural
implications of technology. However, such arguments are not entirely convincing. It seems to me that the world is *genuinely* more
complex at the end of our century than at the end of the last one, and
presents us with more difficult moral, cultural and political dilemmas than Marx (or even Nietzsche) had to deal with. But, more
importantly, such dilemmas are not restricted to intellectuals: with
the ever-growing reflexivity of modern social life, they now form
a part of everyday life for vastly more ordinary people than ever

before. In living with the ambiguities involved, for example, in the routine use of new globalizing communications technologies, we all, I suspect, develop complex and nuanced responses even if these are not always articulated as such.

The very complexity of localized and distanciated, immediate and mediated cultural experience in the high-modern epoch then – and the uncertainties of identity and values that this produces – is one general way of explaining the opposing tendencies towards unicity and fragmentation. But we can take the debate further by looking more closely at one of the principal sources of contemporary scepticism over the possibility of an emergent global culture: that of the grip that *national identity* has upon our cultural imagination.

The Global from the Standpoint of the National

One very well articulated sceptical position in current discussions of the possibilities for a global culture is that of Anthony Smith (1990, 1991, 1995), a sociologist who, significantly, is known for his work on ethnicity and national cultures. Smith places at the centre of his discussion a picture of the sort of global 'cosmopolitan' culture that he says we may extrapolate from, on the one hand, the growth of new communications, information and computer technologies and, on the other, the 'western experience of postmodern cultures':

> A global culture would . . . be composed of a number of analytically discrete elements: effectively advertised mass commodities, a patchwork of folk or ethnic styles and motifs stripped of their context, some general ideological discourses concerned with 'human rights and values' and a standardized quantitative and 'scientific' language of communication and appraisal, all underpinned by the new information and telecommunications systems and their computerized technologies. (Smith 1991: 157)

Clearly Smith doesn't warm to the picture he paints. He goes on to describe this potential global culture as 'fundamentally artificial', 'shallow', 'capricious and ironical', 'fluid and shapeless' and as 'lack[ing] any emotional commitments to what is signified'. One reason for this negative view seems to be that Smith rather conflates the category of the 'postmodern' with that of *any* potential communications-mediated global culture. But if we separate out his obvious distaste for the pastiche and bricolage that has been associated with postmodern culture, and his suspicion of an accompanying –

'quantitative and standardizing' – technological rationality, we are left with a more focused scepticism about the general prospects for a global culture. This can be summarized in the related charges that a global culture is necessarily a 'constructed' culture and that it is ahistorical, timeless and 'memoryless'.

Something of what he means by calling this culture 'constructed' can be seen in the description he gives of its contents. Nothing really binds together the features he describes – for example the global promotion of consumer goods and the discourse of universal rights and values – other than that they are global issues which seem to exist simultaneously. Here is a sense, then, of global culture having to be deliberately constructed out of the various discrete features and consequences of the globalization process, and yet having nothing really to bind them together as common integrated cultural experience. The understandable scepticism here is over the possibility of manufacturing a 'culture' to coincide with the diverse manifestations of the globalization process.

However, as Smith is quick to recognize, there is an important sense in which national cultures too are constructs – 'imagined communities': 'Nations were "built" and "forged" by state elites or intelligentsias or capitalists; like the Scots kilt or the British Coronation ceremony, they are composed of so many "invented traditions" ... '(Smith 1990: 177). In the light of this, he concedes that the need to construct a global culture 'along with global economic and political institutions' should not seem surprising. There is nevertheless a crucial difference for him between the cultural constructions involved in the projects of nation-building and those he associates with the idea of a global culture. For all that they are constructs, Smith argues that national cultures remain obstinately 'particular, timebound and expressive'. By this he means that the deliberate construction of national identity was necessarily parasitic upon deeper senses of collective identity shared by people situated in a particular location and involving 'feelings and values in respect of a sense of continuity, shared memories and a sense of common destiny' (1990: 179). It is these attachments – which Smith associates with pre-modern ethnic identity, 'the community's ethno-history' – that are the subjective 'core' upon which he believes the purposive construction of modern national identities is able to elaborate.

Given this view of the nature of collective identity, Smith's scepticism over the possibilities for an emergent global cultural identity crystallizes into the argument that a global culture necessarily lacks the vital ingredients of common historical experience, a sense of temporal continuity and, crucially, shared memories. There are, he argues, no 'world memories'; at least those that there are – of colonialism and world wars – are not recommended to produce feelings of global unity. He concludes that 'the project of a global culture, as opposed to global communications, must appear premature' (1990: 180). Since he takes such a dim view of the ersatz nature of 'postmodern' cultural production, this might seem no bad thing. However, he does also recognize that, from the point of view of both global security and the higher ideals of cultural coexistence and mutuality, the continued – and often aggressive – assertion of ethno-nationalist cultural division that this implies is a 'bleak conclusion'.

Smith's arguments are to a certain extent persuasive. In particular he is right to stress the necessary aspect of popular involvement in any cultural identity, the elements of it which escape formal structured projects (from the state) and the fact that cultural images and traditions 'do not descend upon mute and passive populations on whose *tabula rasa* they inscribe themselves' (1990: 179). This recognition of reflexive cultural agency, as we have seen, is also an important critical perspective from which to view pessimistic claims about global cultural domination. It is also difficult to dissent much from the contrast that he draws between the *longue durée* of the establishment of national identities and the notion of a global identity as an instant, immediate construction. For all that the symbolic forms of national culture were in part deliberate projects, he is surely correct to stress the work of time and popular memory in their 'rootedness'.

There is, however, a more general scepticism implicit in his account, and this relates to the way in which the very presence of national cultures themselves may act to inhibit the emergence of a global culture. As Smith recognizes, there is nothing necessarily exclusive about cultural identifications; indeed it is quite common for people to feel, for example, 'Yoruba, Nigerian and African in concentric circles of belonging and identity' (1991: 175, cf. Tomlinson 1991: 78). There is perhaps no reason, then, why one's repertoire of identities may not also comfortably embrace the global. He none the less claims that national identity has a particular power *vis-à-vis* other forms of identity, that 'It provides the sole vision and rationale of political solidarity today, one that commands popular assent and elicits popular enthusiasm. All other visions, all other rationales, appear wan and shadowy by comparison. They offer no sense of election, no unique history, no special destiny' (Smith 1991: 176).

This argument is made to support the case for the continuing resilience and relevance of national cultural identities in a globalized world, a point with which, in general, it would be foolish to disagree. However, a corollary to this might be the idea that the continuing existence of national identities inhibits the emergence of a global, cosmopolitan identity, if only in the way they preoccupy people's cultural imagination to the point of defining its horizons. Further, it might be argued that all the cultural-ideological work put in by nation-states in the establishment and maintenance of national identifications is in no way matched by any deliberate symbolic constructions of a global home for humankind. If visions of global solidarity appear 'wan and shadowy' it is, arguably, for the prime reason that they have little in the way of an institutional sponsor. The United Nations and all its subsidiary bodies which spring to mind in this connection are, of course, primarily *international* as distinct from global bodies, dependent for their existence on the continuing structure of the nation-state system. Thus, though a rhetoric of global unity informs UN discourse, this is always precariously balanced against the need to assert the principles of national sovereignty and cultural difference (Schlesinger 1991; Tomlinson 1991). The interests in a national as opposed to a global cultural identity might then be construed as a potential 'zero-sum game'. Viewed thus, it seems unlikely that much serious global identity-building will be forthcoming from the international institutional bases that currently exist. So when looked at on the level of political institutions and their orchestrations of cultural attachment (as well as from the ethno-historical point of view) the prospects for a global culture again look dim. Smith's scepticism therefore appears well founded.

There are however some important qualifications to be made, and the most significant one relates to his central critical strategy. For what informs the whole of Smith's scepticism is, of course, the contrast he draws between our *present* experience of national cultures and possibilities of a global culture. Now at one level this seems a perfectly reasonable strategy to adopt, but it does have the effect of inflecting the argument towards one particular model of collective identity, one style of cultural imagining. National cultures we may agree *are* historically situated, time-bound, particular and so forth. But this fact in itself is not sufficient to undermine the potential for the emergence of *any* sort of global cultural identification, but only one after the style of the nation-state. What Smith's scepticism really relates to is the emergence of a global culture as, in Mike Featherstone's words, 'the culture of the nation-state writ large' (1993: 173). This is something which we can readily agree with. Globalization does not look set to usher in a single global culture on the model of particular, historically specific national cultures. However, once we recognize this specificity, then other ways of thinking about the idea of global cultural identity might begin to suggest themselves.

Beyond 'Embedded Statism'

There is in fact a good case for looking beyond the centripetal pull exercised by the nation-state and its culture. Against all the arguments that take as their point of reference the resilience of national identities, there are others that suggest we should not allow the shadow of the nation-state to eclipse everything.

In the first place we can situate the influence that the nation-state exercises over cultural imaginings within the broader debate about 'state-centric 'conceptualizations in the social sciences more generally. For example the geographer Peter Taylor has recently criticized the 'embedded statism' that he claims characterizes mainstream social sciences and has had the effect of 'nationalizing social knowledge'. That is to say: 'In terms of the ontology upon which social science has been built, the key spatiality has been the sovereign territories that collectively define the mosaic that is the world political map' (Taylor 1996: 1919). Taylor argues that disciplines like sociology, political science and economics have until quite recently failed to recognize (much less, problematize) the extent to which they are actually the 'creatures of the states', owing their very conceptions of 'the social', 'the political', 'the economic' to a particular historical configuration that accompanied their emergence at the end of the nineteenth century.

The central consequence of 'embedded statism' in the social sciences that Taylor identifies is the way in which its long taking-for-granted of *one* form of spatiality has marginalized alternative spatial conceptions of the social world. This is the point at which his argument has particular relevance to our discussion, since he makes the point that the symbiotic relationship between state as political 'power container' and nation as source of cultural identity (having a supposed primordial ethnic core) had the effect of 'naturalizing' the nation-state so that it came to be regarded in almost the same way as other 'natural' spatial features like 'rivers, mountain ranges and coastlines'. Thus, 'being "natural", states precluded all other social worlds and the spatiality of fragmented sovereignty became ingrained in modern society' (1996: 1920). The implications of this for the limited cultural imaginings of territorial identity beyond the nation-state are obvious.

However, Taylor argues that the impact of globalization is now undermining the credibility of this social-scientific orthodoxy and that a 'new heterodoxy' is emerging in all sorts of cross-disciplinary inquiry – including cultural studies – which is 'opening up to new spaces '(1996: 1928).

It is in this broad context that we can consider alternative ways of thinking about globalized culture that do not keep us continually in the shadow cast by national cultures. We need to consider those factors related to the globalization process that reduce or otherwise compromise the grip that the nation may exercise on the cultural imagination of its population. These factors will include the influence of what one might call the global 'culture industry' – the 'commercialized mass commodities' that Smith so disparages – but in a rather more complex way than he recognizes. Rather than seeing cultural commodities as simply images of a depressing global standardization or homogenization, we can recognize the way in which their use contributes to the general experience of 'cultural disembedding' – or, as I shall describe it in the following chapter, 'deterritorialization' – typical of modern societies. This sense of deterritorialization will include many other aspects of mundane experience – our everyday use of globalizing communications and media technologies, the 'transnational' dependencies people may have in terms of their employment (working for a foreign-based multinational company), the increasing sense that, because of globalizing processes, the nation-state is no longer able to 'deliver the goods' to its population in economic terms (full employment, stable currency and interest rates) or in terms of control of the quality of the physical environment.

At the risk of labouring the point, there is little here to support the idea that a single, unified global culture in any conventional sense is about to emerge. On this point at least, the present analysis coincides pretty much with Smith's sceptical position. Neither do I want to deny that national cultures are likely to remain very significant poles of cultural identification for the foreseeable future. However I do believe the style of cultural experience and identification is bound to be affected by the complex and multiform interrelations, penetrations and cultural mutations that characterize the globalization of our current stage of modernity. In the process, not merely different, more complex identity positions, but also different *modes* of cultural identification are arising. It is to these – the complex constituents of what we can call a deterritorialized, *globalized* culture – rather than to the monolithic imagining of a *global* culture, that we now turn.

4

Deterritorialization: The Cultural Condition of Globalization

The previous chapter addressed the most 'obvious' though, as it turned out, least plausible implication of globalization for cultural change – the question of the prospects, viewed either with anticipation or foreboding, for the emergence of a single, unified global culture. This chapter adopts a rather more oblique approach. Here we explore a broad conceptual category through which we might think about the cultural implications of globalization. This category grasps a number of aspects of a globalized (as distinct from a global) culture as it is lived in daily experience, but it relates these to one key assumption, namely that globalization fundamentally transforms the relationship between the *places* we inhabit and our cultural practices, experiences and identities. 'Places', Morley and Robins provocatively claim, 'are no longer the clear supports of our identity' (1995: 87). In employing the concept of 'deterritorialization' we will try to understand why this might be so.

The Concept of Deterritorialization

Several theorists have used the term 'deterritorialization' in relation to globalizing processes (e.g. Appadurai 1990; García Canclini 1995; Mlinar 1992; Lull 1995; Featherstone 1995; Mattelart 1994; Morley and Robins 1995; Latouche 1996) while others have preferred related terms such as 'delocalization' (Thompson 1995) or 'dis-placement' (Giddens 1990) to grasp aspects of the process. Though there are several differences of emphasis between these usages,[1] I think it is possible to identify a *general* sense of the concept which can help us understand broad transformations in the place–culture relationship in the context of global modernity. So I want to use the term 'deterritorialization' in this very broad, inclusive, way to grasp what García Canclini calls, 'the loss of the "natural" relation of culture to geographical and social territories' (1995: 229). To approach this I want to return, briefly, to Giddens's account of the implications of time-space distanciation and disembedding for our experience of place.

As we saw in chapter 2, a central aspect of Giddens's argument is that modernity frees social relations from the constrictions of face-to-face interactions in the localities of pre-modern societies, allowing for the stretching of relations across time and space which is, for him, the core of globalization. But, of course, the disembedding involved does not mean that people cease to live their lives in 'real' localities. So from the point of view of cultural experience, what becomes important is the way in which this stretching of social relations affects the character of the localities that we typically inhabit. As will be recalled from the earlier discussion, Giddens grasps this transformation by describing modern places as increasingly 'phantasmagoric'. The comforting, familiar character of the cultural settings we routinely move amongst conceals the influences of distant social forces and processes.

However, he argues against the familiar claim that modernity means the loss of the existential comforts and assurances of local communal experience in the face of increasingly 'abstract' social forces which structure our lives. Rather, he argues that we retain a sense of familiarity in our day-to-day experience of local contexts, but that this familiarity no longer derives from 'the particularities of localized place'. People may still be 'at home' in their localities but they are at some level aware that these are 'phantasmagoric' places in which familiar features are often not unique to that locale and part of its 'organic development' but, rather, features that have been 'placed into' the locale by distanciated forces:

> The local shopping mall is a milieu in which a sense of ease and security is cultivated by the layout of the buildings and the careful planning of public places. Yet everyone who shops there is aware that most of the shops are chain stores, which one might find in any city, and indeed that innumerable shopping malls of similar design exist elsewhere. (1990: 141)

So the experience of 'displacement' in modernity is not one of alienation, but of ambivalence. People 'own' their local places phenomenologically in a sort of *provisional* sense, recognizing, at some level, the absent forces which structure this ownership. And, of course, this perception is linked to the reality of a steadily declining local ownership of public spaces in a direct material sense linked to the globalization of capital. The small retail businesses – 'corner shops' – run by local families which were once ubiquitous in the United Kingdom, as in many European countries, have been largely replaced in the last forty years by supermarkets[2] and the rather anachronistically named 'high street' chains located in shopping precincts. Such shops in the 'mall' – itself an ambivalent public/private space unknown in the UK before the 1960s – appear and disappear at the behest of global market forces, not, primarily, as the expression of local will, other than in the formalities of planning provisions.

But the argument is not simply one about the transformation of public communal spaces. As we saw in chapter 2, we can contrast the most intimate locales of modernity – our private living spaces – with the dwellings of pre-modern societies in terms of their relative degree of 'openness to the world', particularly as a consequence of the routine use of domestic communications technologies. So the link between our mundane cultural experience and our location is transformed at every level. As Giddens has it, 'the very tissue of spatial experience alters, conjoining proximity and distance in ways that have few parallels in prior ages' (1990: 140).

This is the experience that I shall try to understand here through the category of deterritorialization. This experience is fundamental to the way we live our daily lives in modern societies: it touches nearly all aspects of our mundane practices, it has become 'naturalized' and taken for granted in the routine flow of experience and yet it is a complex and ambivalent cultural condition. It is important to stress this ambivalence and therefore to distinguish the condition of deterritorialization from the claim that global modernity, in its massifying, centralizing moment, is *destructive* of real localities. I don't believe this is the case, however much similar terms – 'displacement', 'de-localization'– might at first glance suggest it. To make this important distinction we can consider the idea that modernity replaces real localities with 'non-places'.

Non-places

The French anthropologist Marc Augé describes 'non-places' as follows:

If a place can be defined as relational, historical and concerned with identity, then a space which cannot be defined as relational or historical, or concerned with identity will be a non-place. . . . A world where people are born in the clinic and die in hospital, where transit points and temporary abodes are proliferating under luxurious or inhuman conditions (hotel chains and squats, holiday clubs and refugee camps, shantytowns . . .); where a dense network of means of transport which are also inhabited spaces is developing; where the habitué of supermarkets, slot machines and credit cards communicates wordlessly, through gestures, with an abstract, unmediated commerce; a world thus surrendered to solitary individuality, to the fleeting, the temporary and ephemeral, offers the anthropologist (and others) a new object. (Augé 1995: 78)

Augé argues that contemporary capitalist modernity creates a distinct mode of mundane locational experience which he describes as 'supermodernity', defining our increasing interactions with these 'non-places'. His examples are of airport departure lounges, supermarkets, motorways and service stations, street-corner cash dispensers, high-speed trains. These supermodern locales are, for him, 'non-places' in distinction from the 'anthropological places' that 'create the organically social' (1995: 94).

As an instance of an 'anthropological place' – one that provides cultural identity and memory, binding its inhabitants to the history of the locale through the daily repetitions of 'organic' social interaction – he offers the following generalized description of the centres of typical small French provincial towns, 'as they appeared under the Third Republic . . . the leading cafés, hotels and businesses . . . concentrated in the town centre, not far from where the market is held':

At regular intervals, on Sunday or market day, the centre 'comes to life'. [It is a place] where individual itineraries can intersect and mingle, where a few words are exchanged and solitudes momentarily forgotten, on the church steps, in front of the town hall, at the café counter or in the baker's doorway: the rather lazy rhythm and talkative mood that still characterize Sunday mornings in contemporary provincial France. (1995: 66–7)

There is undoubtedly something of the nostalgic in Augé's depiction of these 'real' places. But, interestingly, he doesn't think of them as part of a disappearing world of 'traditional life', but as characteristic of an earlier period of modernity itself – what he calls

'Baudelairean' modernity (p. 92), in which the link between the present and the past, the old and the new, is still visible and the link between place, memory and identity is preserved in routine interactions. Baudelairean modernity, as he says, is still alive in contemporary France, but it is threatened by the incursions of 'supermodernity'. In these 'non-places', 'talkative' organic inter-actions are replaced by mute signs: the instructions on the VDUs of automatic cash dispensers – 'Please withdraw your card. Thank you for your custom' – or illuminated signs on motorways – 'Two-kilometre tailback on A3.' In contrast to the conviviality of the market square, the supermarket shopper engages in a silent, solitary congress with labels, instructions and self-weigh machines. Even real 'anthropological places' can become transformed into non-places for outsiders as their real lived-history becomes 'textualized'. As an ex-ample of this he describes the experience of driving along autoroutes which bypass provincial towns and yet advertise their attractions as heritage sites on sign boards: 'drivers batting down the *autoroute du sud* are urged to pay attention a thirteenth-century fortified village, a renowned vineyard, the "eternal hill" of Vézelay . . . '(p. 97). The non-place of the autoroute is defined for Augé precisely by its routing round real places whilst fixing these in signs aimed at commodifying them. The theme is pursued in his treatment of motorway service stations, 'adopting an increasingly aggressive role as centres of regional culture, selling a range of local goods with a few maps and guide books '. His point is that the anonymous, ersatz, non-place of the service station – probably as close to the 'real place' as most travellers get – is a sort of simulacrum of anthrop-ological place. The same argument is applied to travel on the high-speed TGV trains, where images in the rail company magazines provided for passengers stand in for the real places no longer clearly visible – even the names of stations now impossible to read as the train flashes by. Places are therefore increasingly 'invaded by texts'.

Non-places are, as we can see, bleak locales of contemporary modernity: places of solitude (even in the presence of others), silence, anonymity, alienation and impermanence. They are places where interaction is instrumental and 'contractual' – the apotheosis of *Gesellschaft* – lifted out of any organic relation with a community existing in continuity through time. Augé's argument is also one that privileges the 'local' as the site of the genuine. The efficient 'connec-tivity' of the TGV and the autoroute are contrasted with '*local* [rail-way] services and the roads of *local* interest ' which 'used to penetrate the intimacy of everyday life'. The local railway, in particular, as it passes slowly around backs of houses, 'catches provincials off guard in the privacy of their daily lives, behind the façade, on the garden side, the kitchen or bedroom side '(pp. 98–9).

The immediate critical response might be to see this as another version of anti-modern 'alienation theory', conjuring a comparison with a mythical *Gemeinschaft*. But this would be to miss the main point: that non-places, however problematically marked off against the 'authenticity' of anthropological places, are none the less genuinely new, peculiar cultural-spatial phenomena, unique features of our late twentieth-century cultural landscape. Augé brings the ethnographic eye to these new salient features, and argues, I think plausibly, that 'some experience of non-place (indissociable from a more or less clear perception of the acceleration of history and the contraction of the planet) is today an essential part of all social existence' (p. 119).

The experience of non-places, then, is certainly an *aspect* of what I want to understand by deterritorialized culture. However it is important to keep their significance in proportion. In the first place, the sort of locales Augé describes do not, as he concedes, map the totality of modern cultural-spatial experience: 'real' places and non-places 'intertwine and tangle together' in modern societies (p. 107). As we saw in chapter 1, the 'world' of the international air terminal coexists spatially and culturally with the neighbourhood pressed up against its perimeter fences. The danger, then, is that we come to think of deterritorialization as *only* applying to this world of transit and impermanence. One feature of Augé's discourse that encourages this is his standpoint as the eternal *passenger*, always viewing locales as one passing through them – on trains, in cars, on planes. This perspective accentuates the alienating, individualizing, contractual aspect of non-places.

Take the example of the processing of passengers through Roissy 1 airport that runs as a leitmotiv through his book. Stressing the contractual nature of relations here – as instantiated in the routines of documentation that establish the 'validity' of the passenger's presence in the locale – the checking of tickets, boarding passes, passports, visas – he contrasts these interactions with 'the complicities of language, local reference, the unformulated rules of living knowhow that apply to 'anthropological place'. So, he challenges: 'Try to imagine a Durkheimian analysis of the transit lounge at Roissy! ' (p. 94). But what he does not account for here is the entirely different experience of Roissy that belongs to its more permanent denizens – the check-in clerks, baggage handlers, cleaners, caterers, security staff and so forth who work there. For these people the non-place of the terminal is clearly a 'real' place – their workplace. And we must assume that it is experienced by them with all the anthropological richness, the tacit rules of 'living know-how', the subtleties of daily interpersonal contact, the friendships, rivalries and so on that apply to any other place of work.[3] So the designation of places as non-places is clearly not an absolute, but one that depends, crucially on *perspective*.

What this also implies, of course, is that non-places are not necessarily so intrinsically alienating, but can be places where social relations can be re-embedded. Compare Augé's description of the instrumental interaction at the supermarket checkout, 'The customer . . . hands his credit card to a young woman as silent as himself – anyway not very chatty – who runs each article past the sensor of a decoding machine . . .' (p. 100), with this very different account from a British lesbian woman of her social use of supermarket shopping:

> It is funny going to Sainsbury's . . . I never go there without seeing a lot of dykes . . . which is nice! And people you haven't seen for ages, so you kind of end up – what was going to be like twenty minutes nipping in getting a few things, you know, you end up chatting to people and that's quite – I do enjoy that. (Bell and Valentine 1997: 138)

Just how different, we may ask, is this from encounters on the church steps or the *mairie* of Baudelairean modernity? Well different, admittedly, in terms of the overall texture of 'late modern' social relations, but not intrinsically different on some axis of organic versus contractual relations. The point is that non-places can be seen as particular, distinct instances of 'deterritorialized' locales, embodying distanciated relations, but this does not necessarily render them socially or culturally sterile. Mike Featherstone makes a similar point in a discussion of the small, subtle but taken-for-granted social routines and rituals that pick out the unique cultural character – the 'at homeness' – of *any* 'locality' for those who live and work there: 'the little rituals of buying a round of drinks in a particular way . . .' Citing Gertrude Stein's famous remark about Oakland, California – 'There's no there there' – he shows how this could be read as registering, 'the apparent absence of . . . affective and symbolic sedimentation into the material fabric of the buildings and the environment and the embodied practices of social life' (Featherstone 1995: 94). But of course this is to view the locale from the cultural exterior: Stein's quip, as Featherstone says, was referring to a dearth of 'recognizable cultural capital', whilst for the actual inhabitants of Oakland, no doubt, the place was experienced as a meaningful and affectively rich – if perhaps not a vivid – locality. For the residents, the 'there' of Oakland lies in the fact that 'they're there.'

The concept of deterritorialization, then, has to be able to grasp the novelty of the contemporary transformation of place – its positive as well as its negative features – without yielding to the temptation to read this as simply the impoverishment or, indeed, the dissolution of cultural interaction. We can get a little further in understanding this intrinsic ambivalence of deterritorialization by considering a hypothetical case of the 'lived experience' of global modernity.

The Mundane Experience of Deterritorialization

Raymond Williams provided the basis for this (actually before most people had begun to talk about globalization) in the following little vignette of bourgeois 'cosmopolitan' western lifestyle:

> There was once this Englishman who worked in the London office of a multinational corporation based in the United States. He drove home one evening in his Japanese car. His wife, who worked in a firm which imported German kitchen equipment, was already at home. Her small Italian car was often quicker through the traffic. After a meal which included New Zealand lamb, Californian carrots, Mexican honey, French cheese and Spanish wine they settled down to watch a programme on their television set, which had been made in Finland. The programme was a retrospective celebration of the war to recapture the Falkland Islands. As they watched it they felt warmly patriotic, and very proud to be British. (Williams 1983: 177)

Williams uses this sketch to launch a discussion of the contradictory nature of contemporary national identity, and we *could* pursue this by thinking about how the globalization of mundane experience may make a stable sense of 'local' cultural identity (including national identity) increasingly difficult to maintain, as our daily lives become more and more interwoven with, and penetrated by, influences and experiences that have their origins far away. But we can equally take the experience of this (rather complacent) couple to illustrate the broader substance of deterritorialization, without being drawn too much back to the discourse of nationality which we tried to escape from in the previous chapter.

Since part of the argument about globalization is that it is a rapidly accelerating process, it might be interesting to bring this hypothetical couple quickly up to date from the early 1980s to the late 1990s. There is, first, a context of rapidly developing 'world events' to be considered here. As these fifteen or so years fast forward across their TV screen, our couple will witness enormous and unpredictable changes, many of which are directly connected with the broad process of globalization: both resulting from and contributing to it. So, for example: Chernobyl and its (literal and metaphorical) fallout, the fall of the Berlin wall and the collapse of the communist world, the movement towards closer European unity represented in the Maastricht Treaty and the single European currency, the deregulation of global capitalist markets exemplified in the 'Big Bang' of the London stock exchange, global summits on environmental pollution and climate change, and of course, other wars – Beirut, the Gulf, Somalia, Bosnia, Rwanda – all played out with increasing technical sophistication and 'immediacy' in their living rooms.

There are at least two senses in which such global events may relate to the cultural experience of deterritorialization. First, some of them will have direct effects on people's immediate material conditions and environments. For example, European Union regulations may impact (positively or negatively) on the working practices of small local businesses, or EU regional development grants may transform the local built environments of depressed inner city areas. The way in which local people experience these interventions (as either unjustified interference and a threat to 'our British way of life', or the promise of a new, if rather vague, European identity and 'communal' project) will clearly depend, largely, on the degree to which they benefit or are disadvantaged. But underlying this is surely the growing awareness of the significance of 'remote' forces beyond what, at a rather fundamental level and over an extended period of historical time, we have come to think of as our 'natural' and valid polity – the territorial boundaries of our nation-state.[4] In the case of the impact of European Union legislation, the experience of distant determinations can be related to definite (if arcane) international political/economic processes and to identifiable agents and loci of power (Brussels 'Eurocrats'). But other events create more dramatic and seemingly random impacts – for example the effects on domestic economies of fluctuations on world capitalist markets. The most spectacular of these are the periodic international stock market or currency crises – the 'Black Days' referred to in chapter 3. People experiencing the impact of such events – on their jobs, their mortgage payments or their savings – are of course liable to feel generally more insecure in planning their lives and less confident in their national government's ability to control events. But, more broadly, such events may add to the extension of the individual's 'phenomenal world': people probably come to include distant events and processes more routinely in their perceptions of what is significant for their own personal lives. This is one aspect of what deterritorialization may involve: the ever-broadening horizon of relevance in people's routine experience, removing not only general 'cultural awareness' but, crucially, the processes of individual 'life planning' from a self-contained context centred on physical locality or politically defined territory.

Of course such effects will be uneven in their impact – distant wars, for example, may not have the same direct impact on people's mundane experience as economic crises. But there is another sense in which conflicts are more immediate, loom larger in daily experience than ever before and this is, of course, in the way they are 'delivered' to our homes by globalizing media technologies, particularly by television. We shall discuss the media's role in cultural globalization in more detail – including the specific 'phenomenology' involved – in chapter 5. But it is important here to outline the broad significance of the media in the process of deterritorialization. And we can begin by considering the sheer ubiquity of media and communications technologies in modern mundane experience – and the way in which, as a consequence, mediated experience becomes imbricated with 'immediate' experience.

So, to return to our time-travelling couple. As successful and affluent business people, they have acquired lots of new communications technology since the early eighties to keep them 'in touch' with the world: satellite or (more discreetly) cable TV, cellphones, paging machines, fax machines, computers and 'laptops', modems to connect with the internet, and so on. They now routinely pick up and send their e-mail and maybe will even surf the internet as an alternative to watching the television. One of the interesting things about the way they use this communications technology is how quickly they take it for granted, how it soon loses its wonder and becomes integral to everyday life. But how do they experience the way in which their home is now more 'open' to information? In one straightforward sense they are, at least potentially, much better informed. For example they can now choose between the coverage of news events not simply of different national 'terrestrial' broadcasters (the BBC or ITN) but of commercial satellite channels like

BSkyB, international news specialists like CNN or even, allowing for the language problems, of other national stations in Europe or beyond. Not only this; they can now check this coverage against information from specialist websites on the internet. So, for example, they might want to check the BBC's coverage of some environmental issue against the version provided on Greenpeace International's website.

There is a sense, then, in which this very *choice* provided by new media technologies contributes to deterritorialization. Being 'better informed' implies having available a range of perspectives on events beyond that of the 'home culture', being able to situate oneself at a distance from the (national, local) 'viewpoint'. Whatever this may promise for the development of cosmopolitan cultural dispositions, it also represents a loss of the cultural certainty, even of the existential 'comfort' involved in having the world 'out there' presented to us from the still point of an unchallenged national/local perspective. Deterritorialization in this sense of opening up to the world and expanding cultural horizons via globalized media may thus be an ambiguous condition.

This sort of ambiguity is also suggested in the way communicational technologies can be conceived of as, simultaneously, 'exits from' and 'entrances into' our intimate living spaces. The corollary to 'keeping in touch' might be the sense that our attention to the outside world is more constantly in demand, that we are continually 'on duty' as communicational agents. This is, of course, a perception now widely distributed in relation to the telephone: simultaneously a blessing and a curse, the ubiquitous (indispensable?) tool of social convenience, and the alien presence always ready to summon us, imposing its own implacable priority over our chosen activities of the moment. But now there are also all the faxes and e-mails to be responded to, the answerphone messages to be 'got back to', the cellphone or the pager that accompanies us even while on the move, the TV programmes to remember to video and then to find the time to watch. In all these ways media and communications technologies have cultural significance not only in terms of the messages and representations they carry, but in their capacity to structure our experience and use of time and space. Communicational connectedness, being 'plugged into' the global media and communications network has implications for our experience of the distinction between a public and a private sphere: our couple might sense that the information affluence they enjoy also means their home is no longer quite their castle. Joshua Meyrowitz (1985) quotes John Ruskin to good effect here:

This is the nature of home – it is a place of peace; the shelter not only from all injury, but from all terror, doubt and division. In so far as it is not this, it is not home; so far as the anxieties of the outer life penetrate into it, and the inconsistently minded, unknown, unloved, or hostile society of the outer world is allowed by either husband or wife to cross the threshold, it ceases to be a home; it is then only a part of the outer world which you have roofed over and lighted a fire in. ('Of Queen's Gardens', quoted Meyrowitz 1985: 222)

Meyrowitz uses Ruskin's romantic notion of the sacrosanct private space of the home to illustrate how media technologies have contributed to disclosing the gender politics of the private sphere and thus 'politicizing the personal' in family life.[5] However the quotation can equally be taken to reflect a more general point. Ruskin's paternalist sexual politics aside, his anxieties over the disconcerting intrusion of the outer world into the domestic sphere have a peculiar resonance in the mediated culture of the late twentieth century.

What is at stake here is a shift in the phenomenology of that space which defines the house as the home. This, for Ruskin, depended on the notion of a 'shelter' both as the figure of physical protection – 'roofing over' a space – and as psychological and emotional protection, the forming of a boundary – the 'threshold', the liminal space – separating the outer world from the inner world of intimacy and subjectivity. This is a spatial distinction which, as Marc Augé points out, can be traced to the classical mythological figures of Hestia and Hermes: 'Hestia symbolizes the circular hearth placed in the centre of the house, the closed space of the group drawn into itself (and thus in a sense of its relations with itself); while Hermes, god of the threshold and the door, but also of crossroads and town gates, represents movement and relations with others' (Augé 1995: 58).

Thinking along the lines of this classical dualism, we could imagine the penetration of the modern domestic space as the triumph of Hermes over Hestia. After all, Hermes was also the god of communications – in the Roman version of the myth, Mercury, the messenger of the gods and now, inevitably, a telephone company. The mythology reinforces the gender politics of course. Hestia was Vesta in Roman myth, the enclosed (virginal) guardian of the sacred domestic flame. But again there is more at stake in the figures of the hearth and the threshold than this sort of (gendered) dualism. The incursions of the world 'out there' are ambiguous in their implications, grasped by the figure of Janus – the Roman god of the threshold – who famously faced two ways.

We can find some interesting parallels to Ruskin's view in Gaston Bachelard's *Poetics of Space* (Bachelard 1969). As Ann Game (1995) shows, Bachelard's attempts to describe the phenomenology – the affective and imaginative experience – of houses, centred precisely on the notion of shelter and protection, on 'the intimate values of inside space', the 'immediate well-being, the inhabiting, a dwelling encloses' (Bachelard, quoted in Game 1995: 200–1). But this 'sheltering' is not merely (as it might be read in Ruskin) about the exclusion of a potentially threatening, divisive 'hostile society'; in Bachelard the house is conceived as imaginatively constituting an aspect of the human self as 'dweller' – indeed the house becomes part of the embodied self – 'the house is in the body' (Game 1995: 202). As Game argues, 'protection' and 'shelter' point to the self-constitutive principles of 'integration' and 'binding', and so 'the house provides continuity, a counter to the dispersion of the subject' (p. 201). So it is not merely the privacy of bourgeois family life that is threatened by the penetration of the outer world into the inner: there is also an implied challenge to the 'boundary' which constitutes the self. This however does not necessarily have to be imaged as a *threat* to self-identity, but perhaps as a movement in the placing of the boundary between the 'private self' (say, the self of the insular familiar structure) and the self imagined in relation to a wider horizon of human belonging. The shifting of this 'threshold' produced by the penetration of the enclosed space of the house by globalizing technologies – to an extent unthought of in either Ruskin or Bachelard – thus becomes a way of thinking the ambivalent effects of deterritorialization on self-identity.

But, of course the domestic setting is by no means the only one in which the cultural effects of deterritorialization are felt. Our couple don't sit at home every evening. For example, since the new multiplex arrived in the 1980s they go to the cinema more, and this in itself is an oddly deterritorialized experience. The cinema complex is on an 'out-of-town' site on the edge of the business park and trading estate and so surrounded, as they arrive in the twilight, by dark warehouses rather than the pubs and shops and restaurants around the old city-centre Odeon or Gaumont. But it is, of course, so much easier – and safer – to park here. Once inside, the sense that this is an environment that has been artificially 'placed into' the locality continues – this is clearly an *American* cinema, evident from the transatlantic voice-overs in the trailers and the slightly jarring terms in the screened announcements ('candy', 'please deposit trash') to the giant buckets of popcorn being consumed.

And unsurprisingly, of the dozen or so movies on offer, the great majority will be Hollywood movies, since the multiplex is 'vertically integrated' with the American companies producing the films. What images of locality, what landscapes and what linguistic cadences will they find here as backdrops to the narratives? With the odd exception such as *Four Weddings and a Funeral* and *The Full Monty* or adaptations of classic novels like *Sense and Sensibility* or *The Wings of the Dove*, probably mainly ones from the US. Does this alienate them? Do they feel the victims of cultural imperialism? Or aren't these distant locations – the actual physical landscapes of America, from the great open spaces of the western or the road movie, to the cityscapes of the thrillers or the TV cops series – somehow, paradoxically, rather familiar? Think of how effortlessly we can relate to these environments without ever, most of us Europeans, having experienced them at first hand. Don't we very easily feel as much 'at home' with Meg Ryan and Tom Hanks in Seattle, as with Elinor Dashwood and Edward Ferrars in Devonshire? For where *are* these places except in our cultural imagination, our repertoire of 'textual locations' built up out of all the millions of images in films, TV programmes, books and magazines that we have encountered? And do we really *require* any of them to correspond all that closely with our 'real' locality?

A further aspect of deterritorialization, then, is the lifting out of locality that occurs in this intertextual realm of the imagination. One way of thinking about this is to compare the routine consumption of images of distant places, and their normalization in the mediated lifeworld of the individual, with the processes Michael Billig describes as *Banal Nationalism* (Billig 1995). What Billig means by banal nationalism is the routine reinforcement, through the steady tempo of everyday life, of images which attach the citizen's identity to the nation-state. This is the process, which he contrasts with the 'hot nationalism' of 'waved or saluted flags', by which, 'Daily the nation is indicated, or "flagged", in the lives of its citizenry' (Billig 1995: 6). The sorts of example Billig gives – pursued in a subtle social-psychological discourse analysis – are the routine rhetorical forms of address of national politicians, or the deixis – the 'rhetorical pointing' – of the delivery of news in national daily newspapers. It is not just in the coverage of politics, but of home news, sport, popular culture ('The Great British Pub') and even reporting the weather that the subtle positioning of the reader (or viewer) as a member of the nation that is 'home' is achieved.

Now the comparison I want to draw with the thesis of banal nationalism is not at all one that challenges it. Billig also discusses

the idea, which he associates with a postmodern take on globalization, that banal nationalism is being replaced by 'banal globalism'
(1995: 129ff). He rejects this – rightly I believe – on the basis of the
demonstrable persistence of strategies and practices of national identification – both in its hot and banal forms – in the contemporary world.
Here his position is close to that of Anthony Smith discussed in chapter 3. And I agree with him. However, the point I want to make is
that the more or less deliberate ideological promptings of banal
nationalism compete on the same phenomenological terrain with a
whole range of more random deterritorializing imagery. The embedded familiarity of the distant 'alien' cinematic landscapes and
scenarios I described above is just as much part of the mundane
mediated process of identity-formation as the rhetorical forms of
address that bind identity to (national) locality. It is not as though
these distantiated images act as a direct counterpoise to the processes Billig describes; but they clearly do have a significant role in
the constitution of imagined belonging. To take one 'banal' example,
we could consider the dress code of the young people pouring
into the multiplex – the 'American-international' sportswear that is
almost the uniform of a globalized youth culture.[6] Work done to
anchor identity to the nation thus has to be seen *as work*: as a process
which does not unfold effortlessly out of a popular culture securely
rooted in geographical place. Rather it is achieved against the grain
of a broader tendency for imaginary identification fairly effortlessly
to escape the constructed boundaries of locality.

Global Food and Local Identity

Modern lived culture is not, of course, *exclusively* mediated culture and
there are other ways in which deterritorialization may be experienced.
For instance, Raymond Williams pointed out the international provenance of the food his couple put on their dinner table in the early
1980s. Today they will find an even wider range of 'foreign' foods on
the shelves of the supermarkets. Some of these – pastas and pizzas for
example – have long since ceased to be regarded as unusual and are
now marketed on a mass scale as everyday family foods, while on the
other hand there has been a huge expansion in the range of foods marketed precisely on their attraction as exotic: Mexican tacos, Thai cur-
ries, Italian ciabatta and polenta, Swedish gravadlax, and so on. And
in addition, of course, imported fruit and vegetables, both familiar and
exotic, are now more or less constantly available, regardless of season.

One obvious way in which this transformation in British food culture could be interpreted is in terms of the globalization of the food
industry itself, beginning with what Jack Goody (1997) refers to as
the global production of 'Industrial Food'. Goody shows how
developments in preserving, mechanization, retailing and transport
during the nineteenth century transformed the diet of the mass of
the population in the West by making available an 'industrial
cuisine' of mass-produced food often sourced from the colonies and
former colonies. Examples like the rise of the beef canning industry
at places like Fray Bentos in Uruguay show how this industrialization transformed the diets of the First World and the economies of
the countries of the Third World as they became 'geared to supply-
ing those ingredients on a mass scale' – and later how these Third
World countries *themselves* came increasingly to rely upon industrial
food (Goody 1997: 338).

This process has of course grown immensely in both its scope and
its technical sophistication in the twentieth century and generated
economic dependencies in the Third World that have been widely
criticized (see for example, George 1982; Goodman and Redclift 1991;
Tansey and Worsley 1995) not just in terms of relations of economic
domination, but also in their environmental effects. Such critiques
have now made evident the connections between the provision of an
increasing consumer choice in the affluent West, and conditions
forced upon workers in the transnational agribusinesses that produce the Zimbabwean mange-tout peas, the Kenyan runner beans,
the Guatemalan carnations and so on.

In cultural terms there has also been plenty of discussion of the
'abstraction' of consumption in the West from production in the Third
World: the way in which the complex connectivity of the global food
industry causes these commodities to appear, as Marx might have
put it, 'as if by magic' on the shelves of our local store. David Harvey,
for instance, discusses the rise of a global food culture as an example
of 'time-space compression': the way in which, on supermarket
shelves or in the range of ethnic restaurants to be found in any
moderate-sized western city, 'the whole world's cuisine is now
assembled in one place'. This cultural assembly, he suggests, is a
parallel to the assembly of images of the world available via television or in theme parks. Following Baudrillard, he thinks of global
food culture as part of a range of 'simulacra' by which we now
'experience the world's geography vicariously'. But, he adds, this
occurs, 'in such a way as to conceal almost perfectly any trace of
origin, of the labour processes that produced them, or of the social

relations implicated in their production' (Harvey 1989: 300). Susan Willis expands on the theme of abstraction and commodity myst-ification in her fascinating analysis of the ambience of the supermar-ket. For example, she links the themes of refrigeration, chilling and air-conditioning as they are experienced in the walk around the supermarket aisles, with the temperature control used in shipping technologies that brings tropical fruit to us:

> Maintained in a constant bath of refrigerated air, these fruits are in-capable of producing scents, harbouring bugs, growing moulds, and becoming decayed. Air conditioning is a medium of abstraction which severs the agricultural production of the Third World from the heat of labour and the heat of the marketplace . . . It swaddles the product in First World antiseptic purity and severs the connection with the site of production. The shopper who enters the air-conditioned super-market and chooses between its papayas, mangoes, pineapples, bananas . . . is as unaware of the factors and labour force behind their production as the tourist whose experience of Mexico is in an air con-ditioned hotel lobby. (Willis 1991: 51)

But, important as this sort of abstraction is in cultural-political terms, I want to focus on another order of abstraction – that involved in the severance of the experience of food from the experience of the local-ity of the consumer. So the question is, how does the simple wide availability of all these 'global foods' – pastas, pizzas, burgers, cur-ries, chillies, stir-fries, kebabs – as everyday diet options contribute to the general experience of deterritorialization for our hypothetical British consumers?

We might suppose that it has clearly undermined, for most people, a strong sense of connection between the food they eat and their immediate cultural location: Indian take-aways now outnum-ber fish and chip shops in Britain (James 1996: 81). However the issue is a complicated one since it rests upon the assumption that there is a fairly simple relationship between diet, cuisine and sense of cultural belonging in the first place. However this is a problematic assumption. As Bell and Valentine argue, there is no easy *essential* connection here, and the marking of locational belonging by refer-ence to food habits is largely built upon cultural mythologies, con-cealing complex syncretic histories:

> [T]here is no essential *national* food; the food we think of as character-ising a particular place always tells stories of movement and mixing . . . all there is is a menu of naturalised foods . . . modified, adapted

and hybridised over time. Furthermore, the foodstuffs we think of as definitionally part of a particular nation's sense of identity often hides complex histories of trade links, cultural exchange, and especially colonialism. (Bell and Valentine 1997: 169)

Apart from this big question of the constant historical flux of food (as of all other) culture, it is clearly difficult in a multicultural, multi-ethnic society like Britain in the 1990s to represent the 'traditional' national diet as roast beef, suet puddings, fish and chips, tea and cucumber sandwiches. For *whose* traditions are we talking about? And this question applies not only to the ethnic mix of national populations but also to class-related differentials in diet.

However, given all of these caveats, there remains a significant transformation to be accounted for here, linking food culture with the progress of global modernity. In the first place we can under-stand this as a continuation and acceleration of the process of the simultaneous industrialization and globalization of food that Goody records. These industrial processes – canning, drying, freezing, pack-aging – mark a significant *material* rupture in the routine sourcing of foodstuffs which is surely a part of the general process of 'disem-bedding'. Before these institutional-technological developments, there was obviously a far greater reliance on locally produced food. Exotic imports were mostly restricted to the luxury commodities – available to a small elite – that were relatively easy to preserve in transit: tea or spices for example. So globalization, from its early impact, does clearly undermine a close *material* relationship between provenance of food and locality. And this particular transformation of modernity must surely have been generally counted as a good thing: an improvement in diet, not only in terms of variety, but of constant availability.

However these advances have also had a more ambiguous cult-ural impact. For today the year-round availability of imported fresh foods (along with the increasing use of processed foods) dissolves what might be seen as a positive, particular connection between diet and locality determined precisely by *restriction* – by the *limits* of avail-ability of local produce. Conditions of constant undifferentiated sup-ply do away with the limited availability of fruits and vegetables 'in season' and so weaken the subtle connection between climate, sea-son, locality and cultural practice. Prior to the industrialization of food, as Delamont reminds us, 'Harvest time, lambing, the start of the hen's laying season, the arrival of the first fruits of summer and so on were the determinants of diet' throughout Europe (Delamont

1995: 28ff). And so the rhythms, anticipations and differentiations of a 'food calendar' of summer abundance, provision for winter shortages, Harvest Festivals, Christmas and Easter specialities, that contribute to a sharp particular sense of local culture are at risk of disappearance.

In the second place we have to be able to account for the impact of the striking *acceleration* of the industrialization-globalization of food in the supermarket culture of the last thirty years. Here I think we can detect something quite new: a different *order* of transition in which deterritorialization works *on the ground of the myths of food culture*, as much as on actual consumption practices. What I mean by this is that the very cultural stereotypes that identify food with, say, national culture become weakened. Take the example of roast beef and 'Britishness'. Though this is clearly, in the multicultural Britain of the 1990s, an identity preserved more at the level of myth rather than of actual practice, it none the less continues to have some degree of cultural purchase. This is evident, for example, in the continuing 'risk crisis' of the infection of the British beef herd with BSE and the possibilities of transmission of a form of the disease (CJDV) to humans. Reactions to this crisis seem to demonstrate something more than just anxieties about health risks (Lupton 1996), bringing to the surface insecurities in national identity. Evidence of this can be found in the popular-media representation of the European Union ban on British beef exports as more than just an economic threat, as part of a wider popular discourse of British culture under siege from the hostile distanciated forces of Brussels bureaucrats. The recent (1997) British government ban on the sale of 'beef on the bone' has prompted further expressions of the resilience of this food-identity myth. For instance, examples of the deliberate flouting of the legislation by some butchers and restaurateurs was rationalized as defiance not just of the state's intrusion into 'civil liberties', but of its attack on a 'tradition' linking the stereotyped bluff independence of the English character with the 'cultural rights' to a traditional diet of beef ('Beefeaters', 'John Bull' and so forth).

And yet we have to place this sort of reaction in a context in which the eating of 'British beef' is now just a small part of an otherwise entirely *pluralized* food culture in Britain, demonstrated in supermarket food, in the range of cosmopolitan cookery books to be found near the checkouts, in the burgeoning quantity of ethnic or 'hybrid' restaurants. Stephen Mennell puts the cultural implications of this point very well when he says that this 'culinary pluralism is the counterpart of something which is more familiar in the arts: the loss of a single dominant style' (Mennell 1985, quoted in Lunt and Livingstone 1992: 98). This, I think is a key point. The 'traditional' British diet of 'roast beef dinners ', fish and chips and jam roly-poly has not disappeared. However, whereas up until the 1950s and 1960s it may have formed a fairly uniform 'style' for the mass of the population, today it exists as a consumption choice amongst a wide range of others. The connection between such foods and a particular 'British way of life', it may then be argued, is at the very least attenuated – remains only in the sense of an explicit lifestyle *choice* amongst others – 'eating British' as opposed to eating American, Italian, Chinese, Thai, Spanish or Indian; Harry Ramsden's as opposed to McDonalds or Prêt à Manger.[7] And this is not just a matter of the 'style' of social-recreational eating – 'eating out'. It is also evident in some of the best-selling practical cookery books of the 1990s, aimed at an expanding market which takes cosmopolitan food for granted as everyday convenient options. A good example is Nigel Slater's *The 30 Minute Cook*, subtitled *The best of the world's quick cooking*. Slater's style is one that demonstrates (and appeals to) an easy, taken-for-granted familiarity with a wide range of different ethnic ingredients and food styles. For instance, eschewing authenticity in favour of a no-nonsense, 'please yourself' eclecticism, he writes: 'Does it really matter that I eat my spiced lentils on naan bread with a knife and fork like beans on toast? [or] if I choose to eat my Chinese noodles with a spoon and fork, Italian style, rather than dribbling juice down my chin and over the table using chopsticks?' (Slater 1994: 9). What is striking about this is the underlying assumption of a *routine* cosmopolitan taste in his readers, extending to the slight anxiety that some may have scruples about preserving the cultural authenticity of *alien* eating styles even within their everyday domestic cuisine. This is, surely, worlds away from any simple assumption of food reinforcing national identity.

The way such mundane cosmopolitan eclecticism 'eats into' the myth of national food might even be thought of in broader terms, as an instance of the transformation of 'tradition' in reflexive modernity. The equation of 'Beef and Britishness' in the 1990s is thus at a double jeopardy: from the threats of contamination of the beef herd with BSE – signalling a symbolic 'contamination' of the myth of national purity; but, more significantly, from the precarious nature of food-identity myths themselves. In the context of the plurality of style that Mennell identifies, food–nation identifications surely exist today not as an unexamined 'second nature', but as 'self-conscious traditions' – traditions, as Giddens (1990: 38) puts it, 'in sham clothing'.

This sort of generalization has, of course, to recognize different levels of specificity in different national-cultural – and even regional – contexts. The impact of accelerating deterritorializing forces today may be experienced less forcefully in countries – or even cities – where food culture has been historically more eclectic and open to influence: for instance in the long-standing hybrid mix of street food associated with an integrating mercantile tradition and waves of colonial migration that Hannerz (1996) describes in the case of Amsterdam. This case contrasts sharply with the deep and persistent investment of cultural/'spiritual' significance in a symbolic staple that can be seen in the centrality of rice eating to Japanese cultural identity as described by Ohnuki-Tierney (1993) (Bell and Valentine 1997: 179–81). However, despite these differing historical contexts of the receiving cultures, it remains clear that deterritorializing forces are present in the food culture of all western nations and are rapidly spreading to the more affluent sectors of the Third World (Classen 1996).

In common with the other aspects of deterritorialization we have mentioned, the transformation in food culture involves a complex mixture of experienced benefits and costs. Few probably would choose to return to the monotonous, unimaginative and probably rather unhealthy British diet – and, indeed, the periodic food shortages – of earlier days (Drummond and Wilbraham 1991). In the 1990s, only those very few who attempt to be self-sufficient or to rely only on locally produced fresh foods experience what was once a regular feature of food culture – the 'hunger gap' in spring after many of the stored foods had run out and before the new season's crops arrive. And along with this increasing availability and choice in food there might – although this is admittedly a hopeful speculation – also have been a certain breakdown in cultural insularity: as food prejudices (foreign muck!) gradually dissolve, so might broader chauvinisms and even perhaps elements of the hostility to the cultural practices of ethnic minorities.

But on the other hand the globalization of the food industry, as it shifts the locus of control from the local to the global, introduces new areas of anxiety and uncertainty. For example, the general sense of risk involved in consumption has certainly increased – from periodic crises over contamination of the food chain ('Chernobyl lamb', 'BSE beef', new strains of influenza species-migrating from Chinese chickens in Hong Kong, new strains of the E. coli bacterium appearing in Scotland, antibiotic-resistant American maize products) to the background uncertainty about the widespread use of pesticides in agribusiness, food irradiation and other preservative methods. Perceptions of food risk are of course scarcely restricted to modern globalized societies. The risk of food poisoning through ignorance about hygiene was endemic in pre-modern societies, and the deliberate adulteration of food by suppliers dates back at least to ancient Greek and Roman societies (Goody 1997: 351).

But what is new is both the loss of local control over food and diet and the way this periodically becomes culturally marked as a 'crisis' – a threat to the normality of life lived amongst distanciated 'expert systems' (chapter 2). A good example of this was Oprah Winfrey's famous address to her afternoon chat show audience in April 1996, on being told of the practice of feeding rendered cattle remains to beef cows, and the consequent risks of BSE in American herds: 'Now, doesn't that all concern you a little bit? It has stopped me cold from eating another hamburger. Stopped me cold! '(quoted in Coles 1998: 3). Oprah Winfrey's remark – famously credited with precipitating a collapse in the sale of beef in the United States and the subject of a high-profile law suit – could be read as a rupture in the routine trust relations of global modernity that, without too much exaggeration, can be compared with the incidence of sudden 'catastrophic' financial crises. For if it is no longer safe to eat hamburgers – more than the US cultural equivalent of roast beef – then what can we trust?

Indeed incidents such as this (which incidentally also illustrate the complex intertwining of the cultural with the other dimensions of global modernity) need to be seen as irruptions out of a more chronic background process of the precarious negotiation of trust relations with distanciated expert systems. Another example of this is the issue of the use of genetically produced foodstuffs – tomatoes and tomato paste, soya – as they are gradually being introduced into supermarkets in the United States and Europe. Witness here the growth of the practice of providing product information leaflets about such controversial products in supermarkets as a means of reassuring consumers. And, indeed, such anxieties have also contributed to various practices of 're-embedding' in food culture: for example the organic farming movement oriented to local production and delivery ('local box schemes'), the search for alternatives to supermarket shopping, food co-operatives and so on (Belasco 1993).

Without extending this discussion any further, I think it can plausibly be argued that a distinct mode of deterritorialized cultural experience exists across a range of everyday activities in late twentieth-century 'developed' industrial societies like Britain.

Although, as we have seen, it has different aspects, a central defining characteristic of deterritorialization is the weakening or dissolution of the connection between everyday lived culture and territorial location. However this is not typically experienced as simply cultural loss or estrangement but as a complex and ambiguous blend: of familiarity and difference, expansion of cultural horizons and increased perceptions of vulnerability, access to the 'world out there' accompanied by penetration of our own private worlds, new opportunities and new risks.

But what I have also tried to stress is the *mundane* nature of this experience. It seems to me that, for all that these are profound transformations in cultural experience, they are not, typically, experienced as dramatic upheavals but are, on the contrary, rapidly assimilated to normality and grasped – however precariously – as 'the way life is' rather than as a series of deviations from the way life has been or ought to be. To this extent, some of the attempts to describe the general experience of cultural modernity – for example Marshall Berman's (1982) images of the dissolution – the 'melting' – of cultural solidity taken from Marx, or the imagery of the modern maelstrom or the *"tourbillon social"* taken from Rousseau, are rather misleading in their dramatization. Whilst they may describe the *conditions* of (global) modern social experience, it seems to me that the experience itself is (in the West at least) generally rather less fraught or dramatic, the rapidity of transformations – even the intermittent 'crises' – something which ordinary people often take in their cultural stride.

Objections to Deterritorialization

Having sketched some aspects of what might count as deterritorialization, I want now to address some objections that could be raised, both to the idea itself and to its broad general application to the analysis of cultural globalization.

The Myth of Pre-modern Localism

The first of these objections relates to the principal grounding assumption of the concept itself: *de*territorialization obviously assumes the existence of a close connection between culture and location prior to the globalization process. But this is perhaps in certain ways disputable. Morley and Robins (1995) for instance point to a critical literature in anthropology which questions what might be called the 'localist bias' of the discipline,[8] born to some extent out of the exigencies of its fieldwork methods. This localism consists of a set of assumptions about the boundedness, 'rootedness', insularity and 'purity' of (particularly) pre-modern cultures. Morley and Robins cite challenges to such assumptions in, for example, James Clifford's arguments (which we encountered in chapter 1) that cultures need to be seen as 'travelling cultures' which 'negotiate themselves in external as much as internal relations' (Clifford 1992, cited in Morley and Robins 1995: 129) – as much as collectivities 'centred' on the villages that field anthropologists tend to study. Implicit in this is a criticism of the connotation of the term 'native' with the idea of fixity of location, something Arjun Appadurai unequivocally rejects: 'natives, people confined to and by the places to which they belong, groups unsullied by contact with a larger world, have probably never existed' (quoted in Morley and Robins 1995: 128).

As Morley and Robins summarize them, the broader implications of this critique of anthropological localism are that we should reject all images of 'pure, internally homogeneous, authentic, indigenous culture[s]' and recognize that 'every culture has, in fact, ingested foreign elements from exogenous sources, with the various elements gradually becoming "naturalized" within it' (pp. 129–30).

This is a valid and important criticism which, as we shall see later, also has significance for the way in which cultural hybridity is formulated. Its force in the present context is to make us sensitive to the possible implication that deterritorialization involves a fall from grace from an original, innocent 'natural' relationship between culture and place. Indeed our use of García Canclini's formulation – 'the loss of the "natural" relation of culture to geographical and social territories' – might seem particularly culpable in this respect, were it not for the significant scare quotes.

However, I think this is an implication that we can avoid. The deterritorialization that we have instanced certainly implies a movement away from a prior state in which cultural experience was linked more closely to place, but this need not involve the sort of myths of indigenousness that are rightly criticized. Where this criticism has most force is in the retrospective theoretical gaze across the divide between modernity and 'tradition'. And, while it is true that the theory of global modernity based in time-space distanciation attributes greater constraints of place on social interaction, and so more local determinations of cultural experience in pre-modern

societies, as we saw in chapter 2, this is not incompatible with a recognition of the (often remarkable) relative mobility of sections of these
societies. So to talk of close links between culture and territory does
not mean to imply insularity or to discount exogenous influence as,
more or less, constants of cultural practice and experience. But the
point, nevertheless, is that these were different *orders* of society
in which some of the 'openness to the world' available to us was
simply not a possibility. 'Locality' in the sense of the significance
of local physical environments and climates, features of landscape,
customs and practices, linguistic dialects, food culture, particular in-
flections of wider religious belief systems and so on clearly *did* figure
much larger in such cultures. In resisting myths of indigenousness
we must not go to the other extreme and discount all these obvious
examples of the significance of locality within pre-modern societies.

To this extent, then, deterritorialization does seem to me a valid
way of grasping a mode of cultural experience which is *particular* to
global modernity and distinct from the *general* properties of fluidity,
mobility and interactivity that can be attributed to all historical cultures. It may be further objected that the instances of deterritorialization
we considered above are, in any case, very much contemporary ones
– movements *within* modern societies rather than examples which span
the modernity/pre-modernity distinction. Does this in any way compromise the theory of modernity as a globalizing epoch marked off
against previous ones? Well, I don't think so. To think of deterritorialization as something particular to modern societies is to see it as a
cultural condition *set in train* by the transition to social modernity.
This does not, however, imply that modernity is an accomplished process, and it makes more sense to see it as an ongoing, developing one,
in Therborn's sense of epoch as an expanse 'open at all ends' (chapter
2). So the changes we have noted can be seen as evidence of the accelerating pace of globalization transforming our own modern cultural
localisms. The concept of deterritorialization is at once, then, a way
of theorizing the underlying 'enabling conditions' of global-modern
culture, and of describing and making sense of the empirical cultural
phenomena which face us in the perplexingly rapid transformations
of our stage of modernity.

The Unevenness of Deterritorialization

But there is another important set of questions that can be posed to
the idea of deterritorialization and these centre on asking *whose* experience we are describing? Who partakes of globalized culture and

who is excluded from it? Is the idea of deterritorialization in fact in any useful way generalizable?

In following the imagined trajectory of Williams's caricatured cosmopolitans – affluent, educated (white?), western, middle-class, 'information-rich' – we have hardly taken a broad section across socio-economic position and cultural experience. There is a risk, then, that talk of deterritorialized experience may be rather exclusive. This point is made very well by Doreen Massey, who argues that there is a distinct 'power geometry' to globalization in which 'some people are more in charge of it than others; some initiate flows and movement, others don't; some are more on the receiving-end of it than others; some are effectively imprisoned by it '(Massey 1994: 149). The privileged players in the globalization process for Massey are, 'the jet-setters, the ones sending and receiving the faxes and the e-mails, holding the international conference calls . . .' But against this elite group, Massey contrasts all those vast numbers who are affected by globalization but not in control of the process, from labour migrants and favela dwellers in the Third World to 'The pensioner in a bed-sit in an inner city in this country, eating British working-class-style fish and chips from a Chinese take-away, watching a US film on a Japanese television, and not daring to go out after dark. And anyway the public transport's been cut' (Massey 1994: 149).

Globalization is an *uneven* process, not just in that it involves 'winners and losers' or that it reproduces many familiar configurations of domination and subordination, but also in the sense that the cultural experience it distributes is highly complex and varied. It is important, then, not to mistake one narrow band of cultural experience for the whole of it, by becoming fascinated (a particular temptation, as Massey hints, for academics) with the technology and the associated lifestyle available to the 'information-rich'. A similar caveat is issued by Morley and Robins who argue that for some social groups, without access to new technologies of communication and transport, modernity, far from offering a widening of horizons may actually involve a narrowing and localizing of experience, 'as their life chances are gradually reduced and they increasingly remain stuck in the micro-territories in which they were born' (1995: 219). Moreover the example they have in mind is not that of isolated British pensioners, but American Black and Latino youths – as represented in films like John Singleton's *Boyz N the Hood*, for whom 'locality is in fact destiny, where the horizon, far from being global, extends only as far as the boundary of "the Hood"' (ibid.).

As Doreen Massey stresses, these are not simply moral/political points but *conceptual* ones. For unless there is some basic level at which the idea of deterritorialization generalizes across various social, economic and geographical divisions, it loses a lot of its power and interest as an approach to the cultural implications of globalization. If deterritorialization is *only* a description of the experiences of the affluent, mobile and information-rich sectors of the most economically developed parts of the world, it does not thereby become an invalid cultural description, but, in one sense, it loses much of its claim to be a description of *globalized* cultural experience. For ought not globalization to be global in its scope?

Well, I think these objections *can* be answered in a way that preserves, though within certain limits, the more or less general applicability of the idea of deterritorialization. In the first place we can readily agree with the main thrust of this sort of criticism – that globalization in all its aspects is an uneven process: privileging some, disadvantaging others, reproducing old and introducing new patterns of domination and subordination. But notice that this is to recognize that globalization has a basic *applicability* to most people living in the world today. Massey's argument about the 'power geometry' of globalization, for instance, is not about people being excluded (exempt?) from the process, but about the differential access to control over events *within* the process.

If this is so with the political economy of globalization, it is also true about its cultural aspect. We can recognize that deterritorialization is extremely wide in its applicability whilst being uneven in its effects. Thus, to take social differentiations (of race, class, gender and age) within developed societies, it is clear that some are going to live a deterritorialized culture more intensely, actively and (on balance) enjoyably than others. The distance between Williams's 'yuppie' couple and Massey's pensioner is illustrative of this. But it would be a mistake to see the experience of deterritorialization as something which only arrives at a certain threshold of socio-economic advantage, above which is a switch to the 'hyper-space' of a 'cosmopolitan' lifestyle and below which there is a simple exclusion from the whole process of globalization and a different *order* of experience.

This sort of mistake is liable to be made where we over-emphasize the *technologies* of globalization – where, for example, we think of it as something that can be 'bought into' by purchasing the latest communicational hardware (and software). But, as we have tried to emphasize, the use of such technologies is only a part of what deterritorialization involves. Just as significant might be, for instance, the experience of the transformation of the local cultural environment brought about by the closure of old heavy industrial plants in working-class areas as such industries relocate to other parts of the world. Or, as part of the same process, the 'placing in' of new industries with different work cultures into these same areas (Japanese car plants in European countries). Or again, the transformation of a predominantly white working-class district into a multi-ethnic one brought about by labour immigration. All of these examples will involve aspects of the removal of cultural experience from local determinations, but none is directly connected with the use of communications technology and, clearly, none is an experience which is 'bought into' at a certain level of affluence. In this regard, we might consider that a white British person in a multi-ethnic working-class community may have as much direct contact with global food culture by shopping in the local Asian store which has replaced the 'corner shop', as a middle-class person cruising the ethnic foods aisle in Sainsbury's or Waitrose.

A second point to make in relation to the access to technology issue is that, arguably, deterritorialization is associated with relatively low levels of technological development which are now very widely distributed (in the developed world at least) and so part of daily life for the majority. So those excluded on this count would be the tiny proportion who never make a phone call or never watch TV. This is a point Dick Hebdige makes:

> We are living in a world where 'mundane cosmopolitanism' is part of 'ordinary' experience. All cultures, however remote temporally and geographically, are becoming accessible today as signs and/or commodities. If we don't choose to go and visit other cultures they come and visit us as images and information on TV ... Nobody has to be educated, well-off or adventurous to be a world traveller at this level. In the 1990s everybody – willingly or otherwise, whether conscious or not – is more or less cosmopolitan. (Hebdige 1990: 20)

Without exaggerating the potential of this 'mundane cosmopolitanism' we can at least agree that even those marginalized groups for whom 'locality is destiny' experience a *transformed* locality into which the wider world intrudes more and more. They may in all sorts of ways be the 'losers' in globalization, but this does not mean that they are excluded from its effects, that they are consigned to cultural backwaters out of the mainstream of global modernity. Quite to the contrary, it seems to me that the poor and marginalized – for example those living in inner-city areas – often find themselves daily closest to some of most turbulent transformations, while it is the affluent who can afford to retire to the rural backwaters which have at least the appearance of a preserved and stable 'locality'.

So, to summarize, I think it can plausibly be argued that deterritorialization in western developed societies is not an experience exclusive to the most privileged groups, but involves a certain basic level of commonality. Disadvantage within globalization may be experienced in many ways, including that involved in 'information poverty', but it doesn't imply exclusion from the underlying cultural transformations which lift lived experience out of its rootedness in localities. Furthermore as we have argued throughout, the experience of deterritorialization is a deeply ambiguous one, mixing enpowerment with vulnerability, opportunity with risk, in complex combinations. It should not therefore be thought of as a simple issue of access or resource distribution in relation to a set of incontestable social goods.

This of course all refers to the experience of the 'First World'. But the question of the unevenness of globalization clearly has sharp relevance for the cultural experience of people in the Third World – many millions of whom indeed have never made a phone call, never watched TV. Are things utterly different here? Can it convincingly be argued that these people – the majority of the world's population after all – experience a deterritorialized culture which has anything in common with that experienced in the 'developed' world?

Well, this raises many complex and difficult questions, some of which go beyond our present scope. In the first place, there is a whole range of vexed empirical issues involved, which extend to definitions of what today counts as the 'Third World'. The concept itself is now in some senses an unstable one as a result of globalization and uneven patterns of economic development. For example, it is often observed that the developmental trajectory of the newly industrialized countries (NICs) of the Third World – the 'Asian Tigers' or Latin American countries like Brazil and Mexico – make them now scarcely comparable with those of some of the poorest countries in the world – Chad, Mauritania, Bangladesh and so on. The degree to which one might think of the Third World as becoming integrated into global modernity (in both political economic and cultural terms) clearly depends on where along this wide continuum one would place its contemporary centre of gravity.

But against examples of recent rapid development often instanced as evidence of the fruits of globalization, we would have to place the current economic crises in many of the Asian NICs, along with the much more sceptical accounts of theorists like Hirst and Thompson (1996) referred to in chapter 3. In short, the situation is inherently complex and fluid. To add to these complexities (particularly in moving from political economy to culture) we would need to consider that the range of lived experience within Third World societies – from subsistence farmers in remote rural areas to affluent urban elites – is obviously far greater than in the developed West, even to the extent of spanning the modernity/'pre-modernity' divide. All this clearly makes generalization about the common experience of deterritorialization a rather risky business.

But, picking our way cautiously, we can, I think, assume the following. First, that at present substantial sectors of populations in the Third World *are* in effect excluded from the broad experience of the globalization process. Indicators such as the United Nations Human Development Index, which combine measures such as literacy, educational attainment, longevity and utility derived from income (Thomas et al. 1994: 22) clearly show how great the gulf is between the life experience of those in countries at the top of the scale (like Canada) and those at the bottom (like Guinea). And we scarcely need to consult these data to realize that for many millions in regions like sub-Saharan Africa and south Asia, life simply does not involve any of the routine experiences of deterritorialization that we have described in relation to the developed world. Indeed the sorts of cultural anxieties described in relation to deterritorialization seem rather trivial when compared to the global coexistence of millions of lives lived at 'subsistence' levels. Here I think 'threshold' arguments do probably apply.

But on the other hand we have to avoid building an unrealistic picture of the contemporary Third World as *predominantly* isolated, marginalized, rural, 'pre-modern'. For even in the rural economy we would have to place alongside subsistence farmers those large numbers of agricultural workers employed in transnational 'agribusiness' in the Third World. Such people are clearly in one sense integrated into global modernity, work with its industrial technology, have distanciated relations with the ultimate determinants of their livelihood, are part of the production base of global capitalism. Of course an important part of the critique of global capitalism lies in recognizing that such people's 'involvement' may be little more than as (exploited) workers. The agribusiness operatives who may suffer health problems from the effects of the intensive chemical farming used to produce the foodstuffs in European and North American supermarkets probably don't shop in supermarkets themselves. None the less, they are no doubt acutely aware of the distanciated forces that control their livelihoods.

One interesting instance of this awareness is found in Mark Phillips's fascinating (1997) film *Mange Tout* [9] which documents the economic–cultural linkages established through the production of mangetout peas on a Zimbabwean farm growing the vegetable on a prized exclusive contract for the British supermarket chain Tesco. One of the revealing aspects of this film was the relative levels of information about, or ignorance of, the other displayed by the producers and consumers. As might be expected, the supermarket shoppers interviewed had hardly any idea where the peas originated, or indeed of where Zimbabwe actually was, and scarcely any interest in the conditions of production of the commodity. By contrast, the farm workers interviewed showed a sharp sense of the distanciated exchange relationship which is central to their lives. This extended from a subtle sense of the hierarchy of demand to be satisfied in the transnational operation and the importance of maintaining the exacting standards of quality of the product 'demanded' by the unseen consumer, to a sophisticated awareness of the importance of bringing foreign exchange into the Zimbabwean economy. But there was also evident a rich, imaginative mythical construction of what life for the inhabitants of the 'Kingdom of Tesco' to the north must be like, which contrasted sharply with the relative imaginative poverty of the British consumers. As with subordinate groups in the First World, then, disadvantage here is not a matter of exclusion from globalization, but of being unequally positioned within it. And this 'inequality' does not work itself out in a way that maps cultural-imaginary resources neatly on to economic advantage.

At this level of 'involvement' in globalization however, one could still argue that there is little comparison between the mundane cultural experiences of the First and Third Worlds. But then we would have to broaden our imagination of what the Third World is today to include the rapid growth of urbanization and industrialization, and the availability and use of communications technologies found there. Trends towards urbanization suggest that by the year 2000 half the population of the world will be living in cities, and this is expected to rise to two-thirds by the year 2020 (Thomas et al. 1994: 70; see also Vidal 1996: 4). This pattern is clearly going to make most impact in the Third World, where already most of the world's largest cities in terms of population are to be found. And this trend is of course connected with the movement away from wholly agrarian economies and towards employment in the industrial and service sectors which is a feature, though at different rates, of all Third World countries. To this can be added a trend towards steadily increasing access to media technologies like television. Although there remains a huge gap between the virtual saturation of television ownership by households in the most developed countries and the radically sparser distribution in the developing world (Sreberny-Mohammadi, 1991), the *rate* at which ownership of communications and media technologies is growing there is none the less rapid (Winseck 1997; Abercrombie 1996: 75). And underlying all this, there is evidence of a slow general improvement in levels of development as measured on the Human Development Index in nearly all developing countries (Thomas et al. 1994: 73).

Now of course all this must be qualified by saying that such general long-term trends may disguise all sorts of current and (possibly) future disparities. Globalization does not imply levelling out. It is not the case that gaps between the First and Third World are gradually closing, and there remain all manner of structural inequalities involved at the level of political economy, access to technologies, 'information poverty' and so on. It would clearly be foolish, then, to try to argue for comparability in cultural experience if this is simply dependent on an argument about gradually converging levels of general material affluence or standard of living. *Some* sectors in *some* parts of the Third World *do* have comparable standards of living to those experienced by affluent groups in countries like the UK, and the sort of lifestyle described in relation to our hypothetical British couple would not be entirely alien to many other affluent couples in Bombay, São Paulo, Seoul or Mexico City. But this sort of comparison alone will obviously not support the claim to the general global applicability of deterritorialized cultural experience.

However, neither does it have to. For, beyond the 'threshold point' recognized earlier, what is at stake in experiencing deterritorialized culture is not, crucially, level of affluence, but leading a life which, as a result of the various forces of global modernity, is 'lifted off' its connection with locality. This is not something restricted to the populations of the First World. And, indeed, it is possible to argue that some populations in the contemporary Third World may, precisely because of their positioning within the uneven process of globalization. actually have a sharper, more acute experience of deterritorialization than those in the First World.

Deterritorialization at the 'Margins'

To illustrate this I want to focus on some of the arguments of the
Mexican cultural theorist Néstor García Canclini, whose definition
of deterritorialization we adopted (and slightly adapted) at the
beginning of this chapter.

What is particularly interesting about García Canclini's work is
that it approaches the complexities of Latin American cultures[10] not
from the familiar perspective of dependency models, but in terms of
a global modernity in which these societies are ambiguously located:
'where traditions have not yet disappeared and modernity has not
completely arrived' (García Canclini 1995: 1). García Canclini encap-
sulates this ambiguity – which, as we shall see later, he grasps in
various senses as cultural *hybridity* – in the following question: 'How
can we understand the presence of indigenous crafts and vanguard
art catalogs on the same coffee table? What are painters looking for
when, in the same painting, they cite pre-Columbian and colonial
images along with those of the culture industry, and then reelaborate
them using computers and lasers?' (1995: 2).

This is not the Third World in which pre-modernity is starkly and
irreconcilably juxtaposed with modernity: the urban enclave against
the vast unchanging rural hinterland, a cultural version of the
'structural duality' argument (Cardoso 1982) in which peasant and
urbanite confront each other as though across history in mutual
incomprehension. Rather, García Canclini is trying to understand
the sort of culture that arises precisely out of the rapid if uneven
growth of urbanization, industrialization and mass communications
that is dissolving sharp distinctions between rural and urban culture and making these societies the sites of so much literal and metaphorical movement and encounter. These are societies in which
tradition and modernity have a complicated, forced coexistence at
all sorts of levels: from the bricolage of *objets d'art* in middle-class
living rooms, to that of migrant street vendors who, 'install their
baroque stands of regional candies and contraband radios, medi-
cinal herbs and videocassettes' on city street corners – cultural as
well as geographical 'intersections' (1995: 3).

In interpreting this cultural experience, García Canclini rejects
the sort of thinking that maps the modernity–tradition relationship
on to a core–periphery model ('the abstract expression of an ideal-
ised imperial system' (1995: 232)), in favour of a view of modernity
as, 'a condition that involves us [all] in the cities and in the country-

side, in the metropolises and in the underdeveloped countries' (1995: 268). Thus when he speaks of deterritorialization, although he describes phenomena which are in certain senses specific to the Latin American context, he none the less refers these to an under-lying *condition* which is recognizable as the common source of deterritorialized cultural experience in both the 'developing' and the 'developed' worlds.

Central to García Canclini's understanding of deterritorialization in Latin America is a fundamental sense of the literal displacement of populations in the processes of labour migration (see also Appadurai 1990): from the countryside to the city and across national borders. So, for him, the most salient sites of deterritorialized culture are those 'spaces on the border' formed by migration.

To illustrate this, García Canclini discusses some ethnographic research he conducted in Tijuana, a Mexican border city that has seen enormous population growth since the 1950s due to the influx of labour migrants from all regions of Mexico. Many of these settlers commute daily to work in the *maquiladoras* or in seasonal agricul-tural work across the border in the US. Others find work in the tour-ist industry which services the millions of American visitors who cross the border to Tijuana to 'see Mexico'. But despite its being a place of recent settlement, of transit, and of cultural intersection and 'marginality', García Canclini describes Tijuana as, 'a modern, con-tradictory, cosmopolitan city with a strong definition of itself'. What is interesting is that the city's self-identity is a product precisely of intense deterritorialization. García Canclini's research in Tijuana involved getting interviewees to identify places and images in the city which they judged most representative of its particular life and culture. The majority of these were

> those that linked Tijuana with what lies beyond it: Revolution Av-enue, its shops and tourist centers . . . the parabolic antennas, the legal and illegal passages on the border, the neighbourhoods where those from different parts of the country are concentrated . . . 'lord of the émigrés', to whom they go to ask that he arrange their 'papers' or to thank him for their not having been caught by *la migra*. (García Canclini 1995: 234–5)

García Canclini goes on to suggest that the deterritorialized nature of Tijuanan culture is also found in other ways: in its bilingualism and in the way its inhabitants have, in a deliberately ironic stance, adopted as their own the ersatz cultural images that litter the tourist city. The juxtaposition of images from all over Mexico – 'volcanoes, Aztec figures, cacti, the eagle and the serpent' – provided for the North American visitors make no claim to local 'embedded' authenticity, and yet provide a sense of what the city is for its inhabitants. Indeed García Canclini even identifies (in an interesting parallel with Giddens's notion of 're-embedding') a process of 'reterritorialization' by which some Tijuanans assert their cultural ownership of the city: 'The same people who praise the city for being open and cosmopolitan want to fix signs of identification and rituals that differentiate them from those who are just passing through, who are tourists or ... anthropologists curious to understand intercultural crossing' (1995: 239). The example Tijuana provides, then, is of a place where identity is complexly forged out of a 'local' experience dominated by its relationship to *other* places: the rest of Mexico, North America, the wider world – it is a 'delocalized locality'.

An even more striking example of a deterritorialized locality that García Canclini gives (citing a study by R. Rouse, 1988) is of the isolated rural town of Aguililla in Michoacán province in the south-west of Mexico. Far from being a border town either physically or culturally, Aguililla has none the less been fundamentally transformed by a pattern of migration, first established in the 1940s, to California – particularly the microelectronics capital of Silicon Valley, Redwood City. As Rouse's study indicates, the Aguilillan migrants who have found work as labourers and in the service industries there have not broken their links with Aguililla but have established and maintained a constant set of flows between their expatriate location and their place of origin. The flow of dollars has supported the declining subsistence farming economy while the labour migrants themselves either return frequently after short spells of work in the United States, or else keep in close contact with their families via the telephone. Rouse argues that these flows have created a single functioning community dispersed across space:

> Through the constant migration back and forth and the growing use of telephones, the residents of Aguililla tend to be reproducing their links with people that are two thousand miles away as actively as they maintain their relations with their immediate neighbours. Still more, and more generally, through the continuous circulation of people, money, commodities, and information, the diverse settlements have intermingled with such force that they are probably better understood as forming only one community dispersed in a variety of places. (Rouse, quoted in García Canclini 1995: 232)

Though different in many ways, Tijuana and Aguililla are none the less both prime examples of the central proposition of deterritorialization – that globalization lifts cultural life off its hitherto close connection with physical locality. They are also both instances which demonstrate that the phenomenon of deterritorialization, far from being exclusive to the centres of affluence in the West, is in certain ways experienced more sharply at the margins. And moreover, the cultures García Canclini describes in Latin America, for all their obvious subordination in the power geometry of globalization and their manifest levels of deprivation, are none the less in some senses *flourishing* cultures. One might even be tempted towards the rhetorical reversal that would place the margins at the centre of globalized culture – something García Canclini hints at when he writes: 'The hybridizations described throughout this book bring us to the conclusion that today all cultures are border cultures' (1995: 261). To see what substance there might be to such a claim we can now move on to examine the idea of hybridization, its relation to deterritorialization and its use as a category for understanding globalized culture.

Hybridization

The idea that globalized culture is hybrid culture has a strong intuitive appeal which follows directly from the notion of deterritorialization. This is because the increasing traffic between cultures that the globalization process brings suggests that the dissolution of the link between culture and place is accompanied by an intermingling of these disembedded cultural practices producing new complex hybrid forms of culture. Though not always related explicitly to the analysis of globalization, this sort of cultural complexity has been a strong theme in writings about post-colonial culture (e.g. Bhabha 1994; Young 1995) and in work on cultural identity more broadly (e.g. Hall 1992; Gilroy 1993; Dodd 1995; Hannerz 1996; Werbner and Modood 1997). Even a theorist like Anthony Smith,who, as we saw in chapter 3, argues for the continuing significance of the ethnic core of national identities admits to seeing 'signs of partial hybridization of national cultures' (Smith 1990: 188), arising from the multi-ethnic mix of most national populations.

But the idea of cultural hybridization is one of those deceptively simple-seeming notions which turns out, on examination, to have lots of tricky connotations and theoretical implications (Werbner 1997;

Papastergiadis 1997). I don't want to become deeply involved in all these here, but we shall have to clear some ground around the concept to see how useful it is for grasping the nature of globalized culture. So let's start with a quotation that establishes much of the spirit of the idea and at the same time introduces some of the problematic elements. This is from an essay by the novelist Salman Rushdie in which he defends his novel *The Satanic Verses* against the charges of blasphemy levelled against it from certain Muslim communities:

> Those who oppose the novel most vociferously today are of the opinion that intermingling with different cultures will inevitably weaken and ruin their own. I am of the opposite opinion. *The Satanic Verses* celebrates hybridity, impurity, intermingling, the transformation that comes of new and unexpected combinations of human beings, cultures, ideas, politics, movies, songs. It rejoices in mongrelization and fears the absolutism of the Pure. *Mélange*, hotchpotch, a bit of this and a bit of that is *how newness enters the world*. It is the great possibility that mass migration gives the world, and I have tried to embrace it. *The Satanic Verses* is for change-by-fusion, change-by-conjoining. It is a love-song to our mongrel selves. (Rushdie 1991: 394)

The whole 'Rushdie affair' – the novel itself, the *fatwa*, the associated debates about freedom of expression, blasphemy, racism, western versus Islamic values, liberalism and fundamentalism and so on – has of course become a particular focus for the cultural politics of global modernity. But without becoming caught up in these specific issues, let us simply take Rushdie's celebration of hybridity on its own terms as a cultural position which proceeds, as he says, 'from the very experience of uprooting, disjuncture and metamorphosis . . . that is the migrant condition, and from which . . . can be derived a metaphor for all humanity' (1991: 394). The idea implicit in this, of course, and echoing García Canclini, is that the hybrid experience is increasingly the global experience.

Perhaps the most basic component of the idea of hybridity is that of simply *mixing* – intermingling, combining, fusion, *mélange*. On the face of it this is straightforward and unexceptionable – hybridity is the mingling of cultures from different territorial locations brought about by the increasing traffic amongst cultures – in Rushdie's version, as in García Canclini's, particularly the processes of migration – that global modernity produces. At this basic empirical level hybridity is a way of describing and thinking through cultural phenomena of the 'hotchpotch, a bit of this and a bit of that' variety that seem to be proliferating. In this sense, it is an attempt to 'come to terms with phenomena such as Thai boxing by Moroccan girls in Amsterdam, Asian rap in London, Irish bagels, Chinese tacos . . .' (Nederveen Pieterse 1995: 53). However, beyond this simple empirical-descriptive use, the concept of hybridity, as Renato Rosaldo suggests, has two distinct polarities:

> On the one hand, hybridity can imply a space betwixt and between two zones of purity in a manner that follows biological usage that distinguishes two discrete species and the hybrid pseudo-species that results from their combination. Similarly, the anthropological concept of syncretism asserts, for example, that folk Catholicism occupies a hybrid site midway between the purity of Catholicism and that of indigenous religion. On the other hand, hybridity can be understood as the ongoing condition of all human cultures, which contains no zones of purity because they undergo continuous processes of transculturation (two-way borrowing and lending between cultures). Instead of hybridity versus purity, this view suggests that it is hybridity all the way down. (Rosaldo 1995: xv)

As Rosaldo points out, the tension between these two positions frequently remains unresolved in writers who, like Rushdie and García Canclini, celebrate hybridity,[11] but there is very often a strong element of the first – what we can call the 'original purity' position. Thus Rushdie, in rhetorically revelling in the 'impurity' of cultural *mélange* might be taken to imply that there were once historically existing pure, original cultures out of which unruly but dynamic 'mongrel' forms emerge. He is ideologically opposed to 'the apostles of purity . . . who . . . have wrought havoc among mere mixed-up human beings', but his version of mixing seems to *imply* this sort of essentialism, if only as something that needs to be overcome. Now it is extremely likely that, being pressed, Rushdie would readily concede that no culture is ever in this pure original state, but that, of their very nature, cultures are all more or less permeable and in constant flux. The problem is that the very structure of the hybridity argument in this form seems to summon up these implicit originary myths.

And the biological imagery in the idea of the hybrid, as Rosaldo also points out, contributes to this. Hybridity is, after all, derived from notions of breeding in plants and animals and is carried over to the cultural sphere via negatively charged notions of racial mixing such as miscegenation and the more ambiguous, though still originally racially derived, notions of *mestizaje* and creolization (Hannerz 1987; Nederveen Pieterse 1995; Friedman 1994, 1995). Now, of course, these terms are today almost always deployed in a celebratory mode deliberately intended to undermine arguments that link cultural strength and destiny with racial purity (Papastergiadis 1997). Indeed there is even the implicit reversal of this idea – the hybrid being seen as the stronger, more vigorous strain. But it might be argued that those who use the notion of hybridity to do this political-ideological work, implicitly accept and reproduce some of the unfortunate connotations of this biologically informed discourse: for instance in Rushdie's ironic acceptance of the label of 'mongrel' or his claim to be 'a bastard child of history' (1991: 394). The notion of cultural hybridity could benefit from jettisoning all this quasi-biological baggage. Jonathan Friedman takes the argument further by tracing the 'confused essentialism'of the discourses of hybridity or creolization to the inappropriate 'substantialization of culture' (Friedman 1995: 82) introduced in the metaphor of mingling itself – where cultures are imagined to 'flow' (as in bodily fluids?) together.

We can see, then, that there are all sorts of conceptual and political pitfalls attending the 'original purity' position. But what of Rosaldo's other interpretation: 'hybridity all the way down'? Clearly this view is to be preferred because it does justice to the now widely accepted view that culture is, of its 'nature', fluid, dynamic, protean, ever-changing – and at no point in history fixed, established, static.[12] This is to see the 'original' state of culture as what Werbner, following Bakhtin, calls 'organic unconscious hybridity' in which, 'despite the illusion of boundedness, cultures evolve historically through unreflective borrowings, mimetic appropriations, exchanges and inventions' (Werbner 1997: 4-5). But the question then arises of what *use* terms like hybridity are in designating something peculiar to the process of globalization. If all historical cultures have always been hybrid – well, what's new? It might be argued that globalization accelerates the process of mixing, but, as Nederveen Pieterse argues, there remains an element of tautology here: 'contemporary accelerated globalization means the hybridization of hybrid cultures.' As Nederveen Pieterse goes on to suggest, it may be that the idea of hybridization 'remains meaningful only as a critique of essentialism . . . as a counterweight to the introverted notion of culture' (Nederveen Pieterse 1995: 64).

Werbner sees a more positive distinction in counterposing 'organic hybridity' with the Bakhtinian idea of 'intentional hybridity', a deliberate deployment in linguistic and other cultural forms of a mixing intended to 'shock, change, challenge, revitalise or disrupt through deliberate intended fusions of unlike social languages and images' (1997: 5). It may be that this sort of shock aesthetic is a distinctive feature of some global modern cultural production, but it scarcely describes the whole gamut of contemporary cultural inter-penetration. Should we infer then that the concept of cultural hybridity remains only of 'strategic' value, and is not really adequate to grasping the broad nature of deterritorialized culture? Well, let's not make our minds up yet, but first consider, briefly, one further set of problems with the idea.

These centre on the apparent neglect of the role of power relations in structuring the hybrid mix. To put it at its simplest, the metaphors of mixing and confluence tend to suggest 'equal measures' and a certain serendipity in the combination – Rushdie's 'hotchpotch, a bit of this and a bit of that'. But the sceptical position points precisely to the unequal balance in the cultural resources that are engaged and to the familiar established hegemonies (the West, multinational cap-italism) that are at work ensuring that newness, in the shape of challenges to their hegemonic positions, *doesn't* enter the world. Aijaz Ahmad is particularly sceptical of the notion of hybridity on this count. Ahmad's particular quarrel is with the way in which writers on post-colonialism, such as Rushdie and, particularly, Homi Bhabha (1994), have tried to use the idea of cultural hybridity (in the broad context of postmodern cultural theory) as a sort of ideological turn-ing-of-the-tables on the West. This implies a privileging – in a way that recalls García Canclini's remarks about border cultures – of the migrant's displaced 'marginal' hybrid experience as the emerg-ing *central* global experience, over that of the decaying cultural hegemony of the West. But these theoretical and discursive moves, Ahmad argues, are unconvincing since they simply fail to engage with the manifest *material* power of (western) global capitalism. Thus those who celebrate hybridity 'in theory' for its anti-essentializing stance finish up rather naively 'endors[ing] the cultural claims of transnational capitalism itself':

> For it is the claim of IBM, CNN etc. that they are indeed the harbin-gers of a culture of global productivities, knowledges, pleasures. Again, it is doubtless true that a global informational regime is being con-structed. But is one to celebrate this process as a globalized hybridity or to conceptualise it as the penetration of far-flung, globally dispersed households by uniform structures of imperialist ideology . . .? (Ahmad 1995: 12)

Ahmad's general position can be aligned here with some of the views suspicious of the globalization process referred to earlier and, more specifically, with the critical stance which we encountered in chapter 3, that reads cultural globalization through the lens of cultural imperialism and homogenization. Despite all the problems which we found with this position, it must be said that Ahmad does pose an important issue of power relations in cultural processes in his insistence that hegemonic structures must be accounted for in any theory of hybridity.

However, recognizing hegemonic structures does not necessarily lead to a rejection of the idea of hybridity out of hand. It is not really a choice between, on the one hand, the hybridity thesis in the simple form of anarchic, unregulated cultural flows creatively combining, or on the other, the 'incorporation' thesis in which cultural hegemons absorb and refigure all subaltern cultures in their own image and to their own ends. Rather as the Chicana writer and poet Gloria Anzaldua describes it, hybrid experience is one which escapes incorporation by remaining marginalized in a 'borderlands' which intrinsically, contradictorily, mixes pleasures and woes:

> I am a border woman. . . . I have been straddling that *tejas*–Mexican border, and others, all my life. Its not a comfortable territory to live in, this place of contradictions. Hatred, anger and exploitation are the prominent features of this landscape. However, there have been compensations for this *mestiza*, and certain joys. Living on borders and in margins, keeping intact one's shifting and multiple identity and integrity, is like trying to swim in a new element. . . . There is an exhilaration in being a participant in the further evolution of mankind . . . (Anzaldua 1987: Preface, no page number).

Anzaldua's work centres on this ambiguity – the living of something new and exhilarating – indeed of being, in García Canclini's sense, in the vanguard of cultural development – within hegemonic structures that constantly 'marginalize' the mixtures they create. As she puts it in a stanza from her poem 'To live in the Borderlands means you':

> To live in the Borderlands means to
> Put *chile* in the borscht
> eat wholewheat *tortillas*
> speak Tex-Mex with a Brooklyn accent
> be stopped by *la migra* at the border checkpoints
> (Anzaldua 1987: 194)

Here the power of hegemonic forces is felt *within* a hybridity which is none the less experienced as having its own independent cultural power. So, as Nederveen Pieterse says, it is a question of recognizing how this complexity of hegemony–hybridity operates: 'Hence hybridity raises the question of the *terms* of mixture, the conditions of mixing and mélange. At the same time it's important to note the ways in which hegemony is not merely reproduced but *refigured* in the process of hybridization' (1995: 57). One way of thinking about this sort of 'refiguring' is to recognize that the movement of populations from the Third to the First World – the 'post-colonial diaspora' – has implications for the cultural identity of erstwhile imperialist nations. As Kevin Robins, puts it, this sort of deterritorialization represents a sense in which the 'Other has installed itself within the very heart of the western metropolis . . . [t]hrough a kind of reverse invasion, the periphery has now infiltrated the colonial core' (Robins 1991: 32). Thus, though we can agree with Ahmad that the creation of hybridity is never a power-neutral process, it does not necessarily proceed on a predictable trajectory reproducing the old hegemonies. Rather, as Robins reasons, the self-confident, stable cultural identity of the West may be becoming threatened: 'Through this irruption of empire, the certain and centred perspective of the old colonial order is confronted and confused' (1991: 33).

Drawing these thoughts together, we can conclude, at a minimum, that the idea of hybridization is a useful way of describing a substantive aspect of the process of deterritorialization. Some term is clearly needed to capture the general phenomenon of cultural mixing that is unquestionably increasing with the advance of globalization. Furthermore, the notion of hybrid cultures may be useful for grasping the sort of new cultural identifications that may be emerging – for example in youth culture built around popular music forms like 'hip-hop' (Gilroy 1993: 33ff) – in the 'transnational' cultural space. These complex transmutations of cultural practices and forms as they pass rapidly and effortlessly across national boundaries through the transnational cultural economy perhaps provide a figure for what a future 'globalized popular culture' may turn out to be like: different, that is, in *character* from the integrating, 'essentializing' nature of national cultures, looser-textured, more protean and relatively indifferent to the maintenance of sharp discriminations of cultural origin and belonging.

However the implications of hybridization as 'simple mixing' are not, as we have seen, straightforward, nor are the political positions to be drawn from it. It may be, for example, that a different term that does not trail behind it all the residual biologism of 'the hybrid' metaphor may be preferable. At any rate, it seems important that the idea of hybridization is kept close to the broader analysis of culture change that is grasped in deterritorialization – and used circumspectly to identify *aspects* of this process – rather than being taken independently as a *general* description of the global cultural condition. Apart from anything else, this is important to avoid overstating the cultural flux of globalization and losing sight of the tendency of cultural mixtures to re-embed themselves, however briefly, into 'stable' identity positions. Including hybridization as a subsidiary concept to deterritorialization allows us the conceptual space to think through this tendency in the dialectically opposed category of reterritorialization.

And this thought brings me to the general conclusion of this chapter. What I have tried to describe in the idea of deterritorialization is something like a general cultural condition which proceeds from the spread of global modernity. No doubt there are other cultural implications of the process of globalization, but those that we have considered under the category of deterritorialization, I have tried to suggest, are centrally significant ones that touch most people in the world and transform their daily life experiences in radical ways. But in concluding, it is important to stress that deterritorialization is not a linear, one-way process, but one characterized by the same dialectical push-and-pull as globalization itself. Where there is deterritorialization there is also reterritorialization.

Although we have met with some examples of reterritorializing practices – for instance in García Canclini's description of Tijuanans' claims to cultural ownership of their city – we have not generally stressed this aspect, since the purpose of the chapter was to focus on the forces that lift us out of our ties to place. But there are at least two good reasons to recognize the strength of this countervailing force. First, as we have stressed, the condition of deterritorialization is an ambiguous one that combines benefits with costs. Amongst the latter are the various existential vulnerabilities that come when our lives are opened up to the wider world and our sense of a secure and circumscribed home – both literally and metaphorically – is threatened. The drive towards reterritorialization can thus be seen in various attempts to re-establish a cultural 'home'. Amongst these there will be examples of very direct collective cultural-imaginative projects – for instance the creation by cultural diasporas of 'invented homelands' such as the Sikh diaspora's claims to 'Khalistan' (Appadurai 1990: 302; Cohen 1997: 106ff). But, more generally there are the numerous small, routine ways in which individual human subjects attempt, as Marshall Berman (1983: 348) says, to make themselves 'at home' in the world of global modernity, to live with its transformations and to generate new identities and narratives of personal meaning out of them. Secondly, there is the simple but important fact that we are all, as human beings, *embodied and physically located*. In this fundamental material sense the ties of culture to location can never be completely severed and the locality continues to exercise its claims upon us as the physical situation of our lifeworld. So deterritorialization cannot ultimately mean the end of locality, but its transformation into a more complex cultural space. Both of these aspects of the countervailing potential of reterritorialization will figure more significantly in the two chapters that follow.

5

Mediated Communication and Cultural Experience

In this chapter we focus on the distinctive contribution of globalizing media and communications technologies to the delivery of deterritorialized cultural experience. Implicit in the approach to deterritorialization adopted in the previous chapter is the idea that, for the majority, the cultural experience of globalization is not a matter of massively increased physical mobility, of notching up thousands of air miles, of 'globetrotting' and having direct experience of distant countries and exotic cultures. Though increased physical mobility *is* an important cultural aspect of global modernity as a whole (chapter 1), it is fair to say that for most people most of the time the impact of globalization is felt not in travel but in staying at home. One rather direct way of posing the issue then is as the distinction between literally travelling to distant places and 'travelling' to them by talking on the telephone, typing at the computer keyboard or watching the television set.[1] Giddens puts the point in the broader phenomenological terms of the impact of globalization on the 'phenomenal worlds' of individuals in their necessarily 'local' contexts:

> In conditions of late modernity we live 'in the world' in a different sense from previous eras of history. Everyone still continues to live a local life, and the constraints of the body ensure that all individuals, at every moment, are contextually situated in time and space. Yet the transformations of place, and the intrusion of distance into local activities, *combined with the centrality of mediated experience*, radically change what 'the world' actually is ... Although everyone lives a local life, phenomenal worlds for the most part are truly global ... in very few

instances does the phenomenal world any longer correspond to the habitual setting through which an individual physically moves. (1991: 187–8 – emphasis added)

But how precisely does our routine interaction with media and tele-communication technologies change our 'phenomenal worlds'? To come at an answer to this I shall first discuss the relationship be-tween the concept of 'mediation' and the idea of the bridging of time and space. Then I shall explore the use of some common mediating technologies, increasingly widely distributed in the developed world and making advances into the 'developing world', in terms of their different characteristic capacities to deliver 'mediated proximity' to users in spatially spread localities. Here, though I shall make some reference to the 'new media technologies' like computer-mediated communications (CMC), I shall mainly focus on very familiar forms of everyday technology – telephones, television. In the first case I shall be concerned with the idea of reproducing local conditions of 'intimacy' over distance, and in this context I shall also try to probe the links between cultural locality and embodiment – the 'constraints of the body' that Giddens implies as a limiting condition of deterritorialization. In the second, I shall try to understand the cap-acity of mediated – particularly televisual – experience to involve us emotionally and morally with distant others, events and social-cultural contexts. This last concern leads us on to the broader issues around the idea of 'cosmopolitan' political culture that we will focus on in the final chapter.

Mediation and Connectivity

What is mediated experience? It might be argued that the term im-plies a redundant distinction. For there is a sense in which almost all human experience is mediated, if we mean by this that experience is given to human beings through the symbolic order of language. Some examples of basic sensory experience such as body states (pain, hun-ger, fatigue and so on) might reasonably be described as 'immediate experiences', though there is of course room for philosophical quibbles even here. But in terms of the social and cultural orders of human existence, language is unquestionably the fundamental 'medium' through which we grasp and relate to the world. And this basic level of mediation is the point of departure for Giddens's reflections on mediated experience.

Giddens argues that 'language is the prime and original means of time-space distanciation, elevating human activity beyond the immediacy of the experience of animals' (1991: 23). Approaching the issue of mediation by way of this philosophical anthropology has interesting consequences, for it trades on a certain conceptual slippage. The notion that language takes us out of the 'immediate' (in the sense of unsymbolized, unrepresented) experience of the animal world is an important one for understanding human action and experience generally, and is closely tied to Giddens's notions of human reflexivity (chapter 2). However here it shades into the idea that the institution of language enables us to handle time and space in ways that are definitive of human existence. Although closely connected, these are not precisely the same ideas. The consequence of eliding them is to set the context for an understanding of the mediation involved in communications technologies that stresses its role in time-space transformation somewhat to the exclusion of other considerations. Giddens thus defines mediated experience as 'the involvement of temporally/spatially distant influences with human sensory experience' (1991: 243). Mediation is therefore seen as, fundamentally, a matter of bridging time and space in communication. And, of course, now we are not simply on the terrain of language, but dealing with the 'mediated experience' provided to us today by modern communications technologies like the telephone and the networked computer and through the 'mass media' of newspapers, cinema, radio, television and so on.

In making this connection between mediation and the transformation of time and space, Giddens broadly follows the tradition of the 'medium theory' (Meyrowitz 1994; Crowley and Mitchell 1994) associated with the work of the 'Toronto circle' of communication theorists between the 1940s and the 1960s. Scholars such as Harold Innis (1951) (here 1995), Marshall McLuhan (1964), Walter Ong (1967) Jack Goody (1968), along with more recent North American writers such as Joshua Meyrowitz (1985) and James Carey (1989), are distinguished within the broad field of communications theory by a concern with the influence of the medium of communication itself, rather than the contents of media messages, on social formations and cultural experience. But for our purposes what is important about their approach is the way in which they foreground the implications of media and communications technologies for our social handling of time and space.

For example, Harold Innis's foundational work The *Bias of Communication* (Innis 1995) argued that different historical epochs could be distinguished in terms of the determination of cultural patterns and political power by their prevalent medium of communication. Most famously (and controversially) he argued that the medium of communication displayed a 'bias' towards either time or space. 'Time-biased' societies were those in which either a simple oral culture dominated, or in which the prevalent medium was heavy and durable but relatively immobile, inflexible and difficult to reproduce: stone or clay tablets in ancient societies, parchment in medieval Europe. The use of such media, Innis (in essence) argued, was directly connected with these societies' orientation towards 'tradition': their emphasis on custom, continuity, sacred revealed knowledge, relatively undynamic social reproduction and so forth, binding the present and future closely to the past. 'Space-biased' societies by contrast were ones which replaced these media with more flexible, portable, easily reproducible ones: papyrus instead of stone in ancient Egypt, paper and print instead of parchment in Europe, and so on. This in turn produced a 'cultural bias' towards space in these societies – the expansion of territorial administrative control (including imperialism) accompanied by the eventual rise of secular institutions, technical expertise, the break with traditional reproduction based on custom and religion and an orientation towards the present and future rather than the past (Heyer and Crowley 1995). As Roger Silverstone (1994: 93) summarizes Innis's argument, whereas time-biased cultures root values and communities in *place*, space-biased ones 'stress land as real estate, voyage, discovery, movement and expansion', thereby producing 'mobile communities of space' connected over distance.

We can see here a certain affinity between Innis's ideas and some of Giddens's notions of the disembedding properties of modernity, for though of course Giddens does not rest his argument on the same sort of 'technological determinism', he does make similar links between the idea of mediation and the time-space distanciation of modernity.

Innis's influence comes through in the more famous visionary and hyperbolic writings of Marshall McLuhan. McLuhan's ideas of the expansionary, 'displacing' effect of communications and media technologies can be seen, for example, in his treatment of such technologies in his book *Understanding Media* (1964) as 'extensions of man'. Here he argued that media technologies should be thought of as spatial 'extensions' of human senses or of the body itself – the book as an extension of the eye; the radio as an extension of the ear. But McLuhan's best-known elaboration of the time-space bridging properties of the media are to be found in his celebrated – some would argue prescient – pronouncement of the 'global village' in which 'Electric circuitry has overthrown the regime of "time" and "space" and pours upon us instantly and continuously the concerns of all other men '(McLuhan and Fiore 1967: 16).

Though McLuhan's work has both benefited and suffered from its hyperbolic and prophetic style it is important to see him within the same tradition as Innis and more recent medium theorists such as Joshua Meyrowitz. For example, Meyrowitz in a text that has become particularly influential, *No Sense of Place*, writes that

> The evolution of media has decreased the significance of physical presence in the experience of people and events . . . Now, physically bounded spaces are less significant as information is able to flow through walls and rush across great distances. As a result, *where* one is has less and less to do with what one knows and experiences. Electronic media have altered the significance of time and space for social interaction. (Meyrowitz 1985: vii–viii)

Now judged as broad theories relating communications media to social interaction and reproduction there are various problems with the ideas of all the 'medium theorists'.[2] However I don't want to pursue these here, but simply to show how the concept of mediation in this tradition is tied very closely to the idea of overcoming distance in communication. This can also be seen in virtually all the etymologies of electronic media forms: the root of 'television', 'telephone', 'telegraph' – from the Greek *tele*, 'far off, distant'; the derivation of 'radio' from the Latin *radius*, 'a ray'; and of course the term 'broadcasting'. This understanding of mediation as essentially 'facilitation' or 'delivery' – bringing distant events into people's localities – is obviously very suggestive for the idea of deterritorialization.

However I do not think it grasps the whole substance of mediation, and to get further in understanding the special, distinctive quality of mediated experience, we need to combine this with a quite different view of the idea. This is the sense of mediation as the process of *passing through a medium* and the consequences for the nature of experience which flow from this intervention. We can grasp what is at stake here quite simply by comparing two dictionary entries under 'medium': 1. 'the means by which something is communicated' and 2. 'the intervening substance through which impressions are conveyed to the senses' (Hawkins and Allen 1991: 902). In the first of these the dominant sense is of mediation as *facilitating* – 'the means by which . . .' – and it is easy to see how this connotes all the technological power of modern media and communications practices to deliver experience with speed, ease and efficiency. There is no sense in this definition of the medium itself *intervening* in the process, making its mark on the communication, producing qualitative changes in the experience of the thing communicated. This is only brought in with the second definition, where the idea of an 'intervening substance' directs attention to all these issues.

Of course mediated communication always involves both of these aspects. The means of communication are never transparent but always intrinsically shape the communication. Televisual experience, for example, is highly mediated not only in terms of the technical determinants of the form (luminous images produced by bombarding a fluorescent screen with a beam of electrons), but in terms of the complex set of semiotic codes, conventions, formats and production values that it employs. There is clearly massive intervention at all levels here – from the strategies of camera work to the organization of experience created in the employment of specific televisual genres and the textual characteristics of the medium: its modes of address, its narrative strategies and so on (Williams 1974; Fiske 1987; Mellencamp 1990; Corner 1995; Abercrombie 1996).

In fact one way of thinking about the development of modern media and communications technologies is as the constant attempt to deliver the promise of the first definition by reducing the problems of the second. The general goal of mediated communication, then, might be thought of, somewhat paradoxically, as the attempt to deliver immediacy. This can be seen most clearly as a technical goal – the improvement of signal quality, the 'instantaneity' provided by satellite links, better image definitions on screens, the now rather old-fashioned-sounding, but none the less telling, idea of 'Hi-Fi' audio ('high fidelity' to the 'real' original performance) and so forth. But it is equally important as a cultural-experiential goal of the media industries: the notion, for example, that events – news, sport, 'historical events' etc. – can be brought to you 'live as they happen' on television (Dayan and Katz 1992).

Thinking about mediation in this way directs us back to the idea of overcoming distance, but with a more problematized sense of the process. 'Immediacy' in the strict sense of the self-dissolution of the medium is clearly never attainable, so the globalizing properties of media experience – the experience of the world in one's living-room – has to be understood as a particular modality of connectivity (chapter

1) different in *kind* from the 'direct' experience of one's own physical locality. Putting this in the language of phenomenology, we have to think of the experience brought to us by telephones, television, networked computers and so on as occupying a distinct, specialized 'space' in the lifeworld of the individual. Mediated experience 'appears to consciousness' in the everyday flow of lived experience in ways that can be distinguished from the face-to-face experience of physical proximity within a locality. So only by paying attention to this distinction will we be able to the assess the significance of 'mediated deterritorialization' in relation to other mundane localized experiences and concerns in the lifeworld of ordinary people. This is, I think, a crucially important consideration since so much seems to rest on the idea of electronic media as vehicles of deterritorialization.

The opposition we are thus pushed towards is one between local direct face-to-face interaction and experience, and a *qualitatively different order of mediated experience* that we, in the developed world, have increasingly routine access to in our localities. This is a valid and useful distinction, but we must be aware if its dangers.

The first of these is that it may mislead us into thinking of direct face-to-face experience as a simple, pure, transparent form of experience just because it is, in a sense, the original 'anthropological' mode of experience. This returns us to our original point that no interaction, communication or experience is ever strictly speaking 'immediate'. As Manuel Castells puts this point: '[W]hen critics of electronic media argue that the new symbolic environment does not represent "reality", they implicitly refer to an absurdly primitive notion of "uncoded" real experience that never existed. All realities are communicated through symbols. . . . In a sense, all reality is virtually perceived' (Castells 1996: 373). And this is not simply to stress the abstract philosophical point about the inevitably symbolized delivery of reality; it is to open up the phenomenological complexity of 'direct' experience. A moment's thought will reveal that this involves a complicated mix of sensory and symbolized experience synthesized with memory and imagination. Face-to-face oral communication itself has a range of different formal and informal modes (receiving information or instructions, listening to lectures, involvement in business negotiations, conversations, phatic communion, intimate disclosures of self, arguments, gossip, jokes, etc.) combined with an ongoing (sometime backgrounded, sometimes foregrounded) awareness of the physical environment, the experience of movement or rest, of time passing, of feeling well or unwell, of sexuality, worrying, daydreaming and so on. So it is not as though the local, face-to-face context of experience can be taken as a simple base line on to which the complexities of mediation are layered.

Where this simplifying of the complexities of face-to-face interaction becomes particularly contentious is when it slips towards the idea that the local face-to-face context is somehow the 'pure' and thus the most *valid* form of communicative interaction. Here the direct and (supposedly) 'immediate' becomes privileged as the high moral ground of cultural interaction from which any degree of mediation seems an inevitable shortfall. This is a position which is often found in defences of the superiority of small-scale political-cultural communities over mass societies. And it is an idea that is vigorously contested, for example by the feminist political theorist Iris Marion Young. Young criticizes some versions of communitarian political thought for the way in which it privileges 'immediacy over mediation'. Those who defend a (romantic) ideal of small face-to-face communities on the grounds of their immediacy – the directness and authenticity of the social relations they promote – are, Young argues, labouring under a 'metaphysical illusion' of the possibility of 'immediate presence of subjects to one another'. She goes on to argue that

> Even a face-to-face relation between two people is mediated by voice and gesture, spacing and temporality . . . [thus] there are no grounds for considering face-to-face relations more pure, authentic social relations than relations mediated across time and distance. For both face-to-face relations and non-face-to-face relations are mediated relations and in both there is as much the possibility of separation and violence as there is communication and consensus. (Young 1990: 314)

In a similar vein, Doreen Massey warns against romanticizing the conception of a community concentrated in space: '"presence availability" does not somehow do away with issues of representation and interpretation. That place called home was never an unmediated experience' (Massey 1994: 163–4).

These are important warnings, but they do not prevent our making the distinction we need to between direct face-to-face experience and the experience obtained from media technologies. The point to be clear about is that this distinction is not one between, on the one hand, the pure and 'immediate' and, on the other, the mediated as 'unreal' or artificial; neither is it one which privileges presence availability as a value. The distinction is simply one between different phenomenological modes, different ways of experiencing 'reality'.

And, indeed, these phenomenological differences do not simply straddle the divide between the 'local-direct' and the 'distant-mediated'. There are clearly different phenomenologies related to different types of media technology. The telephone's ring 'intrudes' into the local situation in a different way from the television's stream of images or the message on the computer telling you that you have a new e-mail. A useful step in understanding mediated connectivity then is to model some of these basic distinctions.

Varieties of Mediated Experience

In his book *The Media and Modernity* John Thompson offers the basis of this in proposing 'a conceptual framework for the analysis of forms of action and interaction created by the media' (Thompson 1995: 82). Thompson suggests three categories of interaction which relate to three distinct communicational modes that are to be found in modern societies (Thompson 1995: 82–7).

The first – 'face-to-face interaction' – is self-explanatory, referring to the direct communication in contexts of co-presence discussed above. It characteristically employs a multiplicity of symbolic cues – not just speech but gesture, body language and so forth – made possible by a shared spatio-temporal reference system. Most significantly, face-to-face interaction is *dialogical*: it involves the two-way flow of communication.

His second category, 'mediated interaction', describes the communicational mode of the letter, the telegraph, the fax, the telephone and, perhaps (though Thompson doesn't mention it) of the most basic forms of computer-mediated communication – say simple e-mail. This type of interaction involves the use of a technical medium – 'paper, electrical wires, electromagnetic waves etc.' – to allow communication between parties distant in either (or both) space and time. According to Thompson, this stretching of the communication across time-space has the following consequences. Participants lack common references of co-presence and so have to consider contextualizing information much more – addresses and dates on letters and faxes, identifications in telephone conversations. They also operate here within a characteristically narrower range of symbolic cues than is possible in face-to-face interaction and thus this sort of communication can have increased levels of ambiguity and greater need for hermeneutic skills by the actors involved. However a key point is that, despite these limitations, mediated interaction remains, like face-to-face interaction, essentially dialogical.

Thompson's final category is the most interesting one for the present discussion. What he calls 'mediated quasi-interaction' refers to the communication of the mass media ('books, newspapers, radio, television, etc.'). This, like mediated interaction, obviously stretches communication across time-space but it has two crucial differences from both of the other categories. First, this type of communication is directed not towards specific identifiable others, but is 'produced for an indefinite range of potential recipients'(it is *mass* communication). Secondly, unlike either of the other categories, it is not dialogical but typically *monological* in character: the communicational flow – be it of print or electronic media – is predominantly one-way. These two distinctions lead Thompson to describe mass-mediated communication as a 'quasi-interaction' for it clearly lacks some of the aspects we associate with 'direct' human interaction: reciprocity and interpersonal specificity. However he rightly insists that it is a *kind* of interaction: it is not merely the transfer of information from source to destination; recipients, though not directly responding, are however not passive in the process but active in the interpretation of the communication and the construction of meaning. And indeed there is an interactional dimension in the sorts of 'relationship' a media audience can establish with media personalities and so forth.

Now all this is, rightly, pitched at the level of interaction – for there is an important sense in which we ought always to think of communications as interactional (or quasi-interactional), rather than as the discrete acts of sending and receiving messages. Furthermore, Thompson's framework is employed to analyse a wide range of social interactions that are related to both the production and consumption of media culture and, beyond this, to issues of the transformation of the public sphere of political engagement entailed in the increasing use of media technologies (see also Thompson 1994). None the less we can, as Thompson recognizes, also talk of *mediated experience* as 'the kind of experience we acquire through mediated interaction or quasi-interaction' (1995: 228), and this is what we really want to get at.

One way of doing this would be to try to build a comprehensive phenomenological analysis upon the distinctions Thompson makes in his interactional analysis. Thompson broaches *some* of these phenomenological issues himself and offers some useful insights which we will return to later in the chapter. But he doesn't attempt to be in any way exhaustive, and it is easy to see why. For we have already seen that even the relatively 'simple' interactional category of face-to-face communication is phenomenologically complex. Extend this just to Thompson's category of 'mediated interaction' and we would need to include a whole range of subtle discriminations: between the phenomenologies of an exchange of letters and a telephone conversation, or between either of these and the 'keyboard interactions' of computer-mediated communication. Is e-mail closer in experience to letter-writing – 'the revenge of the written medium, the return to the typographic mind' (Castells 1996: 363) or is it, 'a new form of "orality" . . . informal, unconstructed writing in real time interaction, in the mode of synchronist chat (a writing telephone . . .)' (ibid.)? The complexity of these questions in relation to 'new media' is exacerbated by their reference back to what we supposed to be 'simple' mediated forms – letters, for example – but which we discover to be phenomenologically complex.[3]

If we add to this range of issues those raised by, for instance, the experience of time-shifted communication made available by answerphone machines, or the different ways in which mobile cellular phones have rapidly integrated with some people's routine lifeworlds, or of how the 'migration' of certain technologies – such as fax machines – from a business context to a domestic one have altered the experience of home life, we clearly have a major undertaking here. And though some of these issues are becoming scrutinized in relation to new media like CMC (Poster 1995; Turkle 1995, 1996) there is very little literature which extends across the range of mediated and 'quasi-mediated experience'.[4]

In the space available here, eschewing any attempt at a comprehensive treatment, I shall focus on just two themes that relate the phenomenology of mediated experience to the broad theme of deterritorialization. Both of these themes can be understood as different expressions of the category of 'proximity' which we discussed in chapter 1 as a cultural elaboration of the connectivity that defines globalization. But, whereas there we focused mainly on the experience of proximity afforded by physical travel, here we try to redeem the promise to understand proximity delivered by media technologies into localities.

Mediated Proximity 1: Intimacy Redefined

The idea of intimacy is related to local experience in a number of interesting ways. First, its dominant sense of 'closeness' is one arguably modelled on the physical embodied proximity of (generally two) people. To be 'intimate' is usually thought of as to achieve a deep level of personal contact with the other. Here the 'face-to-faceness' of local communicative interaction becomes more significantly a 'one-to-oneness' in which the aim is to be present to each other in the fullest way, often involving a degree of bodily contact and usually involving exclusivity of attention. Perhaps the key idea here is the 'innerness' that derives from the etymology of the term – from the Latin *intimus* – 'inmost'. The common, though not exclusive, connotation of intimacy with sexuality gives the clearest sense of this innerness of communication: the sexual act as intimate knowledge of the other, combining physical with psychological closeness and bonding. Understood thus, intimacy is the antithesis of distanciation. And finally the realm of the intimate refers us to specific locales – usually in the domestic sphere rather than the public sphere. Here progressive degrees of intimacy can be understood in spatial-phenomenological terms as levels of 'innerness': from the entrance hall, through the reception rooms to the kitchen and the most private 'inmost' recesses of the home – the bathroom and the bedroom.

If this is the way in which intimacy is most commonly grasped, then the impact of media technologies might be thought of most directly as a *disturbing* of intimacy – the outer world penetrating the inner. This was the sense which we noted in the previous chapter, of communications technologies opening up our private spaces to the outside world and making us constantly 'available'. Marshall McLuhan, for example, insists that the telephone is a *demanding* medium: we generally feel compelled to answer a ringing phone whatever else we are doing. And the comic potential of intimate moments disturbed or frustrated by the intrusive telephone is of course a cliché of popular drama. Joshua Meyrowitz extends this argument noting how such constant availability has become a tacit social norm of modern societies:

> To be 'out of touch' today is to be abnormal . . . for a person to live . . . in a place that has no telephone is often thought to be an implicit insult to friends, relatives and co-workers. Taking one's phone off the hook may be seen as the mark of a misanthrope. In some occupations, people are expected to wear 'beepers' that make them accessible at any time wherever they are and whatever they are doing. (1985: 147)

Meyrowitz goes on to record how even some Trappist monasteries, since the impact of Vatican II in the 1960s, have installed telephones. Although, interestingly, in one that he studied, the monks, though having access to the phone, 'avoid watching regular broadcast television or reading daily newspapers' (Meyrowitz 1985: 353 n. 36) as a way of maintaining their goals of solitude, withdrawal from the world and sustained exclusive intimacy with God.

However we can take a different and I think more interesting approach by focusing not on the disturbance of contexts of intimacy, but on the capacity of media technologies to deliver their own unique *forms* of intimacy, which in the process may be redefining the cultural significance of intimacy for us.

There is a fairly obvious sense in which telephones deliver distanciated 'closeness' in that typically they connect us dialogically with one specific communications 'partner' (Thompson 1995: 84). But is this intimacy? One reason to think it is, is to notice how *relatively close* distanciated telephone conversations are to face-to-face conversations. Despite the limitations imposed by the lack of physical co-presence, it is often observed how 'natural' and unobtrusive the medium is. Again Meyrowitz captures the point:

> Speaking to someone on the telephone . . . is so natural that we almost forget about the intervening medium. (We often say 'I spoke to —— last night', not even thinking to add that it was a telephone conversation. We rarely say, 'I spoke' when we mean that we wrote someone a letter.) Because of the unobtrusiveness of the medium and its code, the telephone conversation is much more spontaneous and much less contrived than most letters. (1985: 109–10)

The seeming 'naturalness' of telephone communication in comparison with letters (or telegrams, or, indeed, e-mail) may be partly accounted for in the difference between the codes of speech and writing, the latter being, as Meyrowitz goes on to note, a much more complexly encoded form. So the peculiar power of the telephone as a 'transparent' distanciating medium is surely, at one level, to do with the way it replicates the face-to-face medium of speech across time-space.

But there is also a sense in which the telephone can actually *enhance* the intimacy of the communication precisely as a function of the lack of presence availability. Giddens (1991: 189) observes the following paradox of distanciated communication: 'A person may be on the telephone to someone twelve thousand miles away and for the duration of the conversation be more closely bound up with the responses of that distant individual than with others sitting in the same room.' We can account for this in terms of an intensified phenomenological focus that the medium elicits: the lack of physical presence and consequent narrowing of the range of symbolic cues available amplifies the exclusive engagement of the dialogical situation of face-to-face interaction. We focus on the telephone partner's voice and give them our full attention because not to do so would mean that the communication would break down altogether. This is what McLuhan (1964: 267) means when he says that telephones 'demand complete participation of our senses and faculties'.

So it is entirely plausible to argue that communications technologies can deliver a form of intimacy; but we begin to see a shift in the meaning of the term. One-to-oneness and innerness are preserved, but first the element of embodiment seems to fall away, followed by the contexts of seclusion and privacy.

Disembodied Intimacy

As the telephone allows intimacy despite bodily separation, one-to-oneness is lifted off face-to-faceness. But isn't this then a sort of ersatz, second-rate intimacy, a weak substitute for the fullness of presence? The rather bland techno-enthusiasm of Bill Gates on this issue might well convince us that it is:

> I used to date a woman who lived in a different city. We spent a lot of time together on email. And we figured out a way we could sort of go to the movies together. We'd find a film that was playing at about the same time in both our cities. We'd drive to our respective theatres, chatting on our cellular phones. We'd watch the movie, and on our way home we'd use our cellular phones to discuss the show. In the future this sort of virtual dating will be better because the movie watching could be combined with a video conference. (Gates 1995: 206)

Struggling against the obvious charges of 'nerdishness' in its corporate guise, it is still rather difficult to take the suggestion of virtual dating very seriously. The sort of bloodless, insipid relationship Gates evokes simply invites the obvious response that 'real' intimacy in human relationships demands close physical contact.

Here sexuality is the implicit standard against which other 'lesser' forms of intimacy become measured. And the idea of telemediated sexual experience is a rather troubling one, conjuring images ranging from the comic wired bodies of virtual sex s(t)imulation to the rather more commonplace, but apparently desperate solitary satisfactions of sex-phone lines. Indeed it would be difficult to find a stronger example of the essential deficit of telemediated intimacy than that of commercial telephone sex. Advertised as one-to-one erotic encounters, the sad reality of these services might be seen to lie in the entire failure to achieve intimacy in its 'fullness'. For this is a business relationship which, governed by its commercial nature, involves bodies only in a pornographic/masturbatory mode focused on the aural stimulation to orgasm of the client. Alienation – separation – rather than intimacy appears as the hallmark of this congress. First there is an abstraction of the 'commodity' registered in the often crudely opposed interests of the parties: speed, hence cheapness, for the client; the opposite for the virtual sex worker whose main task is to keep the client on line. Then the encounter is based on a separation of locale and an anonymity which is crucial to the economics of the business. The client can imagine the encounter in an erotic context which is far removed from the drab functionality of the sex worker's real physical locale, maybe a bleak office, maybe her or his own kitchen. Finally the anonymity of this sort of 'virtual' encounter is, as Castells (1996: 361) says, a function of the riskiness of direct sexual experience in late twentieth-century societies: 'increasingly afraid of contagion and of personal aggression, people search for alternatives to express their sexuality . . . particularly as long as the interaction is not visual and identities can be preserved.'[5]

But if telemediated sexuality suggests alienation (the abstraction of the orgasmic from the organismic) we must be careful not to lay the blame for this at the wrong door. Telephone sex may be more significantly close to conventional (direct) prostitution in its defining context of the commodification of sexuality than it is different from it in its sterilizing distanciation. In this case, maybe telephone (or CMC) sex *could* be a more joyous and intimate imaginary encounter where it is practised in a consensual, non-commercial context between two 'real' lovers.

Furthermore, it might be objected that it is misleading to allow the theme of sexuality to dominate the idea of intimacy. For the sort of 'innerness' that is associated with the close, but not sexualized, relations of family life might provide just as promising a model. A good example of the stretching of this sort of intimacy can be seen in the use of video-conferencing technologies to unite spatially divided families. In one reported case of this practice, a woman living in Bristol is able to maintain routine contact with her three children in Cambridge in a live video link via the worldwide web. The story reports how the woman – separated from her husband – has replaced her intermittent weekend access visits, involving a 300-mile round trip, with daily 'visits' down 'high speed ISDN digital phone lines'. The technology has thus transformed 'the long distance parents to [a] totally wired family': 'The impact has been dramatic. They say it allows them to eat together and lets Gill [the mother] see the children before they go to bed at night. "I can be there to help the children whether it's a grazed knee, a tough piece of homework or boyfriend problems"' (Millar 1997: 5).

The story celebrates the technological restoration of the intimacy of the family circle. Photographs show the smiling children in a cosy, cluttered living-room gathered around the computer screen and a smiling video-imaged mum. This recalls images of earlier media-focused domesticity: the cosy circles around the television in the 1950s or the radio in the 1930s. There is nevertheless the suggestion of a deficit here. The mother admits that it doesn't replace being with the children – bedtime 'contact' does not extend to cuddles and tucking in – and of course the very fact of the family's socio-legal 'separation' cannot be divorced from their physical separation. But despite all this, such examples do seem to offer glimpses of something we can very plausibly think of as distanciated, 'disembodied' intimacy. As these mediated practices become more widespread – with domestic-use videophones linked to wall-sized high-definition screens on the near technocultural horizon – a redefinition of intimacy seems inevitable. The point is to think of telemediated intimacy not as a shortfall from the fullness of presence, but as a different *order* of closeness, not replacing (or rather failing to replace) embodied intimacy, but increasingly integrated with it in everyday lived experience.

And there is yet another way of looking at it: that the intimacy achieved via media technologies could lead to more radical cultural redefinitions – including the idea of 'embodiment' itself. McLuhan's take on this is typically assertive but intuitively insightful. Elaborating his theme of media as body extensions, he approaches the corporeal aspects of intimacy in a way that does not sharply distinguish between bodies and technologies:

> The child and the teenager understand the telephone, embracing the cord and the ear-mike as if they were beloved pets. What we call 'the French phone' the union of mouthpiece and earphone in a single instrument, is a significant indication of the French liaison of the senses . . . French is the 'language of love' just because it unites voice and ear in an especially close way, as does the telephone. So it is quite natural to kiss via phone . . . (McLuhan 1964: 266)

Discounting the casual cultural stereotyping, there is something in the suggestion that phones have a 'natural congruity with the organic' (p. 271) – as extensions of the embodied person – that anticipates some of the work on the human–machine interface that is emerging in the 1990s in relation to CMC. Compare, for instance, this passage on extensionality from Sherry Turkle's *Life on the Screen*:

> Just as musical instruments can be extensions of the mind's construction of sound, computers can be extensions of the mind's construction of thought. A novelist refers to 'my ESP with the machine. The words float out. I share the screen with my words.' An architect who uses the computer to design goes further: '. . . the building . . . comes to life in the space between my eyes and the screen.' (Turkle 1995: 30)

Making a comparison with W. D. Winnicott's psychoanalytical category of the 'transitional object' – objects which, like the baby's blanket, are grasped as simultaneously part of the embodied self and of the outside, 'separate' world – Turkle goes on to argue that the computer can be, 'experienced as an object on the border between the self and the not self'. Turkle's work on the phenomenology of computer use (see also Lupton 1995; Lupton and Noble 1997) opens up perplexing questions about the perceived boundaries between human beings and the technologies we use. And there is a trajectory from this towards the even more challenging ideas about the blurring of the human–machine divide that can be seen in recent theories of 'cyborg' culture (Haraway 1991; Gray 1995; Featherstone and Burrows 1995). In this body of theory the science-fiction hybrids found in, for instance, the novels of William Gibson or films like Paul Verhoeven's *RoboCop*, are conceptualized alongside real developments in prosthetics. As Featherstone and Burrows (1995: 3) put it, 'the mainstreaming of cosmetic surgery, and the rise of biotechnology, genetic engineering and nanotechnology . . . have led some to contemplate that the next generation could very well be the last of "pure" humans.' Without straying too far into this terrain, we can appreciate that to see intimacy as constrained by embodiment – and indeed to see embodiment as the fundamental factor tying individuals to localities – is to think within a particular cultural understanding of the relationship between embodiment and human subjectivity that is, however disconcertingly, open to challenge.

Public Intimacy

In the examples of mediated sexuality and of the spatially extended family circle, intimacy preserves (though from very different motivations) its link with privacy. But another important aspect of the redefinition of intimacy is the dissolution of this link, and the possibility of various kinds of new public intimacy.

One obvious aspect of this is the redefinition of the culturally appropriate spaces for the use of communication technologies. Telephones were once thought of as requiring a particular secluded space for their operation: early 'public' telephone booths provided, in their robust construction, not only quiet but privacy. The increasing openness of their construction reflects not only economies, but a gradual public acceptance of the idea of holding a private conversation in an open public space. The arrival of the cellular phone of course spectacularly accelerated this acceptance and today the commonplace, unselfconscious use of cellphones in (almost) any public situation – on trains, in restaurants, in the street – indicates some dramatic shifts in cultural attitudes to mediated intimacy. It is, for example, apparently easy for many people to blot out the presence of close proximate others (strangers) and to live the relationship with the telemediated other without any great inhibition arising from the lack of privacy.[6]

A different way of approaching the idea of public intimacy is to notice how the idea of one-to-oneness becomes shifted from an exclusive connection with people in our own personal spheres to connections with people only present to us via the public media. A good instance of this is the current (1998) advertising campaign by the mobile phone service provider, 'One-to-One'. In these ads, aimed primarily at the youth market, the idea is promoted of having a 'one-to-one' conversation with a celebrity. In fact the ads feature imaginary 'one-to-ones' by current popular-cultural icons with their heroes of the past: supermodel Kate Moss fantasizes about a date with Elvis Presley, the footballer Ian Wright imagines a meeting with Martin Luther King. These advertisements are complex and sophisticated texts, not least in the way that the promotion of one form of 'intimate' mediated communication (telephones) is parasitic upon others (film, television). What is particularly interesting is the connection established between the cultural values of intimacy as personal contact, innerness and exclusivity (a 'telephone value') and those of access to 'publicly owned' media figures (a 'television value').

Intimacy here becomes 'public' in the sense of the establishment of a mass-mediated lifeworld in which anyone (and any number of people) can live an imaginary relationship of intimacy with public figures they will never meet, but who are none the less intensely real to them in their mediated presence.

Thompson (1995: 219) describes this sort of imagined media relationship, following Horton and Wohl (1956), as 'non-reciprocal intimacy at a distance'. He argues that the peculiar non-reciprocity in the relationship deriving from the monological character of media like television is a distinct but entirely commonplace aspect of 'mediated quasi-interaction':

> In one form or another, most individuals in modern societies establish and sustain non-reciprocal relations of intimacy with distant others. Actors and actresses, news readers and talk show hosts, pop stars and others become familiar and recognisable figures who are often discussed by individuals in the course of their day-to-day lives, who may be referred to on a first name basis and so on. (Thompson 1995: 220)

Probably the most striking recent display of this sort of public intimacy was to be found in the extraordinary reaction to the death of Diana, Princess of Wales – not only in the UK but throughout the world. The experience of genuine personal loss and the expression of intense grieving recorded in the huge crowds of mourners who travelled to London for the funeral, and the vast global 'television community' participating in the event, testified to the 'reality' of this sort of mediated non-reciprocal relationship. It dramatically illustrated how deeply media relationships are woven into the fabric of daily experience for huge numbers of people.

But Diana's funeral also gave a glimpse of another possible aspect of public intimacy. The apparently strong desire of the mourners to share their grief in public – particularly the ones who remained for days camped around the makeshift 'shrines' in Kensington Palace Gardens – could be read as a reaction to what Giddens (1991: 144ff) has called the 'sequestration of experience' in modern societies: the tendency to privatize expressions of grief along with other passionate /intimate experiences. Many of those interviewed expressed the need to extend their participation in communal mourning and linked this with a frustration at the prospect of returning to their ordinary private lives. It is not implausible to connect this to a broader, though generally submerged, cultural desire to escape from the privacy of routine local life into wider, more fulfilling communities of experience. Mass-mediated experience provides models for this in the imagined 'parallel lives' available in relationships with public figures (Chaney 1993; Grodin and Lindhof 1996), or in occasional ritualized-communal media events (Dayan and Katz 1992), and this sort of compromise in the experiential mix of modern lifeworlds is no doubt the most common way this desire is satisfied. But there is also a more radical form evident in some of the new cultural practices emerging with CMC: the desire to be lifted entirely out of the constraints of locality, routine, and even of embodiment and the fixed identity of the self – in fact, the desire to inhabit another person's lifeworld.

The 'Jennicam' website is one rather disconcerting instance of this. The website consists of images of the bedroom of a young woman posted by her every two minutes, twenty-four hours a day, for the last two years. The site attracts 6,000 regular subscribers each paying £10 a year, 'to see Jennifer Ringley sleeping, kissing her boyfriend, putting on make-up or playing with her kitten' (Smith 1998: 3). The popularity of this website is not easy to account for. If we accept that the motivation isn't primarily prurient interest or sexual voyeurism (the site is censored in this respect – 'no nudity or sexual material') then the question remains of why people desire to routinely 'inhabit' another's real, mundane, unretouched intimate space in 'real time'. For this sort of interest has to be distinguished from the more commonplace curiosity about the intimate spaces of celebrities catered for in the glossy, stylized photo-spreads of magazines like *Hello!*.

One way of understanding what is going on here is in terms of a dimly focused desire to escape the constraints of locale. To have routine access to another intimate personal space – to be invited into it – is to have a parallel life which is perhaps more satisfying as an escape from our own reality than those available in the narratives of television. To have access to the intimacy of the bedroom in its real-time ordinariness is in a sense to defeat the seclusion of our own intimate spaces. This could still, of course, be read as a form of prurience, or as the neurotic desire to penetrate or colonize the personal space of the other. It is at the very best a rather dismal sort of transcendence. But judged more charitably, this sort of practice could also be interpreted as a desire for escape from the imposed emotional privacy of modern life (often seen as exacerbated by the privatizing culture of domestic media use) into a fuller connectivity and, at least potentially, a more genuine communion with others.

It has to be admitted, however, that the link between these instances of public intimacy as escape routes from our embodied existential situation, and a more positive sense of cultural connectivity – as the extension of community, as cosmopolitan cultural encounter – is not strongly developed in modern cultures.[7] Indeed the realm of the intimate, even as it is redefined by mediated experience, does not generally open up on a world which challenges parochial cultural assumptions. Telephones, for example, do not (generally) deterritorialize in the sense of exposing us to information or narratives that disturb the cultural taken-for-grantedness of localities. Precisely because they are essentially one-to-one media, they connect us with others in contexts which are, in a certain sense, congruent with our local lifeworlds. It is not that we never meet 'strangers' on the telephone, but that we rarely encounter 'cultural strangeness'.

However other media technologies – television or web-browsers for instance – clearly do have the potential to deterritorialize in a more culturally challenging and morally significant sense. They can connect us with distant others in ways that open up cultural horizons to other practices, values and ways of life. They can reinforce the sense that our localities are connected (for good or ill) with distant parts of the world. They can furnish a sense of the world itself as a meaningful social/cultural/moral context. Of course an awful lot of popular televisual experience is not of this order; quite to the contrary, it is oriented towards providing the 'inward looking' existential comforts of routine, familiarity and cultural inclusion in the local 'television family' (Scannell 1996).

The *potential* for what we might call moral-cultural deterritorialization none the less exists in these forms of mediated experience. And it is interesting to notice how the theme of intimacy recurs in this context. Giddens's (1992) treatment of the transformation of intimacy in modern societies focuses on personal 'face-to face' sexual and love relations and has nothing to say about mediated experience. But he nevertheless suggests a connection between this level of intimacy as the ultra-local and of the sphere of global politics. His argument turns on the way in which the pursuit of autonomy in personal intimate relationships has implications for democratic politics: 'A symmetry exists between the democratizing of personal life and democratic possibilities in the global political order at the most extensive level' (1992: 195–6). Behind this claim lies the intuition that globalization always spans the 'out-thereness' of the world and the 'in-hereness' of our intimate phenomenal 'worlds' (chapter 1). And this connection can be pursued in relation to the mediation of experience. What is at stake here is the specific mode of moral/political engagement that may exist in media forms which are experienced

in the intimate contexts of our local spaces – most commonly, tele-
visions in our living rooms. This is the idea I want to explore in the
following section.

Mediated Proximity 2: Televisual Involvement and the Closing of Moral Distance

To begin with a paradox: as the technological capacity and sophistication of the global media expand, news coverage of foreign events
on television seems to be shrinking. This situation is perhaps most
dramatically illustrated in the case of the United States, the most
information-rich nation in the world, where network news coverage
of foreign affairs has fallen 'by two thirds in two decades' (Culf 1997:
13) and 'by 42 per cent between 1988 and 1996' (Wittstock 1998: 7).
Although the US case attracts the most frequent charges of parochialism and insularity (linked with accusations of trivialization and
'dumbing down' – 'a domestic agenda . . . dominated by the Pres-
ident's anatomy' (Wittstock 1998)), a similar trend is also evident
throughout the developed world. Documentary output on international topics across all British terrestrial TV channels fell by 40 per
cent between 1989 and 1994 (Cleasby 1995: 1). And speaking in 1997,
the chief executive of BBC News, Tony Hall, complained of a wider
international context of journalistic parochialism in which 'most news
organizations are spending less on foreign news, less on correspond-
ents, less on bureaux.' He went on to say that 'at a time when most of
our futures are decided globally, the audience of our broadcast
programmes appears to be less interested in the world. And journal-
ism, in response, seems less interested, more introspective too' (Culf
1997: 13).

The reasons for this trend are controversial, occupying that notoriously contested terrain between perceived audience demand and
editorial and scheduling provision (Morley 1992; Ang 1996). The
policy debate is thus often polarized between a position which holds
to the 'sovereignty of the consumer' in a market conception of the
audience (most robust in the American commercial model) and a
public service ethic which holds that television has an obligation to
provide information and understanding beyond mere entertainment
(Herman and McChesney 1997; Thompson 1997). But however culpable an increasingly commercially pressured media industry is in
the production of cultural parochialism, this alone cannot account
for the phenomenon. Cleasby, commenting on the British case,

attributes the problem partly to broadcasters 'chasing the audience', but he recognizes that the issue of relevance to the lives of viewers is a crucial one: 'The trend towards insularity is clear. It stems in part from a broad assumption that programmes on international affairs are inherently unpopular with the British audience. . . . Viewers want to see more programmes of relevance to their own lives and experiences and this is interpreted as meaning more programmes about Britain' (Cleasby 1995: iii–iv).

Cleasby suggests that broadcasters may be making too hasty and crude assumptions about the perceived lack of relevance of international stories to the domestic audience, and that these assumptions contribute to 'a vicious downward spiral of falling international output, falling audience interest and falling public awareness of global affairs' (ibid.). This may well be true. However there remains the suspicion – struggled against by progressive internationalist-minded intellectuals because of its pessimistic cultural implications – that most ordinary people are simply not interested in events beyond their own (national) localities.

It is notable that within this debate the nature of the *medium of television* itself is rarely considered. The focus on issues of audience ratings and programming tends to obscure the perhaps more fundamental questions of whether and how telemediated experience *itself* can make events which are only structurally (politically, economically) connected to us, relevant and meaningful at the level of experience. The question then becomes one of how telemediation can bring us phenomenologically closer, closing cultural and moral distance and providing a compelling sense of involvement with distant lives and events.

For clearly watching distant events on television is not the same experience as literally travelling to and being present at these events. No one (not even Baudrillard), for instance, would seriously claim that the way in which we are 'touched' by the violent events of a war zone as they are depicted on a screen in our living room equates with being under shellfire. As Roger Silverstone (1994: 30) says, 'it is the quality of the contact – the quality of the touch – that is surely the issue.' And yet some of the more gestural accounts of television's deterritorializing potential – for example, Hebdige's claims about 'mundane (televisual) cosmopolitanism' quoted in chapter 4 – fail to recognize these crucial phenomenological differences and so invite a certain degree of scepticism.

The long shadow of McLuhan's work is often recognized (Ferguson 1991; Silverstone 1994; Stevenson 1995) in the more extravagant claims about television's cultural potential. An early critic of McLuhan, Jonathan Miller (1971), for example, is deeply sceptical of his claims about a televisually constituted 'global village', arguing, amongst other things, that the distant experiences brought to us via television, 'are essentially vicarious and have little or nothing in common with the experiences that define the characteristic collectivism of village life' (Miller 1971: 124). This critique is directed largely at the shortfall of a McLuhanite distanciated/mediated community from the ideal of a local face-to-face community, and it invokes all the familiar notions of the morally and emotionally binding qualities of the latter in contrast with the former. But his scepticism about the power of television to 'involve' us morally and emotionally with the condition of distant others extends to what he calls the 'sensory features of the medium':

Contrary to what McLuhan asserts, TV is strikingly visual and the images which it presents are curiously dissociated from all the other senses. The viewer sits watching them all in the drab comfort of his own home, cut off from the pain, heat and smell of what is actually going on. . . . All these effects serve to distance the viewer from the scenes which he is watching, and eventually he falls into the unconscious belief that the events which happen on TV are going on in some unbelievably remote theatre of human activity. The alienating effect is magnified by the fact that the TV screen reduces all images to the same visual quality. Atrocity and entertainment alternate with one another on the same rectangle of bulging glass. (1971: 126)[8]

This is not just to point to the peculiar characteristics of the medium, but to suggest that these actually *inhibit* the experience of the closing of distance. The intervention of the medium is 'distancing' or even 'alienating': far from connecting us, it 'cuts us off' from distant events. Televisual experience of other places, Miller seems to suggest, only takes place in some essentially mediated phenomenological realm which is 'remote' both from our local space and from the places it depicts. On this account the medium acts as a sort of cordon sanitaire protecting our local spaces from the 'reality' of troubling distant events and alien practices. In a much more recent account, Zygmunt Bauman takes up this theme of 'insulation' from the dangers of cultural encounter in a similarly sceptical comment on the potential of television to produce a real hermeneutic engagement with spatially and culturally distant others:

Contrary to widespread opinion, the advent of television, this huge and easily accessible peephole through which . . . unfamiliar ways may

> be routinely glimpsed, has neither eliminated the institutional separation nor diminished its effectivity. McLuhan's 'global village' has failed to materialize. The frame of a ... TV screen staves off the danger of spillage more effectively than tourist hotels and fenced off camping sites; the one-sidedness of communication further entrenches the unfamiliars on the screen as essentially incommunicado. (1990: 148)

And in a later work still, Bauman extends this idea of the containment of engagement with 'telemediated' strangers in the cultural/phenomenological space of 'telecity'. In 'the telecity' (the ambiguity between an experiential mode and a sort of location is deliberate) strangers are 'gazed at without fear – much as lions in a zoo'. They are 'infinitely close as objects but doomed to remain, happily, infinitely remote as subjects of action – sanitized and safe, like sex with condoms' (Bauman 1993: 178). Televisual experience, for Bauman, is thus not only ersatz experience, it is positively antithetical to genuine cultural/emotional/moral encounters. 'Telecity' is the negative other of the real 'city' in which real people can be encountered in all their fullness as embodied moral agents. In the telecity, we encounter people reduced to an existential mode of 'pure surface', who can be 'zapped out of the screen – and so out of the world – when they cease to amuse' (ibid.).

It is easy to see the drift of this critique towards a sort of manichaeism. The experiential limitations of mass-mediated experience quickly become associated with other ideas of existential and moral poverty, contrasted with the idealized sphere of face-to-face experience and interaction. A similar drift can be seen in some of the critical literature now emerging on computer-mediated communications and 'virtual reality'. For example Brook and Boal, in their preface to a collection they call *Resisting the Virtual Life*, begin by disavowing a bias towards the face-to-face and, 'recogniz(ing) the merits of relationships at a remove' produced by various media technologies. But in the next sentence they claim that: 'face-to-face interactions ... are inherently richer than mediated interactions. Nowadays, the monosyllabic couch potato is joined by the information junkie in passive admiration of the little screen' (Brook and Boal 1995: vii).

One of the problems, it seems to me, with all these criticisms is the precipitate move from phenomenology to moral-existential judgement. It is not that the issues these critics raise are unimportant or misconceived. We can readily agree, for example, that an unrelieved and exclusive diet of screened experience is probably bad for people in all sorts of ways, even including the potential erosion of moral sensibilities. And it may also be true that some developments in the 'customizing' of media technology to suit individual lifestyles[9] might appeal to or encourage an insular, self-centred cultural outlook. There are, then, many genuine anxieties surrounding the way in which mediated experience becomes increasingly integrated with direct experience. But it is also easy to see how these anxieties could become exaggerated in a crude general polarization between 'good' direct experience and 'bad' mass-mediated experience.

To avoid this it will be useful to explore the phenomenology of John Thompson's category of 'mediated quasi-interaction' in a little more detail. In particular I want to draw out two crucial phenomenological distinctions in his account.

The first of these concerns the experiential 'distance' that is maintained between the viewer and the events seen on television. These events are brought, at the touch of a switch, right into our most intimate material spaces and in this sense are close to us. But, none the less, they remain, 'for the most part . . . distant from the practical contexts of daily life' (Thompson 1995: 228). This phenomenological distance derives partly from the fact that the events we see on television – for example distant wars – for the most part do not impinge directly on our own lives. But it is also due, importantly, to our inability to *intervene* in the events we see. As Thompson puts it, these events have a 'refractory' (resistant, hard to influence) character, '. . . that is, they are events which are unlikely to be affected by [our] actions. They are not "at hand" or "within reach", and are therefore not readily amenable to the actions of recipients'(ibid.). This is something which has been noted before in a more political context (Groombridge 1972; Morley 1992) – that is, as an argument about the relative powerlessness of ordinary people in relation to the political events they see depicted on television and their consequent perception of such events as 'remote' from their lives. But here Thompson makes a more general point about the nature of the medium itself.

This difficulty of fully *engaging* with mass-mediated events – which is of course partly a consequence of the monological nature of mediated quasi-interaction (Poster 1990; Tomlinson 1994) – is I think a key issue in understanding the peculiar nature of the televisual experience. It is important to note that this is not a matter of the television audience being 'passive' in the construction of meaning: it is rather that our 'activity' is circumscribed by the intrinsic nature of this deterritorializing technology. Being routinely presented with images and information about events which are remote from our local lifeworld, and over which we have no control or possibility of intervention, means that we *inevitably* experience ourselves as, in a certain sense, outside them. For, in the first place, how could we practically be involved in all the vast number of events that are available to us via television? And, second, these events obviously come to us in the highly mediated and physically 'contained' form of miniaturized pictures on a screen.

Now it is easy to see how recognition of this inevitable phenomenological distance could take on the sort of moral inflection that we saw in Miller's and Bauman's critiques. Thompson's identification of distance can become translated into the idea of moral *detachment*. Kevin Robins's treatment of the issue is a case in point. Robins is interested in the puzzling question of how television audiences respond to the presentation of images of extreme violence and death as they were presented, for example, in coverage of the war in Bosnia. How is it, he asks, that audiences 'appear to be relatively unscathed by their encounters with the violence of war? How is it that . . . such realities can be diffused?' (Robins 1994: 458). As he recognizes, the answers to this puzzle are part of a larger agenda – of 'how our relation to the world is transformed through technological mediation'. Robins offers some subtle and insightful analysis, but he overstates the way in which television may be morally disabling. For instance, he makes part of his case by quoting C. Gallaz on the 'schizophrenic' nature of television viewing, 'allowing us, on the one hand to magically control our position *vis-à-vis* the world and its spectacles, and, on the other, to maintain a distance, never becoming actors in it and never having to assume responsibilities' (Gallaz, quoted in Robins 1994: 461). Posing the matter in this way, as a question of retreat from moral engagement, leads him to a rather bleak encapsulation of televisual experience: 'Dispassionate proximity, intimate detachment' (1994: 461).

But I don't think we are compelled by the phenomenological distance argument towards this sort of moral pessimism. In the first place it seems to me that people do in certain circumstances achieve various levels of moral involvement with issues that are brought to them via the television. Some people are more shocked, more emotionally touched, more moved to compassion and even to action, by the televisual depiction of distant human suffering than Robins allows. There exist, as Thompson argues, a wide variety of responses: 'Some individuals turn away . . . and seek to maintain their distance from events which are, in any case, distant from the pressing demands of their day-to-day lives. Others, stirred by media images and reports, throw themselves into campaigns on behalf of distant groups and causes' (Thompson 1995: 234). Thompson goes on to cite the – admittedly extreme – example of Graham Bamford, a lorry driver from Macclesfield who, in 1993 after watching television coverage of the massacre in Vitez, 'doused himself in petrol and set himself alight in Parliament Square to protest against the British government's failure to intervene in the Bosnian tragedy'. Such incidents are obviously rare and psychologically complex. But put together with many more common cases of people inspired by television coverage to involve themselves in humanitarian efforts – for instance those people who volunteered to load and drive trucks carrying emergency supplies to Sarajevo – they to some extent undermine Robins's thesis of the emotionally and morally anaesthetizing nature of television.

The way to avoid undue moral pessimism is, I think, to recognize how telemediated experience is situated in the human lifeworld. The inevitably 'contained' nature of the televisual experience as it is presented to us in the total flow of everyday lived experience (with its often more 'immediate' moral and emotional demands) means that more moral and emotional *effort* is going to be required to engage with the situations of distant others. This is not technologically induced schizophrenia, but simply part of the peculiar existential condition of global modernity – in which vastly more moral/cultural demands are implicitly made on ordinary people than ever before in history. This implicit 'moral burden' is one of the less obvious aspects of deterritorialization. To explore the way it might generally be managed, we can turn to the other aspect of Thompson's account that I want to consider.

This is the idea of a 'relevance structure' of experience, which Thompson retrieves from phenomenologists such as Husserl and Schutz. The idea is essentially that people do not relate to all the vast number of experiences that are available to them equally, but *selectively* in terms of the perceived relevance of experience to the ongoing constitution of the self. The self is conceived here not as an entity that simply attaches, automatically and unchangeably, to the individual, but as 'a symbolic project which the individual shapes and reshapes in the course of his or her life' (Thompson 1995: 229). We continuously construct and reconstruct our 'selves' across the life-course and, as Giddens puts it, our self-identity is thus a 'reflexive achievement', a 'narrative' which is 'reflexively sustained in relation to rapidly changing circumstances of social life, on a local and global scale' (Giddens 1991: 215).

Thompson's point is that in the conditions of global modernity the project of the self draws selectively on both direct and mediated experience, but the relevance structure is rather different in each case. The relevance of direct experience to the self is, he argues, 'largely unquestioned, for it is primarily through this experience that the project of the self is formed and reformed over time' (Thompson 1995: 229). Thus local direct experience – as the 'immediate environment' within which the self develops – can be argued to have a certain existential priority in people's lives. Mediated experience by contrast, because of its distanciated and 'refractory' nature, 'is likely to bear a rather tenuous, intermittent and selective relation to the self':

> For many individuals whose life projects are rooted in the practical contexts of their day-to-day lives, many forms of mediated experience may bear a tenuous connection to their lives: they may be intermittently interesting, occasionally entertaining, but they are not the issues that concern them most. But individuals also draw selectively on mediated experience, interlacing it with the lived [direct] experience that forms the connective tissue of their daily lives. (Thompson 1995: 230)

Thus, though people do incorporate televisual experience into their routine daily local 'experience mix' – for instance building the evening news bulletin into the structure of the day – it remains, for the majority, stubbornly separate from the experiences that come from 'closer to home'. There are some obvious practical reasons for this. The inescapable material demands of the local world – daily travel, local routine interactions, working, shopping, cooking, caring for a family – obviously impose their own priority not only on our actions but on the constitution of our 'selves'. Thus for the vast majority of people, what we can call, adapting a phrase from Marx, 'the dull compulsion of the quotidian' will usually set the agenda of relevance. To illustrate this we can consider the response of a woman interviewed by David Morley in his study of family viewing practices:

> Sometimes I like to watch the news, if its something that's gone on – like where that little boy's gone and what's happened to him. Otherwise I don't, not unless its local, only when there's something that's happened local . . . national news gets on my nerves . . . I can't stand *World in Action* and *Panorama* and all that. It's wars all the time. You know, it gets on your nerves . . . I don't want to know about the Chancellor Somebody in Germany and all that. What's going on in the world? I don't understand it, and so I don't listen to that. I watch – like those little kids [an abduction] – that gets to me, I want to know about

it. Or if there's actually some crime in [her local area], like rapes and the rest of it. I want to . . . see if they've been caught and locked away. (Morley 1986, quoted in Morley 1992: 251)

This is, as Morley observes, a very cogent justification for a bias of interest towards the local. And I think it illustrates well the active nature of the discriminations that are being made in the appropriation of mediated experience and their relevance to the project of the self. We clearly cannot assimilate this response to the thesis of the anaesthetizing or alienating effects of the medium. Though it is pretty much at the opposite end of the spectrum from the case of Graham Bamford, it is no less a response to televisual experience tied closely – and self-consciously – into the constitution of the self. Although she goes on to dismiss her response as 'complete ignorance really', this woman's use of mediated quasi-experience is a deliberate and *knowledgeable* incorporation of the things that are relevant within the horizon of her lifeworld.

The moral issue here is not therefore one of (media-induced) indifference or detachment, but of the appropriateness of a different moral horizon. It may be tempting to see this woman's response as a form of moral-existential 'nimbyism' – a refusal to let the threatening world 'out there' penetrate the immediate environment of the self. But it is hard to sustain such a moral judgement: for on what criteria *could* we judge how people are to order their sense of existential relevance? A better response may be to see the relevance-structure argument as, curiously, throwing the moral responsibility back upon the media. This is to say that, rather than expecting people to 'rise to the challenge' of moral distance, the 'stories' that frame issues of distant moral concern need to be told in ways which render them congruent with local moral horizons – indeed which translate these concerns into the realm of the personal and the intimate.

As can be seen in examples like the reporting of the death and funeral of Diana, television is actually rather good at framing certain events so as to make them engaging at a personal level. But often television coverage is criticized for making issues *too* personalized – for trivializing them, for obscuring their more challenging aspects in a blur of sentimentality, or for framing them in terms of rather crude and ideological moral stereotypes. Very often this criticism is justified. However, it seems to me that the answer is not to insist that 'serious' issues should be entirely 'depersonalized'.[10] Of course many of the problems that confront us in a globalized world are large, complex and abstract. But if people are to engage with these issues at all – to exercise any degree of moral agency – then ways need to be found to narrate them so that they become congruent with individual, locally situated lifeworlds. A certain degree of 'personalization' may thus be considered essential for a discourse in which the more difficult and 'remote' problems of our time can be 'brought home to us' as moral concerns.

The central question this chapter has posed is that of how the use of media and communications technologies deterritorialize: how they lift us out of our cultural and indeed existential connection with our discrete localities and, in various senses, open up our lifeworlds to a larger world. In the concluding chapter I will try to pursue some of these questions of engagement with the world from their pheno-menological context towards the cultural politics that is implied in the idea of cosmopolitanism.

6

The Possibility of Cosmopolitanism

To coincide with the Fiftieth General Assembly of the United Nations in 1995 a report was published by a body called the Commission on Global Governance. This commission, sponsored by various national governments and national and international foundations, was in effect reporting on how the world has changed in the fifty years since the United Nations was established in 1945, and attempting to sketch out the sort of concerted international political response that these changes demand. The report, which places the globalization process at the core of its analysis of change, took as its title and guiding metaphor the idea of the world as *Our Global Neighbourhood*.

At first glance this title suggests a slightly pious, slightly cosy, *gemeinschaftlich* way of looking at the world, with echoes of McLuhan – or even of Australian soap opera. But in fact it turns out to be rather a clever and appropriate title. For the idea of the 'neighbourhood' grasps something fundamental about the process of globalization: the dialectical relationship between our local lives and cultural experience and the globalizing structures and forces that are rapidly transforming them. What is more, the neighbourhood addressed in the report is not at all a cosy one.

As the report says, neighbourhoods are defined, essentially, by proximity not by communal ties or shared values. So what makes a globalized world a 'neighbourhood' is not the emergence of any of the elusive unities of global modernity: a world community, a global culture, value universalism. Rather, it is the fact that the shrinking of distance and complex interdependence of the globalization process produces what we might call 'enforced proximity'. This has mixed implications. On the one hand, there is the promise of a world of

expanded horizons, of the possibility of increasing political understanding and co-operation and of enriched and diversified cosmopolitan cultural experience. Proximity might mean that global
inequalities are rendered more visible, that common global risks and
threats – most obviously threats to our shared environment – become more focused, and that an agenda of global responsibility
and common interests is established. But on the other hand it is a
characteristic of neighbours that we don't choose them, but have to
live alongside them. And, to quote the report, 'When the neighbourhood is the planet, moving to get away from bad neighbours is not
an option' (Commission on Global Governance 1995: 44). So the all-
too-obvious potential dangers of a global neighbourhood are those
of an increasingly 'crowded' social and cultural space: of the violent
clash of cultures and ideologies and the building of high fences – the
retreat into various entrenched nationalist, ethnic, religious, gender,
sexual or even environmental 'localist' fundamentalisms.

Despite these dangers and uncertainties, the tone of the commission's report is more or less optimistic: what is proposed is not a
framework for world *government*, but a more modest and generally
pragmatic set of proposals for 'governance' seen as 'reforms in the
modes of international cooperation . . . the management of global
affairs . . . responsive to the interests of all people in a sustainable
future . . . that makes global organization conform to the reality of
global diversity' (1995: xvii). So the report proposes certain institutional reforms: in international security policy, in the way the
global economy is regulated, in the framework of international law
and in the organization of the United Nations itself. But what is interesting for us is that these proposals are all subordinate to – in a
sense premised upon – the idea that global governance is not just the
business of nation-states – indeed cannot be left to them – but must
involve the actions of much smaller groupings, even down to the
level of individual people. This is stressed throughout the report and
is indeed central to the metaphor of the global neighbourhood (a
locale defined in the first place as the setting for the interaction of
individuals). Thus the idea of the global neighbourhood is often
used synonymously with the idea of 'the emergence of a global civil
society [which] reflects a large increase in the capacity and will of
people to take control of their own lives' (1995: 335).

Taking this proposition seriously, we can recognize in the commission's analysis a sensitivity to the growth of social reflexivity in
global modernity: that is of a world in which institutions are increasingly attuned to the multiple individual actions and demands of

constituencies of autonomous agents. It probably does not need pointing out that this reflexivity is complex and highly mediated. Although it does represent a potential increase in human autonomy and emancipation, it does not necessarily work itself out in the short term as either a direct simple devolution of power to the people, or even as the obvious 'humanizing' of the institutions that we live within. But what it does grasp is the way in which the complex interconnections of global modernity accentuate the link between individual lifestyles and global consequences (chapter 1). In this sense, what ordinary people think, believe and do in their local situations counts in the sphere of global governance. This is the insight into social transformation that is encapsulated in the famous maxim of the environmental movement: 'Think globally, act locally.' So the repeated call by the commission for a new 'global civic ethic' ought not to be regarded as a piety, but as a plausible political strategy – the grounding of governance in the 'participation' of reflexively consequential agents.

All this is by way of introducing the focus of this final chapter – on the broader 'political' implications of cultural globalization. In chapter 1 I argued that culture matters for globalization in the broad sense that local individual actions undertaken within a culturally ordered 'lifestyle' are frequently globally consequential. This implies a link between the cultural experience of deterritorialization and the political agenda of globalization, the problem of governance of the global neighbourhood.

The way that I propose to think about this – no doubt complex – connection here is via a somewhat simplified formulation of the problem. I want to explore the idea that the globally transformative action of individuals within their situated localities is dependent on the cultivation of a specific cultural disposition – a 'set towards the world'. This, again, is a position that is proposed by the authors of *Our Global Neighbourhood* in their stress on the development of a 'global ethics': 'The most important change that people can make is to change their way of looking at the world' (1995: 47). I think this is broadly correct, though it involves more problems than the commission's authors recognize. Their approach is to move swiftly from the idea of cultural perception and imagination to the recommendation of a core set of universal values (deriving from the norm of reciprocity) to which all human beings could assent, and from this to the stipulation of a set of institutionalizable global rights and responsibilities. This is, of course, a response typical of the discourse of international commissions which are, of their nature, oriented towards concrete policy proposals. But the fairly obvious problem with this is that the 'neighbourhood values' they propose as universal and foundational: 'respect for life, liberty, justice and equality, mutual respect, caring and integrity', appear bland and unexceptionable until forced towards an interpretation within a specific, concrete situation – at which point they often tend to fragment, to take on the moral complexity of the particular context of action and therefore to lose their universally binding qualities.

The complex issue of universalism – as we saw in chapter 2 – is never far from the agenda of global modernity, and we will return to it again later in this chapter. But my point is that the shift in the report to this sort of ethical discourse is, anyway, precipitate. What we could better focus on is the antecedent questions of cultural perception, imagination and disposition. How are people even to *think* of themselves as belonging to a global neighbourhood? This is the problem I want to explore: what does it mean to have a global identity, to think and act as a 'citizen of the world' – literally as a 'cosmopolitan'?

First I shall ask what a cosmopolitan is and whether this is in fact the best way of thinking about global belonging, weighing particularly the ideological connotations the term has attracted. And, second, looking at some arguments that might connect deterritorialization with the cultivation of a cosmopolitan disposition, I shall suggest that we have to think of cosmopolitanism as a cultural resource that needs to operate in a peculiarly unconvivial institutional context. If a cosmopolitan disposition is to have any utility in addressing issues of global concern, it has to be sustainable in a world that lacks, and looks set to lack, any strong formal, centralized global political institutions that might be expected to nourish it.

Cosmopolitanism: Idea, Ideology, Ideal

Idea: Cosmopolitanism as a Cultural Disposition

The etymology of the term 'cosmopolitan' is clear enough: from the Greek *kosmos*, 'world', and *polis*, 'city'. Hence a cosmopolitan is a citizen of the world. Now this idea of citizenship clearly has specific implications in the sphere of politics in the context of globalization. One significant emphasis here – in a discourse that reaches back as far as Kant's international political thought – has been on thinking through the possibility of democratic forms and political institutions that transcend the polity of the nation-state (Held 1992, 1995). The approach I want to take to the idea of the cosmopolitan however is, obviously, as a cultural figure: the *Oxford Encyclopedic English Dictionary* adds to its definition the sense of being 'free from national limitations and prejudices', and this gets nearer to the sense I am after. Being a 'citizen of the world' for our purposes means having a cultural disposition which is not limited to the concerns of the immediate locality, but which recognizes global belonging, involvement and responsibility and can integrate these broader concerns into everyday life practices. It is this sort of disposition that is a precondition for competent 'lifestyle participation' in global governance. Ulf Hannerz puts this well in describing cosmopolitanism as, 'a perspective, a state of mind, or . . . a mode of managing meaning' (Hannerz 1990: 238).

Hannerz's discussion is of particular interest in that it offers some penetrating and subtle insights into the figure of the cosmopolitan as a sort of 'ideal type', whilst at the same time implicitly introducing some of the ideological problems with the idea. He argues that people can relate to the globalization process in broadly two ways: 'there are cosmopolitans and there are locals' (1990: 237). For him, while 'locals' are people whose cultural perspective always remains below the horizon of their particular locality, cosmopolitans are 'footloose' people, 'on the move in the world', who 'tend to want to immerse themselves in other cultures' (1990: 240–1). Thus cosmopolitanism as a cultural perspective is, for Hannerz, 'first of all . . . a willingness to engage with the Other. It is an intellectual and aesthetic stance of openness toward divergent cultural experiences, a search for contrasts rather than uniformity' (p. 239).

Hannerz proceeds to distinguish true cosmopolitans from other groups of globally mobile people – tourists, exiles, expatriates, transnational employees, labour migrants – on the basis of whether or not they have this central cultural disposition. Most he finds do not. Tourists are not interested in engaging deeply with the cultural Other, they simply want 'home plus': 'Spain is home plus sunshine, India is home plus servants, Africa is home plus elephants and tigers' (p. 241).[1] Likewise most labour migrants do not become cosmopolitans: 'for them going away may be, ideally, home plus higher income; often the involvement with another culture is not a fringe benefit but a necessary cost to be kept as low as possible' (p. 243). The other groups he surveys fare little better in his judgement: exiles generally want 'home plus safety', globally mobile employees of transnational companies often encapsulate themselves in their (generally western European and North American) home culture as they travel and thus 'basically remain metropolitan locals instead of becoming cosmopolitans' (p. 245).

Cosmopolitans thus turn out to be quite rare birds of passage for Hannerz. He certainly writes as though they are a significant group of people, with a special cultural role in the globalization process. Yet he seems to suggest that, though some rather special individuals within the groups he surveys may have this disposition, most of us probably do not.[2] Where it comes to actually existing cases of this specific cultural orientation, this may well be true. Hannerz's anthropological eye is useful in reminding us that the sheer increase in mobility that the globalization process produces is not in itself sufficient to engender a cosmopolitan disposition. This is a problem we will return to later.

However, for the present we are more concerned with working towards a stipulation of the cosmopolitan disposition as an *ideal* – as the cultural outlook appropriate to the competent moral agent in the 'global neighbourhood'. Does Hannerz's cosmopolitan fit this bill? Alas, no. For two reasons.

First, because the perspective he is describing is only *part* of the necessary specification. Cosmopolitans certainly need to be freed from the narrow constraints and prejudices of their home culture, to be open to the diversity of global cultures and to be disposed to understand the cultural perspective of the other. But they also – perhaps more importantly – need to have a sense of wider cultural *commitment* – of belonging to the world as a whole: that is, in the sense proposed by both Anthony Giddens (1991) and Ulrich Beck (1992, 1996), of a world in which, particularly in terms of common environmental threats requiring lifestyle adaptation, there are *no others*. Being culturally footloose is not necessarily an advantage here. The sort of delight in cultural difference that Hannerz describes *may* link to an ethical disposition towards global responsibility or it may not. It is possible that the 'wider picture' that his cosmopolitans cultivate might lead them to be more responsible global citizens, having a feeling of being, as Sartre once put it *'embarqué'* – all in the same boat. But equally, they may simply choose to keep on the move, indulging their taste for new cultural experiences whilst remaining, as Hannerz himself suggests, generally uncommitted, 'All the time [knowing] where the exit is' (Hannerz 1990: 240).

The second reason why Hannerz's cosmopolitan ideal type falls short of a moral-cultural ideal is on account of the quantity of ideological baggage he (and Hannerz explicitly writes of a 'he') carries.

Foremost amongst this, as we shall see, is the tendency to denigrate the experience of the local that is implicit in the structure of the dualism Hannerz establishes. So let us now look at some of the unfortunate ideological connotations that have accrued to the concept of the cosmopolitan.

Ideology: Cosmopolitans Privileged over Locals

To avoid misunderstanding, I should say at the outset that these ideological problems are not ones attaching specifically to Hannerz's account, but rather general shades of meaning that the idea of the cosmopolitan has acquired. I shall begin by simply mentioning two of these and spend a little more time on a third one – the idea of the privileging of 'global' over 'local' experience.

A first unfortunate connotation of the term is that of the cosmopolitan as the *homme du monde* – the 'man of the world'. The implicit gender bias is clear: men – as opposed to women – are 'of the world'. There is a Spanish popular saying that illustrates this sentiment nicely: *Hombre en la calle, mujer en la casa* ('Man in the street' – the wider world; 'woman in the house' – the domestic sphere). And just to make quite sure of the requisite immobility of women, the saying continues *con la pata quebrada!* ('with a broken leg!'). As Janet Wolff has argued, not only has travel historically been structured by patriarchy, but both the literature of travel and the metaphors of travel that have been employed in broader cultural theory are intrinsically gendered (Wolff 1993). The idea of the cosmopolitan, then, might have to be 'reappropriated', as Wolff argues for the case of travel metaphors in cultural theory (the 'nomad', 'mapping'), from this implicitly patriarchal discursive context. And indeed, this problem also raises the wider and deeper problem of the 'sequestering' of women in the western conceptualization of citizenship from the Greek city-states down to Habermas's public sphere (Benhabib 1992; Fraser 1987).

Secondly, there is the suspicion that the figure of the cosmopolitan is a (literal and symbolic) figure of the West. There are two levels on which this charge can be brought. Most obviously there is the suspicion of an immediate ethnocentrism: that, in Doreen Massey's words, the idea of cosmopolitanism, along with that of globalization, is 'a predominantly white/First World take on things' (Massey 1994: 165). It is primarily westerners who get to be the globetrotters – by choice, that is, not as refugees; it is the people of the First

World who are the fax senders, and the internet users. We raised this general issue in chapter 4 in relation to the global generalizability of the idea of deterritorialization. But we can add here that there are ways of stipulating the cosmopolitan disposition so as to avoid its appearing merely as the cultural property of the West. Although Hannerz does tend to cast Third World cultures as generally belonging to the localist pole of his dualism, he also makes the important point that most of the 'transnational' cultures of the West cannot be considered properly cosmopolitan *either*, insofar as they generally manifest themselves, globally, as 'occidental cultural enclaves' (Hannerz 1990: 245). Openness to the world in this sense is therefore specifically incompatible with a complacent western global hegemony. Nor is the cosmopolitan disposition, properly understood, something that arrives, culturally, as a bolt-on accessory to western 'technological globalization'. So at this level, it would seem that the ideological thread connecting cosmopolitanism with the West can be relatively easily broken.

However at a different level the issue might become more complex. For there is also what we might call the 'post-colonial suspicion' of the idea: the suspicion that western cosmopolitanism is tied deeply into western 'cosmology'. This is the sense that the very idea of being a citizen of the world inevitably reproduces the deeply rooted intellectual and ethical 'world-view' of the West: its epistemological, ontological and normative assumptions – in Cornelius Castoriadis's terms, its fundamental 'social imaginary significations' (Castoriadis 1987). If this line of critique is pursued, we may be led to be sceptical about the fundamental premises of the cosmopolitan disposition – in both its 'universalizing'and its 'pluralizing' moments – as somehow the dubious legacy of the European Enlightenment that John Gray criticizes (chapter 2). And this of course reopens, if at a different level, the whole issue of the relationship of modernity to the West that we discussed in chapter 3 in relation to Serge Latouche's critique. But this is not a line of criticism I intend to pursue, since I do not believe that the sort of practical cultural-ethical disposition that we are concerned with here needs to be fundamentally compromised simply by its provenance in western thought. To the same degree that the condition of modernity has a general global applicability (chapter 2), even though experienced in different historical contexts of 'entry' ('global modernities'), cosmopolitanism can, I think, be retrieved as a generalizable cultural stance.

My third ideological suspicion of the notion of the cosmopolitan, however, demands rather more attention because it presses to the core of the idea. This is the issue of the denigration, or at least the subordination, of locally situated cultural experience and practice. At the most superficial level this is evident in the common connotation of the 'cosmopolitan' with a degree of social privilege – the sense of a cultural elite with the means to rise above the petty concerns of the everyday. Thus, for example, the familiar contrast between the cosmopolitan (as an amplified form of the 'metropolitan') and the 'provincial'. Really this is a prime example of the ideological force of the binary opposition. So it is not surprising that, where the cosmopolitan is formally opposed as an ideal type to the 'local' – as in Hannerz's approach or in the classic study of small-town America by Robert Merton (Merton 1968) which in some respects he follows – the local comes off badly. The problem with this sort of dualism is that it almost inevitably denigrates local lived experience and practice *by implication* as somehow narrow, benighted, parochial, conservative, incestuous, ill informed, lacking the broader picture and so forth. We can recall here, from chapter 3, Marx's cosmopolitan/modern/urban bias and his famous description in the *Communist Manifesto* of the 'idiocy of rural life' (Marx and Engels 1969: 53). What is even more problematic is the way this cultural distinction can slip towards an *ethical* distinction in which the cosmopolitan might be seen as having a sort of moral advantage over the local, simply by reason of better mobility, increased access to the means of communication and so forth. We might then be led towards the dubious conclusion that socio-economic advantage creates superior moral agents.

If the problem were simply one of connotation or of the logic of binary opposition it could be overcome, and the category of the cosmopolitan could, again, be rescued. For one thing, we could pretty easily distance the required sense of cultural openness from connotations of cultural elitism and construct a more 'democratic' sense based, for example, in the wide access to a globalizing media experience that we discussed in chapter 5. For another, we could cease thinking in terms of antagonistic binary oppositions and try to think about the cosmopolitan disposition as something that does not have to exclude the perspective of the local. This is the course that I shall presently advocate. However, before we can come to this we need to probe the issue a little deeper. For it may be that there is more at stake here than simply the effects of binarism. There may be a genuine cultural–political tension between the perspectives and the *interests* of localism and cosmopolitanism.

This is a possibility that has been raised in an interesting essay on environmental politics by John Vidal. Vidal argues that the politics of the environmental movement are ambiguously distributed across the 'two axial principles of our age': 'localism' and 'globalism'. Localism is expressed, for him, in the increasing number of grassroots political movements in the 1990s protesting against what he calls 'remotism': the imposition of projects or policies which affect a locality, by forces – be they the state, transnational companies or global institutions like the GATT, the WTO or the IMF – that are perceived as remote from and unresponsive to the desires and interests of local populations. Vidal thus gathers into the perspective of localism, Third World struggles like those of the Ogoni people of Nigeria against Shell's pollution of their lands, together with local protests against centralized planning decisions – on road construction, opencast mining, the siting of new supermarkets and shopping malls and so forth – in the developed world. This perspective is for him, indeed, remarkable in that it cuts across the First World/Third World axis: 'When a Hopi Indian from Arizona can visit South Wales miners and be applauded for calling them "indigenous peoples" who should "rise up and take back their raped lands", and when "tribes" of homeless, jobless motorway protesters widely identify with the Zapatistas in Mexico or marginalised Amerindians in Brazil, then something is happening' (Vidal 1995: 57). The guiding principle of localism as a globally distributed cultural-political perspective is thus the maximization of local autonomy and control over the local environment together with the conservation of particular 'ways of life'.

Globalism, by contrast, is 'the mesmeric and deeply seductive' axial that 'offers all Mammon's plums': 'So in the safe hands of transnational corporations and political and economic elites, globalism proffers the best of science, the latest in genetics and computers, glitzy cure-alls for society's new shibboleths ... and messages in global languages about interdependence, interactivity, unlimited communication and universal solutions' (p. 58). Now the interesting point is that 'globalism' is not seen here as simply the ideology of the usual suspects – rapacious transnational corporations or nation-states given to grandiose centralized planning. It is a perspective that has, Vidal argues, equally seduced the environmental movement.[3] For him the maxim 'Think globally, act locally' is not a dialectical strategy so much as a 'paradoxical mantra'. Environmentalists have tried to embrace the localist perspective, in their stress on community action and so forth but, despite this, the environmental movement as a whole has tended to reinforce the globalist perspective. The interests of an increasingly powerful ecological globalism – concern for the 'whole earth' but with its roots in the lifestyle concerns of the affluent First World – have frequently come to dominate over local interests and practices – forbidding Inuit communities from whaling or seeking to deny Chinese people their CFC-emitting refrigerators. Thus, 'the San people can be excluded from the Kalahari, where they have lived for thousands of years, because they are considered by the Botswana government too dangerous for the fragile ecology' (Vidal 1995: 60).

Vidal goes so far as to describe Greenpeace, probably the most successful international environmental group, as 'a transnational corporation by any other name'. What he means by this rather provocative statement is that, despite its (almost defining) goal of waging a publicity war on the polluting practices of transnational industry, Greenpeace's environmentalism shares some of the globalist assumptions and practices of its enemies. It uses 'big science' to define environmental issues in global terms rather than in local, culturally sensitive contexts, it 'depends totally on globalism for communicating its message', and it maintains a freewheeling distanciated relationship from particular localities, 'as it swings into developing countries ... having no mandate to stay and help locals right the consequences of its actions' (1995: 61).

No doubt Vidal rather exaggerates for polemical effect, but he does pose a significant potential divergence of interest here. If the cosmopolitan disposition in the environmental field is to be simply a form of 'globalism' – drawing on what Marjorie Ferguson (1992: 82) calls the 'globalization myth' of 'saving planet earth' – then it is plain to see how it could be in conflict with the interests of localism. For, as Lash and Urry (1994: 305) have it, for most people 'the environment is their locality' and they may not be persuaded that wider (that is more experientially 'distant') concerns should take priority. And this is not merely so in the most obvious cases where there is direct conflict of interest between local practices (perhaps produced by unquestioned traditions or by direct economic material necessity) and a negative global consequence: coal burning and acid rain or global warming; the fishing out of endangered species like that occurring around the Galapagos islands. But it is equally true in the more difficult cultural-political cases where there are different *types* of environmental concern at the local and at the global level: the so-called 'brown agenda' of the polluted and overcrowded environments of Third World *favelas* as opposed to the typical 'green' concern with the 'global commons' such as the Amazon rainforests. And, since the causality of environmental problems is so complex and open to dispute (Goldblatt 1996; Yearley 1996), it is not at all clear that the interventions that may be called for at a global level to address environmental problems can be privileged over the local practices and knowledge bases of environmental sustainability that traditional 'ecocultures' (Dyer 1993) have developed over hundreds of years.

What these considerations bring us back to is the problems involved in aligning the cosmopolitan disposition with political and moral *universalism*. Approaching this issue in a more general way, we can consider, briefly, the position advanced by Nicholas Garnham in relation to the ideas of political citizenship and the public sphere in their global context. Garnham poses these questions explicitly in terms of the need for universal political solutions, asking, 'Are we to conceive of ourselves as citizens of the world or of a nation-state or of what?' (Garnham 1992: 368). He is quite clear that, given the operation of global market forces and other matters of global concern, it must be the first of these:

> In short, the problem is to construct systems of democratic account-
> ability integrated with media systems of matching scale that occupy
> the same social space as that over which economic and political de-
> cisions will impact. If the impact is universal, then both the political
> and media systems must be universal. . . . If, whether we like it or not
> the problem faced has a general impact upon us all, then there can
> only be one rationally determined course of interventionist political
> action. This course of action has to be agreed to consensually or has to
> be imposed, whether by a majority or a minority. If market forces are
> global, any effective political response has to be global. . . . The same
> applies equally strongly to issues of nuclear weapons or the environ-
> ment. (1992: 371–2)

This is a vigorous political and cultural universalism: global problems require global solutions that bind us all. The implication of Garnham's argument is that a 'global public sphere' would consist in a parallel set of global media and political institutions whose function would be to inform and, as it were, culturally empower a global public and to institute its collective will. In a context in which corporate and political actors are constantly making interventions in their own partial interests – in the interests of capital accumulation or of the narrow domestic concerns of individual nation-states – the function of a global public sphere is to render these actions democratically accountable to the universal polity of the 'global community'.

Given the urgency of many of the global issues we face, Garnham's argument may look persuasive. However, as he recognizes, universalism has attracted many criticisms in contemporary social, political and particularly cultural theorizing. It is these various 'pluralisms' with which Garnham takes issue – be it in the postmodern celebration of 'difference', feminist claims about the gendered nature of universal rationality, the critique of Eurocentrism in postcolonial theory or the particularizing arguments of communitarian political philosophers. He is most adamantly opposed to what he sees as the politically disabling cultural relativism that flows from these pluralist positions. The epistemological scruples of (some) pluralists – centred on doubts about the commensurability between cultural discourses, ultimately whether there can be a universal discourse rationality – is an anxiety with which he has little patience. He argues that, given a situation in which systems of global economic and political power determine large areas of our lives and produce a common interest in emancipation – or ultimately in species survival – we need 'to make a Pascalian bet on universal rationality' (1992: 370).

So Garnham's argument is that we cannot afford to indulge radical pluralism – 'a utopian and romantic pursuit of difference for its own sake' (1992: 375) – since our common – universal – human interests are so significant, so urgent. Whilst one may have some sympathy for Garnham's impatience with the more simplistic forms of cultural relativism that have followed in the wake of postmodernism, the sort of robust, single-minded universalism he advocates does not seem very attractive either. This is because the arguments we have considered so far suggest that the problem of pluralism is not that of fashionable relativist theory, but of the real plurality of lived experience that is to be found in the local situations that make up the global totality. People simply do have different cultural perspectives and cultural-political interests, deriving from their location, outside any universal human interests. And we possess neither any superordinate moral criteria which would allow us to hierarchize such interests, giving precedence to the global ones, nor any effective political-institutional mechanisms that could institute such a hierarchy in practical policies. It is indeed, precisely because of this lack that, as the Commission on Global Governance recognizes, issues of global concern need to be addressed in terms of a cultural dialogue between the interests of the global and the local.

It is instructive to compare Garnham's universalism with John Gray's equally forceful anti-universalism (chapter 2) which fetches up in the defence of cultural difference that seems liable to frustrate a cosmopolitan politics.What I argued in relation to Gray's position was that there are 'good' and 'bad' universalisms. The bad forms include that in which particular cultural/political interests masquerade as general ones; the benign forms are found in human values that *may* – through dialogue, through deep hermeneutic engagement – come to be recognized as having purchase across a range of different cultural contexts and related local interests. Now Garnham's universalism clearly does not fall into the 'bad' category, but what seems missing is that degree of cultural pluralism that would make his gesture towards consensus more convincing and that would cause him to remove his reference to the 'imposition' of a 'rational' course of action. The cosmopolitan cultural disposition cannot be one that rejects pluralism in favour of the claims of rationally deduced universal human interests. Cosmopolitan people need to be simultaneously universalists *and* pluralists.

Ideal: Cosmopolitanism as 'Ethical Glocalism'

If we are sufficiently sensitive to all the problematic connotations of cosmopolitanism, I think it can be retrieved in non-elitist, non-ethnocentric, non-patriarchal – and non-'globalist' – terms as the sort of cultural disposition people living in a globalized world need to cultivate.

To summarize this, the cosmopolitan first needs an active sense of belonging to the wider world, of being able to experience a 'distanciated identity': an identity that is not totally circumscribed by the immediate locality, but, crucially, that embraces a sense of what unites us as human beings, of common risks and possibilities, of mutual responsibilities. To put this in more concrete terms we can think of the difference between the local ethics of 'nimbyism' – concern for one's immediate environment and indifference towards others – and that of an ethics of global environmental care. The first characteristic of cosmopolitanism, then, is a keen grasp of a globalized world as one in which 'there are no others.'

But then the second necessary specification is an almost opposite sensibility: an awareness of the world as one of *many* cultural others. What I mean by this is that the cosmopolitan must have a grasp of the legitimate pluralism of cultures and an openness to cultural difference. And this awareness must be reflexive – it must make people open to questioning their *own* cultural assumptions, myths and so on (which we might be otherwise disposed to regard as 'universal'). So the point is that the two parts of the disposition should not be seen as antithetical and antagonistic, but as mutually tempering and thus disposing us towards an *ongoing dialogue* both within ourselves and with distanciated cultural others.

We have, of course to recognize the danger here that this reflexivity could tip over into mere relativism, the 'postmodern cosmopolitanism' that Garnham is so suspicious of. Being sensitive to plural cultural perspectives risks yielding to the rather simplistic but seductive logic that, since all values are contingent 'local' ones, there are, in effect no values. It is easy to see how the cosmopolitan could invoke this sort of logic to renounce commitments, to remain, as Hannerz observes, cultural dilettantes and ironists. But we don't have to fall towards this antifoundationalism and its consequences. Giddens, for example, depicts the cosmopolitan attitude, following Oakeshott (1991), as a form of 'civil association' – an 'intelligent relationship' between equals which respects the autonomy of the other. He goes on to say:

> A cosmopolitan attitude would not insist that all values are equivalent, but would emphasize the responsibility that individuals and groups have for the ideas that they hold and the practices in which they engage. The cosmopolitan is not someone who renounces commitments – in the manner, say, of the dilettante – but someone who is able to articulate the nature of those commitments, and assess their implications for those whose values are different'. (Giddens 1994: 130)

Putting this slightly differently we could say that the cosmopolitan is not an ideal type to be opposed to the local. She is precisely someone who is able to live – ethically, culturally – *in both the global and the local at the same time.* Cosmopolitans can recognize and value their own cultural dispositions and negotiate as equals with other autonomous locals. But they can also think beyond the local to the long-distance and long-term consequences of actions, recognize common global interests and be able to enter into an intelligent relationship of dialogue with others who start from different assumptions, about how to promote these interests.

One way of grasping the texture of this complementary two-sidedness of cultural disposition is in the idea, developed particularly by Roland Robertson, of 'glocalization' rather than 'globalization'. Robertson appropriates the term 'glocalization' from (originally Japanese) business discourse where essentially it refers to a 'micromarketing' strategy – 'the tailoring and advertising of goods and services on a global or near-global basis to increasingly different-iated local and particular markets' (Robertson 1995: 28). Now, of course, Robertson recognizes all the problems with the discursive context out of which the term emerges, but he none the less finds it useful for underlining one of the central themes in his own approach to the globalization process. This is the insistence that the local and the global (or in his terms 'the particular and the universal') do not exist as cultural polarities but as mutually 'interpenetrating' prin-ciples (1995: 30) – obviously a position broadly friendly towards our conception of cosmopolitanism.

Adapting the idea a little further, we may be able to think of cosmopolitanism as a sort of 'ethical glocalism'. One positive aspect of the term in its marketing context is, at least, the sensitivity it displays to the principle of cultural agency. The rather crude perception that 'diversity sells' (Robertson 1995: 29) is also a cultural insight – as well as being one move ahead of the homogenization scenario (chapter 3). As Robertson suggests, the term 'glocalization' – in Japanese *dochakuka* – derives from *dochaku*, meaning 'living on one's own land' (1995: 28). There is the idea here of adapting agricultural techniques to suit local conditions. And this is a good part of what the ethics of cosmopolitanism may need to be about. If what we argued about the local constitution of the human lifeworld in chapter 5 is correct, then wider global com-mitments need to be concretized in terms relevant to this lifeworld. We cannot expect people to live their lives within a moral horizon that is so distant as to become abstract: the cosmopolitan ethic may have to be, in a rather literal, but positive, sense, 'self-centred'.

To illustrate this, we can return again, briefly, to the field of ecol-ogy and consider an image described in an edition of *The Ecologist* that followed the 1992 Rio Earth Summit. This journal adopts a highly sceptical stance towards the whole project of 'global environmental management' implied in the Earth Summit deliberations, seeing this as a prime example of what Vidal would call 'globalism'. It cites as an instance of what it sees as the shallowness of this approach, a photograph that appeared in a corporate-funded 'Global Environ-mental Magazine' called *Tomorrow*:

> The photograph depicts a young, blond Western model in a bathing suit standing waist-deep in a sunlit sea. . . . [S]he is hugging a colour-ful giant inflatable plastic globe . . . her face with its closed eyes and soft smile, communicates passivity and bliss. She is pictured, as her cheek rests on the North Pole and her arm embraces Africa, trying to show love for an abstract 'world' which is in fact connected with her

life only through impersonal mechanisms and expert explanations. (*The Ecologist* 1992: 182)

The article contrasts this image with that of a woman from the Chipko movement in India – 'a village-based movement that takes its name from the Hindi word "to hug", villagers literally hugging trees to prevent them being felled' (1992: 195). The point of this comparison is to contrast the 'non-rooted, impersonal affection which according to the managerial mentality is required to save the world, with the highly particular, personal moral feelings' which characterize local actions to preserve environments (1992: 195).

The stance of *The Ecologist* here – particularist, localist, resolutely anti-managerial and anti-universalising – could easily be read as simply romantic anti-modernism.Their representation of the environment as essentially a set of local 'commons' does, indeed, push them towards a romanticizing of the capacity of local groups to maintain a sort of intuitive environmental equilibrium. And this is an implausible projection of the power of 'localism', given the complex interconnections of globalization.

But what is more interesting is the view of the relationship between moral-political engagement and local situation that is implicit here. It is interesting to compare their stress on 'highly particular, personal moral feelings' with Zygmunt Bauman's decidedly unromantic analysis of the postmodern moral situation. Following the philosopher Hans Jonas, Bauman suggests that

> Morality which we have inherited from pre-modern times – the only morality we have – is a morality of proximity, and as such is woefully inadequate in a society in which all important action is an action on distance. . . . [T]he moral tools we possess to absorb and control [modern technological power] remain the same as they were at the 'cottage industry' stage. Moral responsibility prompts us to care that our children are fed, clad and shod; it cannot offer us much practical advice, however, when faced with numbing images of a depleted, desiccated and overheated planet which our children, and the children of our children will inherit and have to inhabit in the direct or oblique result of our collective unconcern. (Bauman 1993: 217–18)

What *The Ecologist* celebrates as authentic moral dispositions in the Chipko movement, Bauman might characterize as an anachronistic 'morality of proximity'. But both agree on how in fact people *form* moral-political attachments. Though we should not romanticize local communal mobilizations, we can see an important comparison between the Chipko tree-huggers and, say, the tree-top 'tribes' protesting against the Newbury bypass. Though neither movement demonstrates the negative localism, self-centredness and moral indifference to the other of 'nimbyism', both are, none the less, examples of what Bauman calls a morality with 'powerful but short hands' (1993: 218). They both draw the strength of their mobilization from proximate substantive threats. The significance of such movements is not really in their effectiveness, but in their demonstration that issues of universal concern need to be instanciated in the everyday, local experience and 'moral lifeworld' of people.

Cosmopolitan people are, as we have stressed, ordinary people. They do not need to have the single-minded disposition to activism on particular issues that is characteristic of the 'new tribes' (Maffesoli 1996; Melucci 1989) – who may or may not be cosmopolitans. But in the everyday lifestyle choices they make, cosmopolitans need routinely to experience the wider world as touching their local lifeworld and vice versa. They need to act as 'ethical glocalists'.

Cosmopolitans Without a Cosmopolis

At this point, the reader will be justified in asking if all these specifications of the cosmopolitan disposition are worthwhile, and to wonder whether the idea is anything more than a pious aspiration. Are there any signs that this sort of cultural orientation is likely to emerge?

Certainly there are plenty of reasons to be sceptical. In particular there seem few signs, as we approach the millennium, of the strengthening of global *institutional* support for cosmopolitanism. I have stressed throughout this book that the globalization process does not look set to produce a global culture in any unified institutional sense. And this is, indeed, a context which the Commission on Global Governance recognizes. Although it looks to the United Nations to play a continuing role in global governance – and recommends some quite radical structural reforms towards this end[4] – the report recognizes that this is an institution that was 'hobbled from the outset' by the realities of the divergent interests and power plays of its (differentially powerful) member states. So, looked at as an institutional route to the cosmopolitanism implicit in its Charter – 'We the peoples of the United Nations . . .' – the actual institution of the UN as it has developed must be considered a disappointment: its interventions limited and often ineffective, its future uncertain. This is, moreover, not just a problem with the historical constitution of the United Nations, but with the institutional form of *any* global body composed of nation-states. For, as Lash and Urry (1994: 301) put it, the modern nation-state is constantly 'squeezed between local and global processes' and mostly looking towards the sort of short-term popularity with electorates that is not perceived to be bought by expenditure outside the 'locality' of the national boundaries. Hence, also, the reluctance of nation-states to respond significantly in either hard economic[5] or policy terms to common global environmental problems: what has been called the NIMTOO syndrome – 'Not-in-my-term-of-office' (Leggett 1990: 3).[6] For a splendid example of this, one only has to consider the United States' regressive stance on fossil fuel CO_2 emission controls at the 1997 United Nations Kyoto Climate Summit – unintelligible except in terms of a craven capitulation by the Clinton administration to the pressure of the American oil industry lobby.

All these things considered, the prospects for cosmopolitanism built through international governmental institutions look poor. And, though the rise of (international) non-governmental organizations ((I)NGOs) is to be counted as one of the more optimistic political aspects of the globalization process (Hamelink 1994; Waters 1995), their potential for broad cultural change remains, for all sorts of reasons, limited.[7] For all practical purposes, cosmopolitanism as a cultural disposition may need to be established without any strong institutional supports. We probably have to become cosmopolitans without the prospects of a cosmopolis.

Deterritorialization and the Cosmopolitan Disposition

Is there anything in the cultural processes we have considered in this book to encourage this hope? Well, perhaps. If deterritorialization lifts us out of our ties with spatially defined culture there may at least be the hope of a broader global *re-territorialization*.

So, as we saw in chapter 4, there is the possibility that some of the routine lived experience of global modernity might be producing a general cultural disposition of more openness to the world, regardless of the lack of any encouragement by nation-states. The transformation of our localities into 'glocalities' that we discussed in terms of 'mundane deterritorialization' in chapter 4 – changes in our actual physical environments, the routine factoring-in of distant political-economic processes into life-plans, the penetration of our homes by media and communications technology, multiculturalism as increasingly the norm, increased mobility and foreign travel, even the effects of the 'cosmopolitanizing' of food culture – all these transformations hold the promise of vital aspects of the cosmopolitan disposition: the awareness of the wider world as significant for us in our locality, the sense of connection with other cultures and even, perhaps, an increasing openness to cultural difference.

Of course we have also to realize the danger of cultural reaction that accompanies the experience of deterritorialization. The various insecurities that attend the dissolution of the ties to place clearly have the potential for the hostile retreat into imagined communities of the nation or the ethnie, rather than for cosmopolitanism. However, the very fact that we call these 'retreats' might suggest a temporary moment of reaction in a more powerful long-term cultural process. The complex hybrid nature of contemporary global youth cultures organized around music, dance and fashion is suggestive here. Though clearly commercial cultures, these are in many ways also cosmopolitan, paying little heed to the exclusivity of national or ethnic divisions.

So, ought we to be optimistic about the steady underlying cultural drive towards openness to the world? To probe this a little further I want to consider an argument which John Urry makes about the relationship of the growth in popular travel and tourism to the development of what he calls 'aesthetic cosmopolitanism' (Urry 1995). Urry is careful to distance his argument from the rather banal and, as he says, dubious claim of the tourist industry that 'tourism facilitates international understanding'. However he does argue that we can see an enormous popular appetite for the 'consumption' of foreign places emerging in recent years.

He gives as an example the massive flow of visitors to western European tourist centres from eastern Europe following the collapse of the Iron Curtain, and the way in which the *right* to unlimited travel and cultural consumption has become part, not just of the promise of western liberalism, but of a broader notion of globalized 'consumer citizenship'. Along with this increased tourist mobility – and Urry it will be remembered (chapter 2) more generally sees rapid mobility as the 'paradigmatic modern experience' (Lash and Urry 1994: 253) – he suggests a new type of 'aesthetic cosmopolitanism' is emerging, which involves 'a stance of openness towards divergent experiences from different national cultures' and 'a search for and delight in contrasts between societies rather than a longing for uniformity or superiority'. He goes on from this to develop a model of this cultural attitude, similar in many ways to Hannerz's ideal type of the cosmopolitan which includes, apart from this basic cultural openness and curiosity: a 'rudimentary ability to map places and cultures historically, geographically and anthropologically'; a risk-taking attitude in the willingness to move 'outside the tourist environmental bubble'; a level of semiotic skill in the interpretation of cultural signs and, perhaps most significantly, the reflexive ability 'to locate one's own society and its culture in terms of a wide ranging historical and geographical knowledge' (1995: 167).

Urry compares this late twentieth-century aesthetic cosmopolitanism with that cultivated by the British aristocracy and gentry in the late eighteenth and early nineteenth centuries: the practices – such as the 'Grand Tour' of Europe – which enabled them to 'expand their repertoire of landscapes for visual consumption'. The most obvious difference is, of course, the much wider distribution of opportunity to travel today – the massification, popularization and democratization of tourism that began in the 1840s with Thomas Cook. But there is another distinctive feature of Urry's aesthetic cosmopolitanism: that it is – like much of youth culture – firmly anchored in the practices of popular *consumer culture*. It is in the very act of the 'consumption' of places as cultural commodities that the cultural skills, attitudes and even maybe (though it is a big maybe) the ethics of the cosmopolitan are emerging.

Urry's argument is persuasive, but he would, I am sure, agree that the patterns he is describing fall somewhat short of the *ideal* of cosmopolitanism we are considering here. In the first place, there are all the problems of the potential exclusivity of the category that we discussed earlier. The socio-economic spectrum with access to the experiences he describes, though clearly much broader than the elite cosmopolitans of an earlier age, is nevertheless still a restricted one: regular recreational foreign travel is clearly a practice primarily of the West and of relatively affluent groups within the West. Secondly, and by implication, this restriction raises some of the ethical problems mentioned earlier: the sense that affluence and mobility provide privileged access to a realm of superior cultural and ethical judgement, and the consequent denigration of the experience of those who, perforce or by choice, remain local. And thirdly, though aesthetic cosmopolitanism may characterize some tourist activities, clearly much tourism – by whatever socio-economic groups – remains of the type dubbed by Hannerz the pursuit of 'Home plus'.

Despite all such problems, Urry's argument is interesting in its specification of the *aesthetic* aspect of the cosmopolitan disposition. What he is describing is an emergent *taste* for the wider shores of cultural experience, which is perhaps a move in the right direction. The aesthetic is not, of course, to be confused with the ethical and, as we argued in relation to Hannerz's cosmopolitan figure, there is no guarantee that the lifting of general cultural horizons, the honing of semiotic skills and the development of hermeneutic sensibilities will be followed by any necessary sense of responsibility for the global totality. But on the other hand, it is perhaps more likely that such a sense will develop *obliquely* from these popular cultural practices, than that it will be directly cultivated in some sort of abstract global-civic ethic.

The same reasoning could be applied to the sort of 'indirect travel' which Urry (following Hebdige 1990) recognizes is available to people via their television sets. As we argued in chapter 5, the experience connected with the routine use of media technologies must be counted as one of the most significant and widely available sources of cultural deterritorialization. There is *sense* – albeit a restricted one – in which people can, as Hebdige suggests, become 'cosmopolitans' in their living-rooms through the routine exposure to cultural difference and the constant reminder of the wider world beyond their locality. And people receive this experience, not didactically, but simply as the normal pattern of global media output.

But we also noted that the phenomenological 'distance' involved in the 'quasi-experience' of television viewing constituted a certain limitation on its capacity to involve and engage us emotionally and morally. It is not a case of television being 'morally anaesthetizing', but that it provides a different *kind* of cultural experience which is probably not morally sustaining in the same way that the proximate experiences and personal relations close to the core of the lifeworld are. Because of these limitations it is implausible that media experience alone will furnish us with a sense of global solidarity. And so we have to be reasonably, though not blindly, sceptical of the closely related idea of mediated global 'communities' coming into existence, 'organised around issues of universal moral concern' (Hebdige 1989: 91).[8] As I have argued elsewhere (Tomlinson 1994), television audiences cannot properly be conceived of as diasporic 'communities' but should be thought of as having the same relationship to shared experiences as any other audience. A distinction is suggested here something like the one which Sartre makes between the 'series' – an ensemble of people connected by nothing other than their relation to an external object – and the 'group' – defined by bonds of reciprocity and the recognition of the potential for mutual praxis (Sartre 1976). Sartre's most famous example of a 'series' is a queue of people waiting for a bus in the Place Saint-Germain – a random collection of people who are unrelated and indifferent to each other – a 'plurality of isolations' – except in their common relationship to the awaited bus. But he also discusses the example of a dispersed audience for a radio broadcast, arguing that these people constitute a series (in distinction from a group) defined by 'absence'– not simply in their physical separation from each other, but in 'the impossibility of [such] individuals establishing relations of reciprocity between themselves, or a common praxis' (1976: 270–1).

Without following Sartre too far into the complexities of his analysis of social collectivities, it seems important to press the point that the simple fact of common, simultaneous attention to a broadcast event – even though it may be concerned with a universal moral cause, such as the Live Aid concerts of the 1980s – is not sufficient to constitute such ensembles as 'groups' in Sartre's sense or as communities in ours. It is important to preserve the conceptual space between audiences that are *also* communities (for example, church congregations listening to a sermon, students (in some instances) attending a lecture) and those that are not (cinema audiences randomly assembled, witnesses to a road accident, the distanciated mass-media audience) if we are to avoid an over-optimistic assessment of the culturally and morally binding potential of televisual experience.

One of the main reasons for these conceptual scruples lies in the nature of mediated quasi-experience as monological rather than dialogical (a point Sartre also stresses), since the opportunity for dialogue seems to be central, not just to the idea of community, but to cosmopolitanism itself – certainly as thinkers like Giddens conceive it. Given this, it might be argued that there is a straightforward *technological* barrier to mediated community in our present most widely available forms, such as television. And, of course, there is – in the interactive computer-mediated technologies of cyberspace – a putative technological solution to these problems. This is the promise, in Howard Rheingold's words, of a 'Virtual Community' (Rheingold 1994) of globally spread internet users in dialogue through their keyboards and VDUs. It is comparatively easy to dismiss such techno-utopianism for, as several critics have now shown (Stallabrass 1995; Robins 1996; Gray 1997), there are depths of political naivety in claims that on-line interactions can rebuild a disembodied *Gemeinschaft* in a sort of parallel world to the real world. But, on the other hand, we probably need to avoid falling towards the sort of reactive scepticism and, particularly, the form of manichaeism we described in chapter 5 that denigrates mediated experience against an ideal standard of direct experience. However, scepticism is I think justified over the assumption – built into much of the enthusiastic discourse on cyberspace – that political, social and moral problems can in general yield to technological solutions. John Gray, though perhaps overly pessimistic in his approach to cyberspace, is surely correct on this point:

> The appeal of the Utopia of virtual community comes partly from the magical powers it ascribes to technology. But in the real world of human history, new technologies never create new societies, solve im-memorial problems or conjure away existing scarcities. They simply change the terms in which social and political conflicts are played out. The uses to which new technologies are put depend on the distrib-ution of power and access to resources and *on the level of cultural and moral development in society*. (Gray 1997: 120 – emphasis added)

Applying this to the specific question of the global sense of moral involvement demanded of the cosmopolitan – the order of self-regulation in lifestyle practices that is the cultural key to reflexive global governance – it is clear that, here, there can be no technolog-ical fixes. What communications and media technologies *can* give us is a significant degree of access to, and information about the world and even, perhaps, new modes of distanciated interaction. These are not to be despised or underestimated. In this respect John Gray is probably insufficiently demanding of them when he argues that 'they will serve us best if we treat them as modest devices, tools whereby we protect what is important to us'(1997: 121). This is to fail to recog-nize the intrinsically deterritorializing nature of these technologies that is effectively altering 'what is important to us'- for instance in relation to the cultural value attached to embodiment (chapter 5). But, on the other hand, he is right to keep the categories of the technological and the moral quite clear and distinct. The moral-existential effort required to do anything *with* the experiences available via media technologies has to come from other sources – ultimately from within the situated lifeworld of the self. Without this, no amount of technological sophistication can make us cosmo-politans on-line.

Conclusion: Extending Solidarity's Short Hands

So, finally, what sort of answer can we give to the question of the potential of mundane deterritorialization to produce a cosmopolitan disposition? It is difficult to be conclusive. Though all the various forms and sources of global consciousness, of openness to the world, of mobility, of hybridity and so on can make cosmopolitanism a *possibility*, none of these seems to guarantee it. Not even the threats of a global 'risk society' guarantee it. Ulrich Beck argues that 'Global dangers set up global mutualities' and therefore that 'Cosmopolitan society . . . can take shape in the perceived necessity of world risk society' (Beck 1996: 2). But, as he recognizes elsewhere, it is unclear how 'the binding force of anxiety operates, even if it works' (Beck 1992: 49) (cf. Tomlinson 1994: 163).

This uncertainty I think derives from the fact that these experiential factors are underlaid by a more difficult problem of the nature, and possible limits, of human existential-moral engagement. That is to say, we do not really know whether it is possible to extend Bauman's 'morality of proximity' to encompass the massive and extensive complexities that tie us all in with the fate of the rest of the world. We don't know whether the resources of moral imagination that will sustain a cosmopolitan ethical practice are available from the locally situated lifeworld.

So let us end by imagining the worst. Let us assume that it is simply in the nature of moral engagement and human solidarity that it is essentially a local affair. This might suggest that the global-existential condition is a tragic one: that our social and technological capacities to extend relations across distance – to produce the *social* condition of globalization – has simply outstripped our moral-imaginative capacity to live our lives in regard to – with a sense of mutuality with – all the distant others with whom we have necessarily become connected. With the global and the local so profoundly out of kilter, prospects for cosmopolitanism look bleak.

But maybe not. It may be that cosmopolitanism can be conceived in terms other than those of an austere ethical commitment which strains to connect our lifeworld with the distant and 'abstract' generalized others who are our global neighbours.

A first point to bear in mind is the *power* of moral commitment, mutuality and solidarity as it exists in modern societies at the local level. It is not as though the condition of global modernity causes an overall decline in these virtues. Helmuth Berking, for instance (following Wuthnow 1992) cites evidence to suggest that in America – the cradle of modern possessive individualism – 'other-oriented' cultural practices are actually *expanding*:

> What is to be made of a situation in which, week after week, 80 million Americans, or over 45% of the population above the age of 18, dedicate five hours or more of their time to voluntary relief work and charitable activities, work in crisis centres . . . organise neighbourhood help projects, build social networks dedicated to geriatric care . . .? If the data can be believed, for over 75% of Americans solidarity, helpfulness and public interest orientations lay claim to the same prominent relevance that is attributed by them to such motives as self-realization, vocational success orientations and the expansion of personal freedom. (Berking 1996: 192–3)

Berking traces this apparently thriving local mutuality to its source in the ongoing reflexive constitution of the human self. He argues that we see in modern societies the emergence of a 'solidary individualism'– in which the building of self-identity depends on an increasing reflexive awareness of relations with others. This means that to act in one's 'self-interest' is not necessarily to do so in a narrowly utilitarian way, but indeed involves the 'self-justification' that comes from acts of mutuality (here he cites the expanding 'private economy of gift giving' in modern societies). The key point in this argument is that mutuality, solidarity and moral concern are not seen as somehow endangered 'traditional' collective social values, but as dispositions which flow from the very condition of modernity itself: the requirement (recalling Thompson's arguments in chapter 5) for individuals chronically to 'construct' their identities in social interactions rather than to find them in stable social roles and associated subject positions. Moral engagement thus becomes less a case of the formal rational commitment to a set of abstract ideals and responsibilities, than an act of *Bildung*, of self-fulfilment. Thus the modern reflexive subject, 'in the intention of realising itself, acts towards changing the social world' (Berking 1996: 201).

Looking at moral engagement in this way may cause us to be less generally pessimistic about the moral resources of modernity, but it doesn't in itself advance the prospects of cosmopolitanism. Indeed, as Berking recognizes, there is a danger that this sort of mutuality may turn out to be insular, to realize itself in 'morally overheated zones of nearness, and, as closeness diminishes, increasing indifference' (p. 199) (cf. Castells 1998: 352).

But, on the other hand, recognizing the connection between the possibility of a cosmopolitan disposition and the constitution of the reflexive self does shift the argument in a more positive direction. For if it is 'solidary individualism' that drives mutuality, this seems in principle a more flexible dynamic than other accounts of moral localism – for instance that which be might be derived from socio-biology (Wilson 1978). The possibility of cosmopolitanism is not therefore ruled out by any iron logic of localism, but becomes focused on the cultural project of extending the field of relevance of mutuality to embrace a sense of distant others as symbolically 'significant others'. This may not be easy, but as Berking argues, it is not impossible: 'If I know what tropical forests or automobile traffic mean for my health; if I know what love and friendship, empathy and compassion can give rise to . . . what then counts . . . are extended solidarities that are no longer restricted to my own community of shared values' (Berking 1996: 201).

Nothing guarantees the building of cosmopolitan solidarity in the uncertainties of global modernity. But its possibility at least derives from some powerful modern cultural resources: a combination of the deterritorialization of mundane experience that increasingly opens the world to us, along with the drive to self-realization in lifestyles which are themselves 'open' to an expanded mutuality. Seen thus, the cultural condition of deterritorialization is not something which has to be reckoned as separate from or antagonistic towards an essential human moral condition, but something which develops in tandem with it. This rather low-key, modest cosmopolitanism may be a far cry from a heroic ideal of global citizenship, but it does at least seem a disposition to be built upon that is plausibly within our grasp.

Notes

Chapter 1 Globalization and Culture

1 Of course this familiar in-flight routine, along with the professional demeanour of the flight crew, directing attention to the secure 'in-hereness' of the situation, can also be seen as part of the institutional management of trust relations in conditions of routine risk. See Giddens's (1990: 86) reference to the importance of 'the studied casualness and calm cheer of air crew personnel' in reassuring passengers.

2 The total number of passengers passing through the world's busiest international airport, London Heathrow, in 1996 was 55.7 million or an average 152,600 per day. The world's busiest air terminal overall however – boosted by its much higher number of domestic flights than LHR – is Chicago O'Hare with 69.1 million passengers in 1996 (source: BAA plc Forecasting and Statistics, 1997).

3 A prime example of the complexity of the situation is the way in which legislation on CFCs – restrictions in developed countries and exemptions for developing countries – has affected the business of smuggling. Freon gas canisters produced in Mexico are smuggled across the Rio Grande into the United States to supply the demand from US drivers (mostly poorer people driving older vehicles) for their cars' air conditioning systems. This trade is estimated by US customs to be as lucrative as drug smuggling.

4 This outright rejection of the concept has to be distinguished from the sense of globalization as 'myth' found in Marjorie Ferguson's paper 'The Mythology about Globalization'. Ferguson would be equally suspicious of Ohmae, but she is careful to indicate that 'These are not myths *of* globalization as such but myths *about* the objectives and relationships between disparate interests and institutions seeking to ride on the back of the globalizing momentum' (Ferguson 1992: 74). She uses

the idea of myth somewhat in the sense developed by Roland Barthes (1973) to indicate not simple untruths, but complex historically evolving versions of reality which are ideologically inflected.

5   And this separation of domains of course has an ideological aspect. Cultural practices obviously take place within the context of the social power relations of class, race, gender and so on, and are in this broad sense 'political'. There are, for example, 'elite' and 'popular' cultural forms which in certain senses 'express' these power relations and which may contribute to their reproduction, or provide contexts for their contestation. Equally, most symbolic representation in modern societies is conducted within the 'economic' context of the market-place.

6   I have not dealt here with Waters's claims about the 'internationalizing' tendency of the sphere of politics. It must be said that he does appear to have a stronger case here, particularly in the implication that the domain of politics continues to be dominated by the international system of nation-states, rather than a wider and as yet more diffuse 'global' order. However, even here, I remain unconvinced that such clear elective affinities between social spheres and spatial contexts can be sustained. Waters claims that the degree of undermining of the state that can be detected as part of the globalization process should be 'counted as a cultural development', rather than a political one (Waters 1995: 122). This sounds to me suspiciously like 'saving the appearances' of the initial proposition.

7   David Lloyd speaking at the 1995 Edinburgh National Television Conference, quoted in Culf 1995: 2.

Chapter 2   Global Modernity

1   Giddens is careful to point out that not all evolutionary theory is teleologically inspired (1990: 5) but in whatever form, it remains misleading. For a clear and comprehensive critical treatment of evolutionary social theory see Sztompka 1993: 99ff.

2   All such generalizations conceal empirical contrasts. Barber (1992: 45ff) for instance contrasts the typical pattern of sedentary peasantry of lowland England with the much more mobile pastoral lifestyle of shepherds in areas like the Pyrenees during the thirteenth and fourteenth centuries. Cherubini (1990: 133) comments on the expanded worldview of some medieval European peasants that may be attributed to seasonal labour migration.

3   Thrift (1996: 57) describes this nicely as 'the modern world's self image of its own distinctiveness . . . constitut[ing] a sort of orientalism over history'. See also Osborne's (1992: 68) discussion of the problem of modernity as an epoch defined 'solely in terms of temporal determinants'.

4   Giddens dates this 'at the earliest from the late eighteenth century' (1990: 17). Of course mechanical clocks were in limited use much before this time in Europe – and much earlier still in China. As Thrift points out,

church and public clocks began to appear throughout England during the fourteenth century, and were common in most parishes by the seventeenth – though, as he says, 'it is debatable whether these clocks had any great effect on the majority of the populace' partly due to their inaccuracy (Thrift 1990: 107). Up to the mid-sixteenth century timekeeping was a haphazard affair for most, with attempts at accuracy mostly confined to the tradesmen in towns and to monasteries – nicely described by Thrift as 'islands of timekeeping in a sea of timelessness'. Overall Thrift's history roughly confirms Giddens's point about the wider social distribution of clocks: 'Somewhere between 1800 and 1850 a point would be reached where clocks and watches existed amongst all classes'(1990: 112).

5   The Gregorian calendar to which Giddens alludes coexists, of course, with other religious-derived dating systems – for instance the Muslim or the Jewish calendars. Though these latter continue to have cultural significance (dates on letter heads in countries like Iran still use the Muslim calendar), Giddens is right to argue that the Gregorian has 'become to all intents and purposes universal' in co-ordinating modern life. A good example of this is the current anxiety over the so-called 'millennium bug': how the clock-calendars installed in computers world-wide will cope with the digital movement beyond 2000.

6   Letter boxes only began to be installed widely in British houses following the postal reforms of 1840 and the introduction of the adhesive pre-paid postage stamps. Before this, postage charges were generally paid on receipt to the letter carrier and it was the delays in waiting for the householder to answer the door that prompted a government campaign to install letter slits. This campaign (and similar ones, for example, in the United States) went on against a fair amount of public resistance throughout the nineteenth and well into the twentieth century. See Young Farrugia 1969: 145ff.

7   On this point, see also Chris Rojek's discussion of the social implications of the introduction of public street lighting in Europe and North America during the 1870s and 1880s, particularly the impact of this on the distinction between 'interior' and 'exterior' social life in cities (1993: 123–5).

8   Most of Europe had a money economy based on silver coinage by the eighth century, and this developed in complexity during the Middle Ages but retained huge degrees of local variation and lack of standarization (see Brooke 1975: 75ff). But see also Barber (1992: 745ff) on the impetus to international trade provided particularly through the Italian banking houses from the thirteenth century: the use of double-entry bookkeeping and the rise of credit transactions that developed out of the conversion of simple bills of exchange into loan facilities.

9   For example in the Freudo-Marxian critiques of theorists like Christopher Lasch (1980; 1985). See Giddens's critique of Lasch (1991: 171f).

10 Though more critical of the power (particularly class) relations of re-flexive modernity, Scott Lash (1994: 167) argues that 'Giddens's expert systems no longer either dominate or liberate the masses. Instead they *are* the masses.' This refers to the growing proportion of the work force in developed countries (Lash estimates 25 per cent in the UK and USA) employed in expert systems such as the information/communication industry.

11 See here Featherstone's argument (1995: 146) that Giddens's institutional derivation of globalization from modernity 'does not take into account the independent force of cultural factors in the process'. My view how-ever is that his social-ontological analysis has important cultural impli-cations – particularly in the sphere of mediated experience. What Giddens doesn't do is to spell these implications out in any detail.

12 But here we have to recognize how Gray's position meshes with a broad anti-universalizing trend in contemporary thought which is constructed precisely out of 'marginal' cultural experiences which *focus* on differ-ence. This is particularly the case in the field of identity politics where hostility towards the universalizing project of the Enlightenment has arisen – explicitly or implicitly – from all manner of marginalized groups in the West. These correctly point to the tendency to subsume the cul-tural difference that matters to them in broader categories like 'human-ity'. The struggle of these particular identities to find voice and to press their political agendas accounts in large part for the pervasive anti-universalizing intellectual tenor of the times. For an interesting critical-historical discussion of this discourse from a Marxian perspective see Zaretski 1995; for more general discussions of culture and identity poli-tics, see Woodward 1997.

13 Which is not to say that it is uncontentious in its detail. There are, of course, particular and antagonistic constituencies of interest involved even in these global problems (see Sachs 1993). One only has to think of the different perspectives that have arisen in the attempt to regulate the production of ozone-destructive CFC gases referred to in chapter 1: differences between producer and consumer nations and between the developed and the developing world. These genuine and thorny po-litical problems are surely not going to be solved by a facile 'one-worldism'. (For a discussion of these issues in relation to the 'universalizing discourse' of globalization, see Yearley 1996: 100ff). However the point is that *no* solution to this sort of global problem can ever arise unless the universal interest is placed seriously alongside more immediate particular interests.

Chapter 3 Global Culture: Dreams, Nightmares and Scepticism

1 Or even that pluralism and 'cultural relativism' begins with it. For ex-ample see Michel de Montaigne's remarkably 'modern' essay, 'On the

Cannibals' written in the last part of the sixteenth century. Here Montaigne rejects the idea that the 'cannibals '– the people living on the coast of Brazil that he had read of in accounts of the conquest of the New World – should be regarded as 'barbarians': 'I find (from what has been told me) that there is nothing savage or barbarous about these peoples, but that every man calls barbarous anything he is not accustomed to; it is indeed the case that we have no other criterion of truth or right-reason than the example and form of the opinions and customs of our own country' (Montaigne 1995: 8-9).

2   See Thompson (1990: 125ff) for a discussion of Herder's pluralistic concept of culture and his influence on nineteenth-century ethnographers such as E. B. Tylor, and thus on the emerging anthropological tradition.

3   Kant's 'cosmopolitanism' has been perhaps the most influential on modern international political thought. For all his idealism, it would of course be a mistake to describe Kant's ideas of a cosmopolitan political order as 'utopian', for he was quite aware of the huge difficulties posed by national interests (Turner 1990: 349) and proposed what was in essence a federal solution to these. For modern discussions in this spirit see Bobbio 1995, Archibugi 1995 and Held 1995.

4   Marx's speculations about the coming communist society are rather fragmentary and scattered throughout his writings; moreover he generally resisted providing a systematic account so as to distance himself from what he saw as naive 'utopian socialism' not grounded in historical materialism. None the less he does offer many concrete examples of what life in communism might be like. Bertell Ollman (1979) usefully collects these in his essay 'Marx's Vision of Communism'.

5   Quoted in Said 1985:153 – where Said also discusses Marx's ambiguous 'Orientalism'.

6   This quotation is from CNN's Head of Newsgathering, Ed (not to be confused with Ted) Turner, speaking on the television programme *Distress Signals* broadcast in Channel 4's series *Channels of Resistance* in April 1993. But compare Ted Turner's more 'modest' rhetoric in a speech to the 1994 PAN Asia cable and satellite TV conference in Hong Kong: 'We never came out here and told people how to run a television station. We just came out here with our little satellite CNN International, and now everybody's trying to copy it' (Turner 1994: 39).

7   In his book *World Peace and the Human Family*, Weatherford seeks to defend the thesis that 'world peace is both desirable and achievable through a world government and a world culture rooted in the notion of the human family'(Weatherford 1993: x). This is a curious and in many ways idiosyncratic text, but what is of interest in it for the present discussion is the way in which Weatherford maintains a benignly untroubled attitude to the spread of western – and specifically American – culture in the interests of 'world peace'.

8 But as David Crystal (1987: 375) points out, both the hopes and fears of a single dominant world language may be liable to be frustrated because of the very nature of language development: 'As the [dominant] language becomes used in all corners of the world . . . so it begins to develop new spoken varieties . . . In the course of time these new varieties might become mutually unintelligible.' A good instance of the dialectical moment of cultural 're-embedding'.

9 A prime example of this is the famous dispute which arose between the US and Europe in the closing weeks of the Uruguay Round of GATT talks in 1993. This dispute centred on the demand by the Europeans (particularly France) that trade in audiovisuals be excluded from the agreement, allowing them to restrict the flow of American film and television programmes into their countries – a form of 'cultural protectionism' strongly resisted by the Americans. I discuss the GATT dispute further in Tomlinson 1997a. For a comprehensive discussion of the cultural and economic background to the dispute, see the papers in van Hemel et al. 1996. Hamelink 1994 gives a good concise account of the politics involved.

10 Latouche also uses the term 'deterritorialization' (1996: 94–8) but in a more restricted sense than I shall, attaching it almost exclusively to the negative consequences of the transnationalization of national economies.

11 To be fair to Latouche, his indictment of westernization is accompanied by a recognition of its limits, and what he sees as the 'crisis of the Western order' (1996: 85ff). He also offers some interesting discussion of cultural resistances in the Third World to homogenizing tendencies (pp. 100ff). But the many insights of this analysis are confused, partly by initial overstatement of the homogenizing ills of the West and more by the failure to separate out theoretically the principles of social modernity from westernization.

Chapter 4 Deterritorialization: The Cultural Condition of Globalization

1 For completeness we should also note the use of the terms 'deterritorialization' and 'reterritorialization' to denote psycho-cultural effects of capitalism in Deleuze and Guattari's *Anti-Oedipus* (1977). I do not, however, draw on their analysis in what follows.

2 In 1949 there were only ten supermarkets (defined as over 2,000 square feet and with more than three checkouts) in the UK. This rose to 4,764 in 1997 and the 'big four' of these chains - Asda, Sainsbury's, Safeway and Tesco – now control 'more than half of the nation's grocery bill' (Gannaway 1998: 2).

3 Indeed the popularity of the recent genre of 'fly on the wall' television documentaries covering work relations at London Heathrow and Bir-

mingham International airports reveal both the cultural complexity of these milieux and people's interest in these places as rich 'lifeworlds'.

4   In the case of the European Union this awareness is not matched by a sense of the legitimacy of these 'external' forces. A survey conducted by Demos in 1998 found that general support for the European Union amongst the citizens of Europe had fallen to its lowest point ever, with only 41 per cent of respondents feeling that their country benefits from EU membership, only 50 per cent identifying themselves 'with EU institutions or with Europe as a whole' and with 80 per cent admitting 'to being not very well informed' or 'not informed at all' about the EU (Leonard 1998: 6).

5   For a discussion of Ruskin's general gender-political position in relation to the domestic sphere, see Kate Millett's *Sexual Politics* (1971: 98ff) – the source of Meyrowitz's quotation. Here Millett contrasts Ruskin's romantic paternalism with the liberalism of John Stuart Mill's view of women's 'domestic slavery'. For a more recent related debate, see Barrett and McIntosh's (1982) critique of Christopher Lasch's position on the patriarchal family in *Haven in a Heartless World* (Lasch 1977).

6   Though of course such dress styles also become 'indigenized'. Subtle discriminations in the preferred style of trainers for instance can be used to register ethnic or regional differences.

7   We might be tempted to take the current revival of interest in local food specialities – English regional cheeses available from the *Guardian*'s 'Cheese Club', 'bread and butter pudding and tripe on the menus of the more fashionable restaurants' (James 1996: 89) – as signs of 'reterritorialization' in food taste. But we have to distinguish this sort of cosmopolitan 'local sampling' consumption practice (restricted, as James observes, to 'the well-heeled few') from any more widespread and significant reassertion of locality.

8   On the same issue in relation to development studies, see Jane Collins's unpacking of the cultural assumptions and politics of 'grassroots populist' localism (Collins 1996).

9   *Mange Tout* was produced and directed by Mark Phillips for the BBC documentary series *Modern Times* (1997).

10 I discuss García Canclini's work here in general terms which do not do justice to the many nuances and specificities of the Latin American context(s) with which he is concerned. For critical discussions of his work in these contexts, see, for example, Rowe 1992 and the various contributors to the debate on *Culturas Hibridas* in the *Journal of Latin American Cultural studies: Travesia*, 1. 2 (1992), particularly Franco 1992 and Kraniauskas 1992.

11 Rosaldo is writing here specifically in reference to García Canclini. It should be noted that the issue of hybridity has special resonances in Latin American cultural theory, connected as it inevitably is with the racial themes of creolization and *mestizaje* (see Nederveen Pieterse 1995: 54). García Canclini's work breaks free of some of these connections,

but as Rosaldo implies, not always entirely from their essentializing connotations. For a similar argument see Franco 1992.

12 This is the position argued, for instance, in Philip Dodd's (1995) discussion of the politics of British national culture in a paper from the British think tank, Demos. But what we could call Dodd's 'strategic anti-essentialism', intended to undermine (particularly racial) exclusionary identities, ironically falls towards the biological metaphor of 'mongrelism': see his chapter, 'In Praise of Mongrels'.

Chapter 5   Mediated Communication and Cultural Experience

1 I will not try to maintain a sharp division between the deterritorializing properties of 'new' and 'old' media technologies here, though there are clearly some interesting distinctions that could be made. Mark Poster (1995), for instance distinguishes between the 'first media age' of radio, television and the telephone and a 'second media age' of interactive, decentralized computer-mediated communications – the internet, the information superhighway, the realm of 'cyberspace'. This distinction is linked to an analysis of different orders of cultural reception of these media and of different subject positions available from them – in both cases mapped on to a modern/postmodern divide. Although there is much of interest in Poster's analysis, it introduces some of the problems associated with epochal analysis and binarism – particularly as centred on technologies – that we discussed in chapter 2. To be fair, Poster is aware of these problems (1995: 21–2) but does not fully resolve them. For my present purposes it is on balance less useful to stress the differences than the continuities in these technologies. This is particularly so, given the much broader distribution of 'old' technologies globally. As Manuel Castells (1996: 358) argues, 'CMC is not a general medium of communication and will not be so for the foreseeable future. While its use expands at phenomenal rates it will exclude for a long time the large majority of humankind, unlike television and other mass media.' This is not, of course a reason to ignore its specific deterritorializing potential, but it does suggest that it might be more useful to think of CMC in relation to the more common globalizing media forms like television (Turkle 1995: 235) than in sharp distinction from them.

2 Most prominent amongst these are the charges that, in focusing so narrowly on the medium, rather than the broader political-economic and cultural context of communication, they present a view of social-historical change that is based in a 'technological determinism', and a fairly narrow one at that. This charge is typically associated with the criticism that such theories generally ignore issues of institutional and political-economic power and ideology, or the subtleties of cultural difference. McLuhan's work has been most heavily criticized for this

(e.g. Williams 1974; Ferguson 1990, 1991), but the critique also extends to others, notably Meyrowitz (Silverstone 1994: 94–5; Stevenson 1995: 137–8). These criticism are in the main valid ones – though see, for example, Heyer and Crowley's (1995) defence of Innis from the rather crude charge that he does not engage with the contexts of economic and institutional power. However, as Roger Silverstone acutely observes, there is something suggestive in these approaches that derives precisely from their relatively narrow focus: '. . . because, paradoxically, they do insist on isolating and privileging media technologies . . . they raise important questions about their significance in a way that is relatively free from the determinations of the polity or the economy' (1994: 92).

3   Consider, for instance the difference in the phenomenology of time involved in, on the one hand, lingering over a love letter and, on the other, the rush to absorb the contents of a letter bringing bad news – the eye racing ahead in its scanning of the text to 'know the worst' as instantaneously as possible.

4   But see the body of work in social psychology that is now addressing (though not precisely with the phenomenological focus referred to here) the implications of mediated experience for the construction of the self (e.g. Gergen 1991; Grodin and Lindhof 1996).

5   Castells was referring to CMC sex in this context, but the point applies equally to telephone sex. See also his discussion of the rapid growth of sexually oriented chat-lines ('les messageries roses') on the French Minitel system, paralleling the rise of commercial telephone sex lines in other countries, but adding the element of 'spontaneous' (noncommercial) erotic encounters on the general-purpose chat-lines. Castells notes that, at its peak in 1990, this accounted for more than half of the calls made on the system (1996: 344–5).

6   One reason why this phenomenon has not been widely explored is perhaps that the popular-cultural focus has tended to be on the nuisance value of unselfconscious cellphone users. It is interesting to notice that no very clear social etiquette has yet emerged in this respect. This perhaps attests to the contestation of rights within public locales implicit in the use of cellphones. What rights do people have to protection from disturbance by cellphone users in shared spaces like train carriages? How does this differ from disturbance by face-to-face conversations?

7   A similar doubt has to be acknowledged in relation to the various 'virtual communities' – Bulletin Board Systems (BBSs), Multiple User Domains (MUDs) – on the internet that Howard Rheingold famously champions (Rheingold 1994). Sherry Turkle's ethnographic work on MUDs for example, though recognizing the attractions of these disembodied, flexible-identity interactions for their users, none the less remains sceptical about its broader community-building potential: 'It's not hard to agree that MUDs provide an outlet for people to work through personal issues in a productive way . . . And yet it is sobering

to think that the personal computer revolution, once conceptualized as a tool to rebuild community, now tends to concentrate on building community inside a machine' (Turkle 1995: 244). For a more robust critique of the idea of virtual communities in relation to 'real communities' see, for example, Robins 1996.

8   Miller begins by saying, 'Contrary to what McLuhan asserts . . .' because McLuhan had claimed, apparently perversely, that television was essentially a 'tactile' medium rather than a visual one. However, he defined 'tactility' as 'the interplay of the senses, rather than the isolated contact of skin and object' (1964: 314) and so what he seemed to mean was the experience of 'depth involvement' in the viewing experience, rather than simply the visual encounter with the flat surface image on the screen. For example, McLuhan cites medical students watching a televised operation and reporting that they felt they had actually carried out the procedure – that 'they were holding the scalpel' (1964: 328).

9   See here Nick Stevenson's (1995: 141–2) discussion of the possibilities for the erosion of other-oriented sensibilities presented in the development of projects like 'MeTV' – involving the pre-selection of programmes by the TV receiver, tailored to the tastes and lifestyles of the individual viewer.

10 In this connection see my discussion (Tomlinson 1997b) of the moral potential in the media coverage of 'scandals' – generally thought of as emblematic of popular media trivialization, but, as I argue, offering possibilities for moral reflection based on empathy.

Chapter 6   The Possibility of Cosmopolitanism

1   Hannerz takes these instances from the travel writer Paul Theroux (1986). For a similar point, see Featherstone 1995: 98.

2   Hannerz is more or less friendly to the idea that there may exist 'some kind of affinity between cosmopolitanism and the culture of intellectuals' – people with 'decontextualized cultural capital' and a disposition that is 'reflexive, problematizing . . . [and] . . . generally expansionist in its management of meaning' (p. 246). Distant echoes here of the privileging of the perspective of 'socially free-floating intellectuals' in Karl Mannheim's sociology of knowledge? (Mannheim 1960)

3   For sustained criticism of 'global environmentalism' see the contributions to (particularly part III of) Wolfgang Sachs's Global Ecology (1993).

4   The most significant of these being the expansion of the membership of the Security Council and the review of its permanent membership, along with a phasing out of the veto power and a new funding formula to reduce reliance on the major contribution from the US (1995: 301–2, 344–7). But see Held (1995: 273ff) for the argument that even a reformed UN would need to be complemented by a new 'international democratic assembly' which would include, along with states, 'INGOs, citizen groups and social movements'.

5 On this point see Samir Amin's proposal that an embryonic 'democratic world government' might be marked by the introduction of 'a world tax earmarked for ecological operations' (Amin 1997: 22). The remoteness of the possibility of such a progressive taxation regime illustrates precisely the limitations of an approach to cosmopolitanism through currently structured international institutions.

6 On the politics of international co-operation in the environmental field see, for example, Goodwin 1992. Ostrom's (1990) discussion of the institutional governance of 'common pool resources' is relevant to the issue of the global commons. And for a more direct discussion (critically) developing Garrett Hardin's classic analysis of the 'tragedy of the commons', see Lash and Urry 1994: 300ff.

7 For critical discussions of the role of NGOs in the field of global environmental politics, see Jamieson 1996 and Hajer 1996.

8 Hebdige draws on the – rather exceptional – model of global televisual events like the 'Live Aid' and the 'Free Mandela' concerts of the 1980s which seemed to suggest at the time some sort of culturally binding potential. On the broader analysis of the live televising of 'ceremonial media events' like the Olympic Games, royal weddings, papal visits and state funerals, see Dayan and Katz 1992.

Bibliography

Abercrombie, N. 1996: *Television and Society*. Cambridge: Polity Press.

Adam, B. 1990: *Time and Social Theory*. Cambridge: Polity Press.

—— 1996: Re-vision: The centrality of time for an ecological social science perspective. In S. Lash, B. Szerszynski and B. Wynne (eds), *Risk, Environment and Modernity*. London: Sage, 84–103.

Ahmad, A. 1995: The Politics of Literary Postcoloniality. *Race and Class*, 36. 3, 1–20.

Albrow, M. 1997: *The Global Age: State and society beyond modernity*. Cambridge: Polity Press.

Allen, J. and C. Hamnett (eds) 1995: *A Shrinking World: Global unevenness and inequality*. Oxford: Oxford University Press/Open University.

Amin, S. 1997: Reflections on the International System. In Golding and Harris (eds), *Beyond Cultural Imperialism*, 10–24.

Anderson, B. 1991: *Imagined Communities: Reflections on the origin and spread of nationalism* (revised 2nd edn). London: Verso.

Anderson, J. 1995: The Exaggerated Death of the Nation-State. In Anderson et al. (eds), *A Global World*, 65–112.

—— C. Brook and A. Cochrane (eds) 1995: *A Global World: Re-ordering political space*. Oxford: Oxford University Press/Open University.

Ang, I. 1991: *Desperately Seeking the Audience*. London: Routledge.

—— 1996: *Living Room Wars*. London: Routledge.

Anzaldua, G. 1987: *Borderlands/La Frontera: The new mestiza*. San Francisco: Aunt Lute Books.

Appadurai, A. 1990: Disjuncture and Difference in the Global Cultural Economy. In Featherstone (ed.), *Global Culture*, 295–310.

Appiah, K. A. and H. L. Gates (eds) 1998: *A Dictionary of Global Culture*. London: Penguin.

Archibugi, D. 1995: From the United Nations to Cosmopolitan Democracy. In D. Archibugi and D. Held (eds), *Cosmopolitan Democracy: An agenda for a new world order*. Cambridge: Polity Press, 121–62.

Augé, M. 1995: *Non-places: Introduction to the anthropology of supermodernity*. London: Verso.

Axford, B. 1995: *The Global System: Economics, politics and culture*. Cambridge: Polity Press.

Bachelard, G. 1969: *The Poetics of Space*. Boston: Beacon Press.

Barber, B. R. 1995: *Jihad vs. McWorld*. New York: Random House.

Barber, M. 1992: *The Two Cities: Medieval Europe 1050–1320*. London: Routledge.

Barrett, M. and M. McIntosh 1982: *The Anti-social Family*. London: Verso.

Barthes, R. 1973: *Mythologies*. London: Paladin.

Baudrillard, J. 1988: *Selected Writings* (ed. Mark Poster). Cambridge: Polity Press.

Bauman, Z. 1991: *Modernity and Ambivalence*. Cambridge: Polity Press.

—— 1992: *Intimations of Postmodernity*. London: Routledge.

—— 1993: *Postmodern Ethics*. Oxford: Blackwell.

—— 1995: *Life in Fragments*. Oxford: Blackwell.

Beck, U. 1992: *Risk Society: Towards a new modernity*. London: Sage.

—— 1994: The Reinvention of Politics: Towards a theory of reflexive modernization. In Beck, Giddens and Lash, *Reflexive Modernization*, 56–109.

—— 1996: World Risk Society as Cosmopolitan Society? *Theory, Culture and Society*, 13. 4, 1–32.

—— 1997: *The Reinvention of Politics: Rethinking modernity in the global social order*. Cambridge: Polity Press.

Beck, U., A. Giddens and S. Lash 1994: *Reflexive Modernization*. Cambridge: Polity Press.

Belasco, W. 1993: *Appetite for Change*. Ithaca: Cornell University Press.

Bell, D. and G. Valentine 1997: *Consuming Geographies: We are where we eat*. London: Routledge.

Benhabib, S. 1992: *Situating the Self*. Cambridge: Polity Press.

Benjamin, W. 1973: *Charles Baudelaire: A lyric poet in the era of high capitalism*. London: NLB.

Bennett, H. S. 1990: *The Pastons and their England*. Cambridge: Cambridge University Press.

Berger, P. 1974: *Pyramids of Sacrifice*. Harmondsworth: Allen Lane.

Berking, H. 1996: Solidary Individualism: The moral impact of cultural modernisation in late modernity. In S. Lash, B. Szerszynski and B. Wynne (eds), *Risk, Environment and Modernity*. London: Sage, 189–202.

Berman, M. 1983: *All that is Solid Melts into Air: The experience of modernity*. London: Verso.

Beyer, P. 1994: *Religion and Globalization*. London: Sage.

Bhabha, H. K. 1994: *The Location of Culture*. London: Routledge.

Billig, M. 1995: *Banal Nationalism*. London: Sage.

Blackwell, T. and J. Seabrook 1993: *The Revolt against Change*. London: Vintage.

Bobbio, N. 1995: Democracy and the International System. In D. Archibugi and D. Held (eds), *Cosmopolitan Democracy: An agenda for a new world order*. Cambridge: Polity Press, 17–41.

Boulding, E. 1988: *Building a Global Civic Culture*. New York: Syracuse University Press.

Boyd-Barrett, O. 1982: Cultural Dependency and the Mass Media. In M. Gurevitch et al. (eds), *Culture, Society and the Media*. London: Methuen, 174–95.

Brook, J. and I. A. Boal 1995: *Resisting the Virtual Life*. San Francisco: City Lights.

Brooke, C. 1975: *Europe in the Central Middle Ages 962–1154*. London: Longman.

Calloway, C. G. 1994: *The World Turned Upside Down: Indian voices from early America*. Boston: Bedford Books.

Cardoso, F. H. 1982: Dependency and Development in Latin America. In H. Alavi and T. Shanin (eds), *Introduction to the Sociology of 'Developing Societies'*. London: Macmillan, 112–27.

Carey, J. 1989: *Communication as Culture*. Boston: Unwin Hyman.

Castells, M. 1996: *The Rise of the Network Society (The Information Age: Economy, Society and Culture*, vol. I). Oxford: Blackwell.

—— 1997: *The Power of Identity (The Information Age: Economy, Society and Culture*, vol. II). Oxford: Blackwell.

—— 1998: *End of Millennium (The Information Age: Economy, Society and Culture*, vol. III). Oxford: Blackwell.

Castoriadis, C. 1987: *The Imaginary Constitution of Society*. Cambridge: Polity Press.

Cerny, P. G. 1996: What Next for the State? In Kofman and Youngs (eds), *Globalization*, 123–37.

Chaney, D. 1993: *Fictions of Collective Life*. London: Routledge.

Cherubini, G. 1990: The Peasant and Agriculture. In J. Le Goff (ed.), *The Medieval World*. London: Collins and Brown, 113–38.

Classen, C. 1996: Sugar Cane, Coca-Cola and Hypermarkets: Consumption and surrealism in the Argentine northwest. In Howes (ed.), *Cross-Cultural Consumption*, 39–54.

Cleasby, A. 1995: *What in the World is Going on?: British television and global affairs*. London: Third World and Environment Broadcasting Project.

Clifford, J. 1988: *The Predicament of Culture*. Cambridge, Mass.: Harvard University Press.

—— 1992: Travelling Cultures. In L. Grossberg, C. Nelson and P. Treichler (eds), *Cultural Studies*. London: Routledge, 96–116.

—— 1997: *Routes: Travel and translation in the late twentieth century*. Cambridge, Mass.: Harvard University Press.

Cohen, R. 1997: *Global Diasporas: An introduction*. London: UCL Press.

Coles, J. 1998: Oprah Uncowed. *Guardian*, 10 February, 2–3.

Collins, J. L. 1996: Development Theory and the Politics of Location: An example from north eastern Brazil. *European Journal of Development Research*, 8. 2, 56–70.

Commission on Global Governance 1995: *Our Global Neighbourhood: The report of the Commission on Global Governance.* Oxford: Oxford University Press.

Corner, J. 1995: *Television Form and Public Address.* London: Edward Arnold.

Craib, I. 1992: *Anthony Giddens.* London: Routledge.

Crowley, D. and D. Mitchell (eds) 1994: *Communication Theory Today.* Cambridge: Polity Press.

Crystal, D. 1987: *The Cambridge Encyclopaedia of Language.* Cambridge: Cambridge University Press.

Culf, A. 1995: Greenpeace Used Us, Broadcasters Admit. *Guardian,* 28 August, 2.

—— 1997: BBC News Chief Bemoans Slide in Foreign Coverage. *Guardian,* 30 May, 13.

Dayan, D. and E. Katz 1992: *Media Events: The live broadcasting of history.* Cambridge, Mass.: Harvard University Press.

Delamont, S. 1995: *Appetites and Identities.* London: Routledge.

Deleuze, G. and F. Guattari 1977: *Anti-Oedipus: Capitalism and schizophrenia.* New York: Viking.

Dodd, P. 1995: *The Battle over Britain.* London: Demos.

Drummond, J. C. and A. Wilbraham 1991: *The Englishman's Food: Five centuries of English diet.* London: Pimlico.

Dyer, H. C. 1993: EcoCultures: Global culture in the age of ecology. *Millennium,* 22. 3, 483–504.

Eade, J. (ed.) 1997: *Living the Global City: Globalization as local process.* London: Routledge.

Featherstone, M. (ed.) 1990: *Global Culture: Nationalism, globalization and modernity.* London: Sage.

—— 1991: *Consumer Culture and Postmodernism.* London: Sage.

—— 1993: Global and Local Cultures. In J. Bird et al. (eds), *Mapping the Futures: Local culture, global change.* London: Routledge, 169–87.

—— 1995: *Undoing Culture.* London: Sage.

—— and R. Burrows 1995: Cultures of Technological Embodiment. *Body and Society (Cyberspace/Cyberbodies/Cyberpunk),* 1. 3–4, 1–19.

—— S. Lash and R. Robertson (eds) 1995: *Global Modernities.* London: Sage.

Fejes, F. 1981: Media Imperialism: An assessment. *Media, Culture and Society,* 3. 3, 281–9.

Ferguson, M. 1990: Electronic Media and the Redefining of Time and Space. In M. Ferguson (ed.), *Public Communication: The new imperatives,* London: Sage, 152–72.

—— 1991: Marshall McLuhan Revisited: 1960s zeitgeist victim or pioneer postmodernist? *Media, Culture and Society,* 13, 71–90.

—— 1992: The Mythology about Globalization. *European Journal of Communication,* 7, 69–93.

Fiske, J. 1987: *Television Culture.* London: Methuen.

Franco, J. 1992: Border Patrol. *Travesia: Journal of Latin American Cultural Studies,* 1. 2, 134–142.

Frank, A. G. 1969: *Latin America: Underdevelopment or revolution*. New York: Monthly Review Press.

Fraser, N. 1987: What's Critical about Critical Theory? The case of Habermas and gender. In S. Benhabib and D. Cornell (eds), *Feminism as Critique*. Minneapolis: University of Minnesota Press, 31–56.

Friedman, J. 1994: *Cultural Identity and Global Process*. London: Sage.

—— 1995: Global System, Globalization and the Parameters of Modernity. In Featherstone et al. (eds) *Global Modernities*, 69–90.

Fukuyama, F. 1992: *The End of History and the Last Man*. New York: Free Press.

Game, A. 1995: Time, Space and Memory with reference to Bachelard. In Featherstone et al. (eds), *Global Modernities*, 192–208.

Gannaway, L. 1998: Lure of the Aisles. *Guardian Society*, 4 February, 2–3.

García Canclini, N. 1992: Cultural Reconversion. In G.Yudice et al. (eds), *On Edge: The crisis of contemporary Latin American culture*. Minneapolis: University of Minnesota Press, 29–44.

—— 1995: *Hybrid Cultures: Strategies for entering and leaving modernity*. Minneapolis: University of Minnesota Press.

Garnham, N. 1992: The Media and the Public Sphere. In C. Calhoun (ed.) *Habermas and the Public Sphere*. Cambridge, Mass.: MIT Press, 359–76.

Gates, B. 1995: *The Road Ahead*. London: Viking.

Geertz, C. 1973: *The Interpretation of Cultures*. New York: Basic Books.

Gellner, E. 1964: *Thought and Change*. London: Weidenfeld and Nicolson.

George, S. 1982: *Food for Beginners*. New York: Writers and Readers.

Gergen, K. J. 1991: *The Saturated Self*. New York: Basic Books.

Giddens, A. 1979: *Central Problems in Social Theory*. London: Macmillan.

—— 1981: *A Contemporary Critique of Historical Materialism*,vol. I: *Power, Property and the State*. London: Macmillan.

—— 1984: *The Constitution of Society*. Cambridge: Polity Press.

—— 1985: *The Nation-State and Violence*, vol. II of *A Contemporary Critique of Historical Materialism*. Cambridge: Polity Press.

—— 1990: *The Consequences of Modernity*. Cambridge: Polity Press.

—— 1991: *Modernity and Self-Identity: Self and society in the late modern age*. Cambridge: Polity Press.

—— 1992: *The Transformation of Intimacy: Sexuality, love and eroticism in modern societies*. Cambridge: Polity Press.

—— 1994a: *Beyond Left and Right*. Cambridge: Polity Press.

—— 1994b: Living in a Post-traditional Society. In Beck, Giddens and Lash, *Reflexive Modernization*, 56–109.

Gilroy, P. 1993: *The Black Atlantic*. London: Verso.

Goldblatt, D. 1996: *Social Theory and the Environment*. Cambridge: Polity Press.

Golding, P. and P. Harris (eds) 1997: *Beyond Cultural Imperialism: Globalization, communication and the new international order*. London: Sage.

Goodman, D. and M. Redclift 1991: *Refashioning Nature: Food, ecology and culture*. London: Routledge.

Goodwin, R. 1992: *Green Political Theory*. Cambridge: Polity Press.

Goody, J. (ed.) 1968: *Literacy in Traditional Soceties*. Cambridge: Cambridge University Press.

—— 1997: Industrial Food: Towards the development of a world cuisine. In C. Counihan and P. van Esterik (eds) *Food and Culture*. London: Routledge, 338–56.

Gray, C. (ed.) 1995: *The Cyborg Handbook*. London: Routledge.

Gray, J. 1997: *Endgames: Questions in late modern political thought*. Cambridge: Polity Press.

Grodin, D. and T. R. Lindhof (eds) 1996: *Constructing the Self in a Mediated World*. Thousand Oaks, Calif.: Sage.

Groombridge, B. 1972: *Television and the People*. Harmondsworth: Penguin.

Hajer, M. A. 1996: Ecological Modernisation as Cultural Politics. In S. Lash, B. Szerszynski and B. Wynne (eds), *Risk, Environment and Modernity*. London: Sage, 246–68.

Hall, S. 1991: The Local and the Global: Globalization and ethnicities. In King (ed.), *Culture, Globalization and the World System*, 19–30.

—— 1992: The Question of Cultural Identity. In S. Hall, D. Held and A. McGrew (eds), *Modernity and its Futures*. Cambridge: Polity Press, 274–316.

Hamelink, C. J. 1983: *Cultural Autonomy in Global Communications*. New York: Longmans.

—— 1994: *The Politics of World Communication*. London: Sage.

Hannerz, U. 1987: The World in Creolization. *Africa*, 57. 4, 546–59.

—— 1990: Cosmopolitans and Locals in World Culture. In Featherstone (ed.), *Global Culture*, 237–51.

—— 1996: *Transnational Connections*. London: Routledge.

Haraway, D. 1991: *Simians, Cyborgs and Women: The reinvention of nature*. London: Free Association Books.

Harvey, D. 1989: *The Condition of Postmodernity*. Oxford: Basil Blackwell.

Hawkins, J. and R. Allen (eds) (1991): *The Oxford Encyclopedic English Dictionary*. Oxford: Clarendon Press.

Hebdige, D. 1989: After the Masses. In S. Hall and M. Jacques (eds), *New Times: The changing face of politics in the 1990s*. London: Lawrence and Wishart, 76–93.

—— 1990: Fax to the Future. *Marxism Today* (January), 18–23.

Heelas, P., S. Lash and P. Morris (eds) 1996: *Detraditionalization*. Oxford: Blackwell.

Held, D. 1992: Democracy: From city-states to a cosmopolitan order? *Political Studies*, 40, Special Issue, 10–39.

—— 1995: *Democracy and the Global Order: From the modern state to cosmopolitan governance*. Cambridge: Polity Press.

Herman E. S. and R. W. McChesney 1997: *The Global Media*. London: Cassell.

Heyer, P. and D. Crowley 1995: Introduction to Innis, *The Bias of Communication*, ix–xxvi.

Hirst, P. and G. Thompson 1996: *Globalization in Question*. Cambridge: Polity Press.

Holmes, G. (ed.) 1988: *The Oxford History of Medieval Europe*. Oxford: Oxford University Press.

Horkheimer, M. and T. Adorno 1979: *Dialectic of Enlightenment*. London: Verso.

Horsman, M. and A. Marshall 1994: *After the Nation-State: Citizens, tribalism and the new world disorder*. London: HarperCollins.

Horton, D. and R. R. Wohl 1956: Mass Communication and Para-social Interaction: Observations on intimacy at a distance. *Psychiatry*, 19, 215–29.

Howes, D. (ed.) 1996: *Cross-cultural Consumption: Global markets, local realities*. London: Routledge.

Innis, H. A. 1995: *The Bias of Communication*. Toronto: University of Toronto Press.

James, A. 1996: Cooking the Books: Global or local identities in contemporary British food cultures? In Howes (ed.), *Cross-cultural Consumption*, 77–92.

Jamieson, A. 1996: The Shaping of the Global Environmental Agenda: The role of non-governmental organisations. In S. Lash, B. Szerszynski and B. Wynne (eds), *Risk, Environment and Modernity*. London: Sage, 224–45.

Kant, I. 1991: Perpetual Peace: A philosophical sketch. In H. Reiss (ed.), *Kant: Political writing*. Cambridge: Cambridge University Press, 93–130.

King, A. D. (ed.) 1991: *Culture, Globalization and the World System*. London: Macmillan.

Kofman, E. and G. Youngs (eds) 1996: *Globalization: Theory and Practice*. London: Pinter.

Kraniauskas, J. 1992: Hybridism and Reterritorialization. *Travesia: Journal of Latin American Cultural Studies*, 1. 2, 143–51.

Lasch, C, 1977: *Haven in a Heartless World*. New York: Basic Books.

—— 1980: *The Culture of Narcissism*. London: Abacus.

—— 1985: *The Minimal Self: Psychic survival in troubled times*. London: Picador.

Lash, S. 1994: Reflexivity and its Doubles: Structure, aesthetics, community. In Beck, Giddens and Lash, *Reflexive Modernization*, 110–73.

—— and Urry, J. 1994: *Economies of Signs and Space*. London: Sage.

Latouche, S. 1996: *The Westernization of the World*. Cambridge: Polity Press.

Le Roy Ladurie, E. 1978: *Montaillou: Cathars and Catholics in a French village 1294–1324*. London: Scolar Press.

Leggett, J. (ed.) 1990: *Global Warming: The Greenpeace report*. Oxford: Oxford University Press.

Leonard, M. 1998: *Making Europe Popular: The search for European identity*. London: Demos.

Liebes, T. and E. Katz 1993: *The Export of Meaning: Cross-cultural readings of Dallas*. Cambridge: Polity Press.

Lull, J. 1995: *Media, Communication, Culture: A global approach*. Cambridge: Polity Press.

Lunt, P. K. and S. M. Livingstone 1992: *Mass Consumption and Personal Identity*. Buckingham: Open University Press.

Lupton, D. 1995: The Embodied Computer/User. *Body and Society*, 1. 3–4, 76–112.

—— 1996: *Food, the Body and the Self*. London: Sage.

—— and G. Noble 1997: Just a Machine? Dehumanizing strategies in personal computer use. *Body and Society*, 3. 2, 83–101.

Lyotard, J. F. 1984: *The Postmodern Condition*. Manchester: Manchester University Press.

Maffesoli, M. 1996: *The Time of the Tribes*. London: Sage.

Manchester, W. 1992: *A World Lit Only by Fire: The medieval mind and the Renaissance*. London: Macmillan.

Mann, M. 1986: *The Sources of Social Power*, vol. I. Cambridge: Cambridge University Press.

Mannheim, K. 1960: *Ideology and Utopia*. London: Routledge and Kegan Paul.

Martin-Barbero, J. 1993: *Communication, Culture and Hegemony*. London: Sage.

Marx, K. 1973a: *Grundrisse*. Harmondsworth: Penguin.

—— 1973b: *Surveys from Exile*. Harmondsworth: Pelican.

—— and F. Engels 1969: Manifesto of the Communist Party. In L. S. Feuer (ed.), *Marx and Engels: Basic writings on politics and philosophy*. London: Fontana, 43–82.

—— and F. Engels 1970: *The German Ideology*, ed. C. J. Arthur. London: Lawrence and Wishart.

Massey, D. 1994: *Space, Place and Gender*. Cambridge: Polity Press.

Mattelart, A. 1994: *Mapping World Communication*. Minneapolis: Minnesota University Press.

McClelland, D. 1961: *The Achieving Society*. Princeton: Van Nostrand.

McGrew, A. 1992: A Global Society? In S. Hall, D. Held and A. McGrew (eds), *Modernity and its Futures*. Cambridge: Polity Press, 61–102.

—— and P. Lewis (eds) 1992: *Global Politics*. Cambridge: Polity Press.

McGuigan, J. 1992: *Cultural Populism*. London: Routledge.

McLuhan, M. 1964: *Understanding Media: The extensions of man*. London: Routledge and Kegan Paul.

—— and Q. Fiore 1967: *The Medium is the Message*. Harmondsworth: Penguin.

McPhail, T. L. 1987: *Electronic Colonialism* (2nd edn). Newbury Park, Calif.: Sage.

Mellencamp, P. (ed.) 1990: *Logics of Television*. Bloomington and London: Indiana University Press and British Film Institute.

Melucci, A. 1989: *Nomads of the Present: Social movements and individual needs in contemporary society*. London: Hutchinson Radius.

Mennell, S. 1985: *All Manners of Food: Eating and taste in England and France from the Middle Ages to the present*. Oxford: Blackwell.

—— 1990: The Globalization of Human Society as a very Long-Term Social Process: Elias's theory. In Featherstone (ed.), *Global Culture* 359–71.

Merton, R. K. 1968: Patterns of Influence: Local and cosmopolitan influentials. In R. K. Merton, *Social Theory and Social Structure*. New York: Free Press, 441–74.

Meyrowitz, J. 1985: *No Sense of Place: The impact of electronic media on social behaviour*. New York: Oxford University Press.

—— 1994: Medium Theory. In Crowley and Mitchell (eds), *Communication Theory Today*, 50–77.

Millar, S. 1997: Family Enters Wired World. *Guardian*, 27 November, 5.

Miller, J. 1971: *McLuhan*. London: Fontana.

Millet, K. 1971: *Sexual Politics*. London: Virago.

Miyoshi M. and H. Harootunian (eds) 1989: *Postmodernism and Japan*. Durham, NC: Duke University Press.

Mlinar, Z. 1992: *Globalization and Territorial Identities*. Aldershot: Avebury.

Monbiot, G. 1995: Global Villagers Speak With Forked Tongues. *Guardian*, 24 August, 13.

Montaigne, M. 1995: *Four Essays*. London: Penguin.

Morley, D. 1986: *Family Television*. London: Comedia/Routledge.

—— 1992: *Television Audiences and Cultural Studies*. London: Routledge.

—— and K. Robins 1995: *Spaces of Identity: Global media, electronic landscapes and cultural boundaries*. London: Routledge.

Morris, R. 1988: Northern Europe Invades the Mediterranean 900–1200. In G. Holmes (ed.), *The Oxford History of Medieval Europe*. Oxford: Oxford University Press, 165–221.

Mowlana, H. 1996: *Global Communication in Transition: The end of diversity?* Thousand Oaks, Calif.: Sage.

Murdock, G. 1993: Communications and the Constitution of Modernity. *Media, Culture and Society*, 15, 521–39.

Nederveen Pieterse, J. 1995: Globalization as Hybridization. In Featherstone et al. (eds), *Global Modernities*, 45–68.

Nguyen, D. T. 1992: The Spatialization of Metric Time. *Time and Society*, 1, 29–50.

Oakeshott, M. 1991: *On Human Conduct*. Oxford: Clarendon Press.

Ohmae, K. 1995: *The End of the Nation State: The rise and fall of regional economies*. London: HarperCollins.

Ohnuki-Tierney, E. 1993: *Rice as Self: Japanese identities through time*. Princeton: Princeton University Press.

Ollman, B. 1979: *Social and Sexual Revolution: Essays on Marx and Reich*. London: Pluto Press.

Ong, W. 1967: *The Presence of the Word*. New Haven: Yale University Press.

Osborne, P. 1992: Modernity is a Qualitative, not a Chronological, Category. *New Left Review*, 192, 65–84.

Ostrom, E. 1990: *Governing the Commons: The evolution of institutions for collective action*. Cambridge: Cambridge University Press.

Papastergiadis, N. 1997: Tracing Hybridity in Theory. In Werbner and Modood (eds) *Debating Cultural Hybridity*, 257–81.

Poster, M. 1990: *The Mode of Information*. Cambridge: Polity Press.

—— 1995: *The Second Media Age*. Cambridge: Polity Press.

Prendergrast, M. 1993: *For God, Country and Coca-Cola: The unauthorized history of the great American soft drink and the company that makes it.* Toronto: Maxwell Macmillan.

Reich, R. B. 1992: *The Work of Nations*. New York: Vintage.

Rheingold, H. 1994: *The Virtual Community*. London: Minerva.

Ritzer, G. 1993: *The McDonaldization of Society*. Newbury Park, Calif.: Pine Forge Press.

—— and A. Liska 1997: 'McDisneyization' and 'Post-tourism'. In C. Rojek and J. Urry (eds), *Touring Cultures: Transformations of travel and theory*. London: Routledge, 96–109.

Robertson, R. 1992: *Globalization: Social theory and global culture*. London: Sage.

—— 1995: Glocalization: Time-space and homogeneity-heterogeneity. In Featherstone et al. (eds), *Global Modernities*, 23–44.

Robins, K. 1991: Tradition and Translation: National culture in its global context. In J. Corner and S. Harvey (eds), *Enterprise and Heritage*. London: Routledge, 21–44.

—— 1994: Forces of Consumption: From the symbolic to the psychotic. *Media, Culture and Society*, 16, 449–68.

—— 1996: Cyberspace and the World we Live in. In J. Dovey (ed.), *Fractal Dreams: New media in social context*. London: Lawrence and Wishart, 1–30.

—— 1997: *What in the World is Going on?* In P. du Gay (ed.), *Production of Culture/Cultures of Production*. London: Sage/Open University, 12–47.

Rojek, C. 1993: *Ways of Escape: Modern transformations in leisure and travel*. London: Macmillan.

Rosaldo, R. 1995: Foreword to García Canclini, *Hybrid Cultures*, xi–xvii.

Rostow, W. W. 1960: *The Stages of Economic Growth*. Cambridge: Cambridge University Press.

Rouse, R. 1988: Mexicano, Chicano, Pocho. La migración mexicana y el espacio social del postmodernismo. *Pagino Uno*, supplement to *Unomásuno*, 31 December.

Rowe, W. 1992: War and Cultural Studies. *Travesia: Journal of Latin American Cultural Studies*, 1. 1, 18–37.

Rushdie, S. 1991: *Imaginary Homelands*. London: Granta.

Sachs, W. (ed.) 1993: *Global Ecology*. London: Zed Books.

Said, E. W. 1985: *Orientalism*. London: Penguin.

Sartre, J.-P. 1956: *Being and Nothingness*. New York: Pocket Books.

—— 1976: *Critique of Dialectical Reason*. London: Verso.

Scannell, P. 1996: *Radio, Television and Modern Life*. Oxford: Blackwell.

Schiller, H. I. 1979: Transnational Media and National Development. In K. Nordenstreng and H. I. Schiller (eds), *National Sovereignty and International Communication*. Norwood, NJ: Ablex, 21–32.

—— 1985: Electronic Information Flows: New basis for global domination? In P. Drummond and R. Paterson (eds), *Television in Transition*. London: BFI Publishing, 11–20.

—— 1995: The Global Information Highway: Project for an ungovernable world. In Brook and Boal (eds), *Resisting the Virtual Life*, 17–33.

Schlereth, T. J. 1977: *The Cosmopolitan Ideal in Enlightenment Thought*. Notre Dame, Ind.: University of Notre Dame Press.

Schlesinger, P. 1991: *Media, State and Nation*. London: Sage.

Shohat, E. and R. Stam 1994: *Unthinkng Eurocentrism*. London: Routledge.

Silverstone, R. 1994: *Television and Everyday Life*. London: Routledge.

Sklair, L. 1991: *Sociology of the Global System*. Hemel Hempstead: Harvester Wheatsheaf.

Slater, N. 1994: *The 30–Minute Cook: The best of the world's quick cooking*. London: Michael Joseph.

Smith, A. 1990: Towards a Global Culture? In M. Featherstone (ed.), *Global Culture*, 171–91.

—— 1991: *National Identity*. London: Penguin.

—— 1995: *Nations and Nationalism in a Global Era*. Cambridge: Polity Press.

Smith, J. 1998: What's the Problem with Women? *Guardian*, 20 February, 2–3.

Spybey, T. 1996: *Globalization and World Society*. Cambridge: Polity Press.

Sreberny-Mohammadi, A. 1991: The Global and the Local in International Communications. In J. Curran and M. Gurevitch (eds), *Mass Media and Society*. London: Edward Arnold, 118–38.

—— and A. Mohammadi 1994: *Small Media, Big Revolution: Communication, culture, and the Iranian revolution*. Minneapolis: University of Minnesota Press.

Stallabrass, J. 1995: Empowering Technology: The exploration of cyberspace. *New Left Review*, 211, 3–32.

Stevenson, N. 1995: *Understanding Media Cultures: Social theory and mass communication*. London: Sage.

Sumption, J. 1975: *Pilgrimage: An image of medieval religion*. London: Faber.

Sztompka, P. 1993: *The Sociology of Social Change*. Oxford: Blackwell.

Tansey, G. and T. Worsley 1995: *The Food System: A guide*. London: Earthscan.

Taylor, P. J. 1996: Embedded Statism and the Social Sciences: Opening up to new spaces. *Environment and Planning A*, 28. 11, 1917–28.

The Ecologist 1992: Global Management, Special Issue on The Commons, 22. 4, 180–2.

Therborn, G. 1995a: *European Modernity and Beyond*. London: Sage.

—— 1995b: Routes to/through Modernity. In Featherstone et al. (eds), *Global Modernities*, 124–39.

Theroux, P. 1986: *Sunrise with Seamonsters*. Harmondsworth: Penguin.

Thomas, A. et al. 1994: *Third World Atlas* (2nd edn). Buckingham: Open University Press.

Thompson, E. P. 1967: Time, Work-Discipline and Industrial Capitalism. *Past and Present*, 38, 56–97.

Thompson, J. B. 1990: *Ideology and Modern Culture*. Cambridge: Polity Press.

—— 1994: Social Theory and the Media. In Crowley and Mitchell (eds), *Communication Theory Today*, 27–49.

—— 1995: *The Media and Modernity*. Cambridge: Polity Press.

Thompson, K. 1997: Regulation, De-regulation and Re-regulation. In K.

Thompson (ed.), *Media and Cultural Regulation*. London: Sage/Open University, 10–52.

Thrift, N. 1990: The Making of a Capitalist Time Consciousness. In J. Hassard (ed.), *The Sociology of Time*. London: Macmillan, 105–29.

—— 1996: *Spatial Formations*. London: Sage.

Tibi, B. 1995: Culture and Knowledge: The politics of Islamisation of knowledge as a postmodern project? The fundamentalist claim to de-westernization. *Theory, Culture and Society*, 12. 1, 1–24.

Tomlinson, J. 1991: *Cultural Imperialism: A critical introduction*. London: Pinter.

—— 1994: A Phenomenology of Globalization? Giddens on global modernity. *European Journal of Communication*, 9, 149–72.

—— 1997a: Internationalism, Globalization and Cultural Imperialism. In K.Thompson (ed.), *Media and Cultural Regulation*. London: Sage/Open University, 117–162.

—— 1997b: 'And Besides, the Wench is Dead': Media scandals and the globalization of communication. In J. Lull and S. Hinerman (eds), *Media Scandals: Morality and desire in the popular cultural marketplace*. Cambridge: Polity Press, 65–84.

Toynbee, A. J. 1948: *Civilization on Trial*. London: Oxford University Press.

Turkle, S. 1995: *Life on the Screen: Identity in the age of the Internet*. New York: Simon and Schuster.

—— 1996: Parallel Lives: Working on identity in virtual space. In Grodin and Lindhof (eds), *Constructing the Self in a Mediated World*, 156–75.

Turner, B. S. 1990: The Two Faces of Sociology: Global or national? In Featherstone (ed.), *Global Culture: Nationalism, globalization and modernity*. London: Sage, 343–58.

Turner, T. 1994: The Mission Thing. *Index on Censorship*, 4/5, 38–42.

Urry, J. 1995: Tourism, Europe and Identity. In J. Urry *Consuming Places*. London: Routledge, 163–70.

Van Hemel, A., H. Mommaas and C. Smithuijsen (eds) 1996: *Trading Culture: GATT, European cultural policies and the transatlantic market*. Amsterdam: Boekman Foundation.

Vidal, J. 1995: Local Heroes: Is Greenpeace just another multinational? *The Printer's Devil*, Issue G, 56–61.

—— 1996: City Soundings. *Guardian*, 5 June, 4.

Wagner, P. 1994: *A Sociology of Modernity*. London: Routledge.

Wallerstein, I. 1974: *The Modern World System*. New York: Academic Press.

—— 1979: *The Capitalist World-Economy*. Cambridge: Cambridge University Press.

—— 1987: World-System Analysis. In A. Giddens and J. Turner (eds), *Social Theory Today*. Cambridge: Polity Press, 309–24.

Waters, M. 1995: *Globalization*. London: Routledge.

Weatherford, R. 1993: *World Peace and the Human Family*. London: Routledge.

Weber, M. 1977: Science as a Vocation. In H. H. Gerth and C. Wright Mills (eds), *From Max Weber*. London: Routledge and Kegan Paul.

Webster, A. 1984: *Introduction to the Sociology of Development*. London: Macmillan.

Werbner, P. 1997: The Dialectics of Cultural Hybridity. In Werbner and Modood (eds) *Debating Cultural Hybridity*, 1–26.

—— and T. Modood (eds) 1997: *Debating Cultural Hybridity*. London: Zed Books.

Williams, R. 1974: *Television: Technology and Cultural Form*. London: Fontana.

—— 1981: *Culture*. London: Fontana.

—— 1983: *Towards 2000*. London: Chatto and Windus.

—— 1989: *Resources of Hope*. London: Verso.

Willis, S. 1991: *A Primer for Daily Life*. London: Routledge.

Wilson, E. O. (1978): *On Human Nature*. Cambridge, Mass.: Harvard University Press.

Wilson, T. 1993: *Watching Television: Hermeneutics, reception and popular culture*. Cambridge: Polity Press.

Winseck, D. 1997: Contradictions in the Democratization of International Communications. *Media, Culture and Society*, 19. 2, 219–46.

Wired 1995: Premier UK edition, 1.01

Wittstock, M. 1998: Hi There! And Here's Tonight's Non-news. *Guardian Media*, 19 January, 7.

Wolff, J. 1991: The Global and the Specific: Reconciling conflicting theories of culture. In King (ed.), *Culture, Globalization and the World System*, 161–73.

Wolff, J. 1993: On the Road Again: Metaphors of travel in cultural criticism. *Cultural Studies*, 7. 2, 224–39.

Woodward, K. 1997: *Identity and Difference*. London: Sage/Open University.

Woolacott, M. 1995: The Mouse that Soared. *Guardian*, 19 August, 22.

Wuthnow, R. 1992: *Acts of Compassion: caring for others and helping ourselves*. Princeton: Princeton University Press.

Yearley, S. 1996: *Sociology, Environmentalism, Globalization*, London: Sage.

Young, I. M. 1990: The Ideal of Community and the Politics of Difference. In L. J. Nicholson. (ed.), *Feminism/Postmodernism*. London: Routledge, 300–23.

Young, R. 1995: *Colonial Desire: Hybridity in theory, culture and race*. London: Routledge.

Young Farrugia, J. 1969: *The Letter Box: A history of Post Office pillar and wall boxes*. Sussex: Centaur Press.

Zaretski, E. 1995: The Birth of Identity Politics in the 1960s.: Psychoanalysis and the public/private division. In Featherstone et al. (eds) *Global Modernities*, 244–59.

Index